T0330225

The Euro

Dedicated to the memory of two old Europeans:
L/pl Jack Mulhearn, 5th Welch Regiment
and
Philip Maurice Vane, 48th Division Signals

And welcome to a new one:
Layla Moreno Mulhearn

The Euro
Its Origins, Development and Prospects

Chris Mulhearn

Reader in Economics, Liverpool Business School,
Liverpool John Moores University, UK

and

Howard R. Vane

Professor of Economics, Liverpool Business School,
Liverpool John Moores University, UK

Edward Elgar
Cheltenham, UK • Northampton, MA, USA

Published by
Edward Elgar Publishing Limited
Glensanda House
Montpellier Parade
Cheltenham
Glos GL50 1UA
UK

Edward Elgar Publishing, Inc.
William Pratt House
9 Dewey Court
Northampton
Massachusetts 01060
USA

A catalogue record for this book
is available from the British Library

Library of Congress Control Number: 2008927694

ISBN 978 1 84720 051 8 (cased)

Printed and bound in Great Britain by MPG Books Ltd, Bodmin, Cornwall

Contents

Figures

Tables

Abbreviations and acronyms

BIS	Bank for International Settlements
CEEC	Committee for European Economic Cooperation
EC	European Community
ECB	European Central Bank
ECOFIN	European Union Council of Economics and Finance Ministers
ECSC	European Coal and Steel Community
EDP	excessive deficit procedure
EEC	European Economic Community
EMI	European Monetary Institute
EMS	European Monetary System
EMU	economic and monetary union
EPU	European Payments Union
ERM	exchange rate mechanism
ERM II	exchange rate mechanism II
ESCB	European System of Central Banks
EU	European Union
Euratom	European Atomic Energy Community
FDI	foreign direct investment
HICP	Harmonized Index of Consumer Prices
IMF	International Monetary Fund
NCB	national central bank
OCA	optimum currency area
OECD	Organization for Economic Cooperation and Development
SEA	Single European Act
SGP	Stability and Growth Pact
TEU	Treaty on European Union

Preface

Today, university economics students and their teachers can refer to a number of established texts on the economics of monetary union. Given their intended audience, these books are inevitably quite detailed and technically demanding. The main intention behind the present volume is to provide a non-technical but comprehensive overview of the central issues surrounding the euro. Our book is primarily aimed at intermediate undergraduates taking courses not just in economics, but also in business studies, modern economic history, politics and international relations. It should also prove useful to postgraduate students in these disciplines in their preliminary year of study.

Our approach in writing the book is intended to allow students on a range of degree courses to read individual chapters in isolation, according to their interests and needs. Having said this, the book follows a structured path by tracing the origins, development and prospects for the euro. After an introductory chapter on the origins of European integration we examine the first steps in the process of monetary integration (Chapter 2), the economics of the euro (Chapter 3), the euro's architecture (Chapter 4) and euro-area enlargement issues (Chapters 5 and 6), before reflecting on the future of the euro (Chapter 7). Reading individual chapters in isolation can detract from the bigger picture. To help overcome this potential problem we have included a time line of key events in the history of European economic, monetary and political integration. This provides the reader with a useful point of reference, as does the list of abbreviations and acronyms used throughout the book.

In order to help bring the subject matter alive and capture the imagination of the reader, at the end of the first six chapters we have included interviews with leading academics in the field. We are extremely grateful to (listed in the order in which the interviews appear in the book): Nick Crafts, Paul De Grauwe, Niels Thygesen, Charles Wyplosz, Willem Buiter, Patrick Minford and Andrzej Wojtyna for the time and care they took in answering our questions, and in subsequent correspondence. Their illuminating and at times contrasting answers demonstrate the importance of the subject matter of the book.

We hope that readers will find this volume an interesting and informative overview of the main issues surrounding the euro.

Chris Mulhearn and Howard R. Vane

Acknowledgements

The data used to draw many of the figures in this book were obtained from four main sources: Eurostat (the Statistical Office of the European Communities), www.ec.europa.eu/eurostat; the European Central Bank, www.ecb.int; the International Monetary Fund, www.imf.org; and the World Trade Organisation, www.wto.org. In some instances figures have been reproduced directly. In all cases the material may be obtained free of charge from the cited sources.

1. The euro and the origins of European integration

1.1 INTRODUCTION

The euro was launched on 1 January 1999. At the time it was unclear how this ambitious monetary integration project would fare, and there were many grave warnings that it could easily fail. But this did not happen. Indeed, the new currency's emergence was, by any standards, a relatively smooth and comfortable process. This is all the more remarkable because the euro is shared by neighbouring countries that, within living memory, have engaged in the brutal, prolonged and industrialized destruction of each other's populations. Today, war between the nations of Western Europe is absolutely unimaginable and the enmities that once existed have given way, not just to a permanent peace between independent countries, but to deep, shared sovereignty over a range of crucially important economic and political processes. The euro is both the most evident symbol and the deepest material form of this shared sovereignty.

Figure 1.1 depicts the extent of the euro area which presently comprises 15 economies: the 11 that adopted the currency at the time of its launch, plus Greece and Slovenia, which joined in 2001 and 2007 respectively, and – since 2008 – Cyprus and Malta. Currently, the European Union (EU) has 27 members, so the euro area still has considerable scope for enlargement. Table 1.1 sets the euro area in an international context. Although it has a larger population than the United States and Japan – the two other members of the so-called 'triad group' of the world's three largest economies – in GDP terms the euro area is only about three-quarters the size of the US. Note, however, that should the other members of the EU27 join the euro area it would become the world's largest economy in terms of GDP. It is also evident that the euro area is much more open than either the US or Japan, with exports accounting for more than 20 per cent of GDP. As we shall discuss in Chapter 3, sections 3.4 and 3.5, the benefits of a

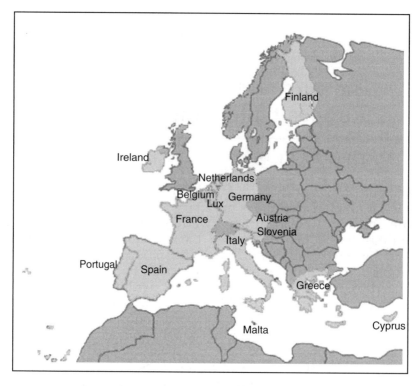

Source: Adapted from European Central Bank.

Figure 1.1   The euro area

Table 1.1   Key characteristics of the euro area, 2005

	€13	EU27	United States	Japan
Population (millions)	316.6	492.8	296.7	127.8
GDP (PPP, € trillions)	8.0	11.3	10.7	3.4
GDP per capita (PPP, € thousands)	25.4	23.0	36.0	26.4
Share of world GDP (PPP, %)	14.9	20.8	20.1	6.4
Exports (goods and services, % of GDP)	20.3	13.4	10.2	14.9

Note: PPP = purchasing power parity.

Source: European Central Bank.

common currency increase the greater the degree of trade integration between member countries. The mutual openness of the euro-area countries – which is likely to be further intensified by the presence of the euro – may be critical to the long-term health of the European integration project.

1.2   THE SECOND WORLD WAR AND EUROPEAN INTEGRATION

What, then, are the origins of the euro? Why did countries such as France, Germany and Italy invent this entirely new currency as a replacement for the franc, mark and lire? To properly understand the genesis of the euro we need to reflect upon the long process of economic and political integration upon which Europe embarked when the European Economic Community (EEC) was created by the Treaty of Rome in 1957. The EEC was a phenomenal achievement. It involved nothing less than the selective pooling of national sovereignties between six independent European countries: France, Germany, Italy, Belgium, the Netherlands and Luxembourg. In one sense, the euro is the logical end of the process that the Treaty of Rome began: it is what Kathryn Dominguez has called the 'diamond head' of European integration.[1] However, the EEC itself did not arise out of the ether. It is rooted in the military, political and economic history of Western Europe and, in particular, is a product of the choices made in Europe and elsewhere at the end of the Second World War (1939–45).

In 1946 in a speech at the University of Zurich, Winston Churchill, who as prime minister had led Britain during the Second World War, reflected on the pitiable condition to which Europe had been reduced by six years of unprecedented and terrible conflict:

> [O]ver wide areas are a vast, quivering mass of tormented, hungry, careworn and bewildered human beings, who wait in the ruins of their cities and homes and scan the dark horizons for the approach of some new form of tyranny or terror.[2]

Churchill then offered what at the time must have appeared an astonishing and even fanciful proposal for the revival and

---

[1] Paper presented at the American Economic Association Conference, Boston, January 2006.
[2] The full text of the speech is available from: www.ena.lu.

transformation of the Continent. He argued that the way forward was:

> to recreate the European fabric, or as much of it as we can, and to provide it with a structure under which it can dwell in peace, safety and freedom. We must build a kind of United States of Europe. In this way only will hundreds of millions of toilers be able to regain the simple joys and hopes which make life worth living.

Britain was not part of this vision. According to Churchill she was embedded in her own Empire-based partnership with the Commonwealth of Nations. But he did identify the essential constituents of the new Europe:

> The first step in the recreation of the European family must be a partnership between France and Germany . . . There can be no revival of Europe without a spiritually great France and a spiritually great Germany.

With notable prescience Churchill also foresaw how the large European nations would combine with the small nations to their collective benefit:

> The structure of the United States of Europe will be such as to make the material strength of a single state less important. Small nations will count as much as large ones and gain their honour by a contribution to the common cause.

In his speech, Churchill was attempting to resolve what was known as the 'German problem'. Essentially this was about the containment of Germany. After the First World War (1914–18) the allied powers had dealt with Germany in a punitive manner, imposing crippling reparations on her that had ultimately proved wholly unsuccessful: in the context of political turbulence and depression in the 1920s and 1930s, the country had eventually turned to fascism, belligerence and, once again, war. By incorporating a reconstructed Germany into a new European family of nations the old mistakes of the past could be avoided, and peace and prosperity assured. This was Churchill's message and, in the end, this is what the Europeans attempted to do; and it worked.

But it was not just European interests that determined the choices made after 1945. The US and the Soviet Union, the senior partners in a wartime alliance with Britain against Germany and her axis allies, both had their own concerns about German reconstruction. The Second World War had cost the lives of at least 25 million Soviet citizens, and the Soviet Union did not intend to risk its security by tolerating the re-emergence of a powerful Germany.[3] On the other hand, the US, fearing the spread of communism in Western Europe and the implications of prolonged Soviet occupation of Eastern Europe, began to envisage German reconstruction as a necessary element in the struggle to develop a prosperous and democratic Western Europe as a key feature of its own security strategy. These differences between the two former allies gave rise in the late 1940s to the Cold War, and conditioned the form that would ultimately be assumed by the process of European integration.

By 1948, the Western powers in Germany – the US, Britain and France – had merged their zones of occupation, and in 1949 this area became the (still occupied) new state of the Federal Republic of Germany (West Germany), with Konrad Adenauer as its first Chancellor. In response, a few months later the Soviet-occupied zone in the eastern part of Germany became the German Democratic Republic (East Germany). The division of Germany meant that there was now a receptive state with which the Western Europeans and the US could begin to do business in attempting to address the German problem in a manner of their choosing. The Soviets, on the other hand, had created a satellite state as a means of resolving their security concerns.

1.3   THE SCHUMAN DECLARATION

The process that began the integration of the newly created West Germany and the other five signatories of the Treaty of Rome was designed by one man – Jean Monnet – and its implementation orchestrated by another – Robert Schuman. Monnet was a French civil servant, the commissioner general of the French National Planning Board. Schuman was the French foreign minister. The signal event which announced the start of the process of European integration is known as the Schuman Declaration. This was delivered in Paris on 9 May 1950.

---

[3] In comparison, French fatalities are estimated at 0.8 million; German fatalities 7 million; British fatalities 0.4 million. In total, the Second World War is estimated to have cost the lives of 61 million human beings.

Schuman's name may figure prominently in the annals of the modern history of Western Europe but it is Monnet who deserves much of the credit for shaping the initial form in which this history unfolded. Monnet's idea was to unify key industrial sectors of the French and German economies. This he supposed would facilitate the reconstruction of both nations, but it would do so in such a way as to deny Germany the material independence to make war on its neighbour in the future. The chosen sectors were coal and steel, then the essential resources for fuelling and arming bellicose nations. The essential strategy was to place the coal and steel industries of France and Germany under a supranational higher authority such that a single market in each commodity would henceforth prevail.

The Schuman Declaration presented Monnet's plan as an invitation from the French government to West Germany to participate in what would in 1952 become the European Coal and Steel Community (ECSC). In fact, the cooperation of West Germany had already been assured through the agency of Konrad Adenauer. Schuman's invitation was also explicitly open to all other European countries and the ECSC membership comprised the 'Six' original partners in European integration: France, Germany, Italy, Belgium, the Netherlands and Luxembourg.

Schuman's Declaration opened by taking up Churchill's theme of the need for a *rapprochement* to overcome the 'age-old opposition' between France and Germany. Schuman continued:

> With this aim in view, the French Government proposes to take action immediately on one limited but decisive point. It proposes to place Franco-German production of coal and steel as a whole under a common higher authority within the framework of an organisation open to the participation of the other countries of Europe. The pooling of coal and steel production should immediately provide for the setting up of common foundations for economic development as a first step in the federation of Europe, and will change the destinies of those regions which have long been devoted to the manufacture of the munitions of war . . . The solidarity in production thus established will make it plain that any war between France and Germany becomes not merely unthinkable but materially impossible.

But it is evident here that Schuman was proposing much more than the shackling of the means to make war. His reference to a higher authority is an acknowledgement that these new arrangements would be about the pooling of state sovereignty. Indeed, ECSC Higher Authority representatives were bound not by the interests of their respective countries but to member states as a whole. Moreover, this was but a first step: note that Schuman's stated intention was to forge a wider federation of Europe and a 'wider and deeper community'.

Schuman did not offer a detailed blueprint for the ECSC but he did sketch out the broad tasks of the Higher Authority that would lead it. These were:

- to modernize the productive capacity of the European coal and steel industries;
- to ensure that coal and steel were supplied 'on identical terms' across national markets;
- to promote Community-based exporting; and
- to improve and equalize the living conditions of coal and steel industry workers in the Community.

In the event, the actual form assumed by the ECSC in 1952 was the subject of a series of negotiating wrangles. On one side was Monnet, who thought that the centralized direction of markets by some higher planning authority – *dirigisme* is the French word for this – was the best way to achieve the objectives outlined by Schuman. On the other stood the entrenched interests of industrialists, who resented the swingeing regulatory powers vested in the Higher Authority. Although in the case of the ECSC Monnet's approach won the day, this was to prove a high-water mark for *dirigisme*: thereafter the incremental sector-by-sector approach to integration in Europe did not flourish. Instead, an emphasis on the interplay of free markets without state-led central direction came to dominate the European agenda.[4] But this is to get slightly ahead of ourselves. To their eternal credit, what can also be claimed by Monnet and Schuman is that their initiative did indeed provide a solution to the German problem. Churchill was right when he said in his Zurich speech that his audience would be astonished by his proposal for a partnership between France and Germany, but by the beginning of the 1950s astonishment had given way to gratitude for the achievement of a permanent peace based on an unprecedented nascent political and economic integration of Western Europe.

---

[4] An extended discussion of the negotiations leading up to the launch of the ECSC can be found in Gillingham (2006).

1.4   EARLY MONETARY COOPERATION IN EUROPE

Integration did not, however, extend to the monetary domain at this early stage. There was some discussion of a single currency in Europe in the early 1950s by France, Belgium, Luxembourg, the United Kingdom and the Netherlands, but this led to nothing. Instead, monetary relations in postwar Europe were heavily conditioned by the general economic imperatives for reconstruction and by the specific influences of three institutions: the Bretton Woods system, the Marshall Plan, and the European Payments Union.

The Bretton Woods system (1944–71) was a fixed exchange rate system designed to stabilize the values of the major Western countries against each other.[5] It was in effect an agreement that governments should intervene in the foreign exchange markets to ensure that currencies were kept within predetermined exchange rate 'bands'. The assumption behind this strategy was that fixed exchange rates – because they stabilize the prices of exports and imports for all participant countries – promote international trade and therefore economic growth. Bretton Woods was a signal that the lessons of the Great Depression (1929–33) – when severe currency turbulence had been associated with a dramatic collapse in world trade, a slump in world output, and rising unemployment almost everywhere – had been learned.

But currency stability alone would not be enough to facilitate the physical and economic recovery of the war-torn countries of Europe. Recognizing this, and mindful of its own security concerns amid the first frosts of the Cold War, the United States agreed a four-year aid package worth $13 billion to underwrite European reconstruction. The initiative became known as the Marshall Plan after the US Secretary of State, George C. Marshall, who proposed it in 1947. To coordinate the distribution of this money, the European recipients established the Committee for European Economic Cooperation (CEEC), the forerunner of today's Organization for Economic Cooperation and Development (OECD).

Marshall aid to Europe was important because it helped to at least address, if not altogether close, a dollar 'gap' that threatened to hold back reconstruction. For at least a decade after the end of the Second World War, the industrial economies were decisively unbalanced. The US emerged from the war in a hugely powerful economic position and found itself producing about half of the

---

[5] Further discussion of the Bretton Woods system can be found in Chapter 2, section 2.2.

entire world's output of goods and services. Although some economies, such as the UK and to a lesser extent France, recovered relatively quickly, the European economies generally were in desperate need of dollars to buy the American and other goods (the dollar was universally acceptable) that would facilitate reconstruction. But Europe itself was initially ill-equipped and unable to export sufficient goods to the US to earn these dollars – hence the dollar gap.

The shortage[6] of dollars had a further consequence: the European economies were loath to make their currencies convertible – that is, free of exchange controls. This was actually required under the Bretton Woods system as a means to promote free and open international trade – one cannot buy an item from a foreign economy without foreign currency – but it proved impracticable until the late 1950s. The British government had made one attempt to institute the convertibility of the pound in 1947, but this was a step it was forced to reverse within weeks as holders of pounds exchanged them in vast quantities for dollars, thus imperilling the pound's value in the Bretton Woods framework.

The absence of convertibility actually left Europe in something of a mess. It was widely agreed that a resumption of international trade was essential to the recovery process, but the European economies were each fearful that their actual trade deficits with the US and potential deficits with each other would sap their gold reserves and call their need for dollars into even more acute focus. The result was an array of intra-European trade control measures – tariffs and quotas on imports – that actively *restricted* trade. Some initiative to unblock European trade and open up foreign exchange markets was sorely needed. An imaginative way forward was agreed in 1950 under the auspices of the CEEC. This, the European Payments Union (EPU), was the first instance of European monetary cooperation in the postwar period.

The EPU allowed economies in trade deficit positions with other members to effectively transfer their liabilities to the EPU itself. These liabilities had to be settled in the end but the EPU extended credit to deficit countries which removed the immediate impulse to engage in trade protection. At the same time, economies in trade surplus received *partial* settlement in gold

---

6 To emphasize the critical nature of the problem, the shortage is sometimes remembered as a 'famine'.

and dollars. Partial settlement was acceptable to economies in persistent trade surplus because their returns were likely to be an improvement on the situation prior to the advent of the EPU when countries were doing all they could to hold on to their gold reserves. In this way the EPU both facilitated currency convertibility and stimulated intra-European trade; a notable achievement at a difficult time. Although it was dissolved in 1959 after a steady improvement in economic conditions allowed the introduction of the general convertibility of Europe's currencies, as the pioneering instance of European monetary cooperation the EPU has been effusively praised: 'It achieved its aim, functioned efficiently . . . and was perhaps the most successful international financial institution ever created' (Scammell, 1987, p. 130).

1.5   INTEGRATION STALLED AND REVIVED IN THE 1950s

Despite the creation of the ECSC and the progress signalled by the EPU, the process of European integration stalled in 1954 over the proposal for a common European Defence Community. The French government had originally introduced the possibility of a European army but then refused to ratify the treaty that would have created it, amid concerns over German rearmament and the lack of British participation in the project. It was at this stage that a joint initiative from the Benelux (Belgium, the Netherlands and Luxembourg) countries rejuvenated the process that within a short space of time would lead to the signing of the Treaty of Rome and the creation of the EEC.

In May 1955 the Benelux group submitted a memorandum to the governments of France, Germany and Italy that proposed using the ECSC model to develop the transport and atomic energy infrastructures of Europe. The scale of investment required in both these areas suggested that a shared approach to their development was the right one. At the same time the memorandum made the case for an economic community defined by a common European internal market. These proposals found a receptive audience in Germany and Italy in particular, and they formed an agenda for a conference of the Six at Messina, Italy in June 1955 which would prove pivotal in shaping the future direction of Europe.

At Messina the Six agreed that their collective interests would best be served by the development of common institutions, the gradual fusion of national economies, the creation of a common market and the harmonization of social policies. These aspirations were fleshed out by an intergovernmental committee chaired by the Belgian foreign minister, Paul-Henri Spaak. The Spaak Committee included British representation for a time, but Britain eventually elected to withdraw before the Committee completed its work.

The Spaak Committee's principal focus was on the detailed and precisely timed measures required to create a customs union for the Six. This would eventually pave the way for a higher level of economic integration – a common market. A customs union involves the elimination of all internal barriers to trade between member states and the establishment of a common external tariff which means that, to the rest of the world, the customs union appears as a unified economic space in the sense that identical trade controls are present at each of its borders. On the other hand, a common market is a customs union that *also* allows the free internal movement of capital and labour: it is, effectively, a fully integrated economy as firms and workers enjoy the same freedoms in other parts of the market as they do in their own national economies. This means, for example, that for a French citizen in a common market of the Six, the economic difference between Paris on the one hand, and Brussels, Milan or Amsterdam on the other, is greatly reduced. His or her rights to invest and work in each are the same.

In 1957, two Treaties of Rome were signed by the Six. One created the European Economic Community (EEC) – Spaak's customs union. The other established the European Atomic Energy Community (known by the abbreviation Euratom), a collective means to secure the development of atomic power for peaceful purposes. Ultimately, Euratom proved rather a disappointment and has recently been dismissed as little more than a 'talking shop' (Gillingham, 2006, p. 76).

The EEC on the other hand has been the undoubted driver of European integration since 1957. Following Spaak, the Treaty of Rome was permissive in the sense that it both established the immediate timetable for the customs union but also looked forward to future developments in the integration process, particularly the creation of a common market. What of monetary integration? The Spaak Committee had not been entirely silent on monetary matters. It had determined that the Six should, in the context of the potential problems posed by balance-of-payments imbalances, 'establish a closer cooperation among their central banks'.[7] This theme was developed in Article 105 of the Treaty of Rome which laid down, in addition, that member states of the EEC 'shall coordinate their economic policies', while Article 107 decreed that the Six should regard their exchange rates as 'a matter of common concern'. To facilitate deeper economic cooperation, the Treaty also established a permanent intergovernmental Monetary Committee. The detailed form that such cooperation might assume was left undetermined but – as we shall discuss in Chapter 2 – by the end of the 1960s the contours of monetary integration in Europe would begin to become more clearly and much more ambitiously defined.

The creation of the EEC was a remarkable achievement for countries that had previously demonstrated only a deep and lasting mutual hostility. European integration clearly has its genesis in politics – as a means of reaching accommodations with neighbours that had often previously been imposed through grievous conflict. By 1957 it was clear that Europe was looking to its *economic* future, too. Yet the ECSC had resolved the German problem, so why go further? The answer lies in the aspirations of the Continent for growth and prosperity. The Benelux initiative which led to the revival of the integration process at Messina and through the work of the Spaak Committee was as much about forging a better economics in Europe as it was about politics. The customs union – leading to a common market – would be a way for Europeans to collectively assert their economic presence in the postwar world and thereby enhance their prospects for economic growth and higher living standards. This would of course take time but in the end a greatly enlarged Community would have within its grasp a common market and, moreover, one topped off with the ultimate material imprimatur of economic singularity: a common currency. We consider the first concrete steps taken towards the latter in the next chapter.

The present chapter concludes with an interview with the renowned economic historian Nick Crafts.

---

[7] Information Service High Authority of the ECSC (1956), *The Brussels Report on the General Common Market*, Luxembourg: ECSC, p. 16 (unofficial translation, unofficially referred to as the Spaak Report).

NICK CRAFTS

Nick Crafts is Professor of Economic History at the University of Warwick, UK. He is generally recognized as one of the world's leading economic historians and has written on a wide range of subjects including economic development and growth in Europe, and the world economy, in the nineteenth and twentieth centuries.

We interviewed Professor Crafts in his office at the University of Warwick on 15 January 2007.

To what extent does the key to understanding the origins of the long process of European economic and political integration since the end of the Second World War lie in Europe's war-torn history?
I think that it is fairly clearly the case that the pioneers were interested in doing a better job of making the peace than had been achieved after World War I. The Treaty of Versailles, for example, was not a great result. Aside from reining-in Germany, people also recognized that they needed German economic success in order to make a success of the reconstruction of postwar Europe. They wanted something that would increase the chances of peaceful behaviour by Germany and also involve economic growth, not reparations. That was not the attitude of the communists, but it was the attitude of the West. I also see it as a reaction, more generally, to what I call the interwar globalization backlash. This involves recognition, by quite a lot of people, that the Depression and the protectionism that it had given rise to was basically economically damaging. People were looking for structures to try to obviate that and to move away from that as peace progressed.

How significant was the establishment of the European Coal and Steel Community in 1952?
I think it was important in so far as it represents an important piece of cooperation and one that seems to have been successful. I think that in all these reform processes it is important to start with a winner if you possibly can. Having said that, in terms of anything that is massively transformational as far as Europe is concerned, it is more of a footnote to history. It was much more important as a harbinger of other things to come rather than being important in and of itself.

You have referred to the period 1950–73 as the 'golden age of economic growth in Western Europe' (Crafts, 1995). To what extent was this

period of unusually rapid growth and catch-up contingent on circum-
stances at the time?
I do think that it is reasonable to think of those years as the golden age of European growth. Growth was very rapid and, this time, Europe did catch up with the US. Again the contrast with the post-World War I period is quite marked. The scope for catch-up is clearly enhanced by the fact that Europe has fallen further behind and there are a number of changes which will give rise to quite big productivity growth. These are again along the lines of correcting the mistakes of the past. That includes the fact that protectionism had left a large agricultural sector that could be reduced by sensible policies. Labour could be transferred elsewhere in the economy, and so on. The potential for catch-up also involves an element of institutional reform. It certainly involves the adoption of what we might broadly call 'good policies'. Although the evidence is a bit thin, I think that catch-up is significantly advanced by good macroeconomic arrangements. The Bretton Woods agreement was, broadly speaking, capable of promoting trade and it did help avoid any repetition of 1929. That was important to achieving and sustaining catch-up. I don't believe myself that catch-up is automatic. It has to be contingent on something. I think, as you say, the initial circumstances have some favourable elements. The policy decisions that are made are broadly better than on the previous occasion and are capable of increasing the incentive to invest. Investment has to be a key feature of the catch-up process. Broadly speaking, circumstances also start to be more conducive to technology transfer into Europe than they had been earlier.

The process of European market integration began when the six found-
ing members of the ECSC signed the Treaty of Rome in 1957. To what
extent was the driving force for European unity as much political as eco-
nomic at this time?
I'm not sure that I'm well qualified to answer that. Other people have better expertise than me on this issue. I think that the features we were talking about a little while ago are there: the desire to enmesh Germany, especially in close relations with other countries; and seeing things like trading relations as some kind of way of reducing the chance of future conflict. I think there is also, however, clear recognition that Europe has not been well served by protectionism and that this is a way, on a regional basis, of reducing protectionism. Then what you have to think about is the

sort of deal which would do that in terms of keeping both France and Germany there. A deal that involves a reduction in French industrial protectionism. But in return we got what eventually became the Common Agricultural Policy and recognition that there would be no free trade in agriculture.

To what extent do you think that market integration in Europe in the 1950s and 1960s contributed to the growth of the 'Six' during this period?
I think that it did, but I'm not sure that at this point in time we have great quantification of exactly what the numbers are. The best papers recently include ones by Badinger [Badinger and Breuss, 2004; Badinger, 2005]. Those papers suggest that the long-run story, over say three or four decades, is that various forms of trade liberalization – including things which were more under the GATT [General Agreement on Tariffs and Trade] than simply European arrangements – might have raised European income levels by something like 25 per cent. The argument is that it is more a level's story than a growth rate story. But nevertheless that will certainly show up in extra growth over some measured, finite period of time. If you think about what the story is that we want eventually to quantify then I don't think that it is just the simple textbook stuff that I was taught as an undergraduate in international economics, where you've got welfare triangles, gains from comparative advantage and so on. I think that quite an important part of the story in Europe is intensification of competition. In other words it is much closer to a new international economics story. I'm thinking about books like John Adams's (1989) book on French industry and the importance he attaches to greater competition as trade barriers come down in putting a lot of pressure on sleepy firms to become more efficient.

Looking at it the other way I think it is quite striking how high price–cost margins were and how high tariff barriers remained in Britain, which stayed outside the Six until the 1970s. If I were telling a story about Britain's relative failure during the golden age I'd include that as part of the story. The problems you look at in Britain include badly managed firms, where the shareholders aren't good at controlling managers. You ask yourself: what are the market processes of competition which might limit the scope for managerial failure? I think they are weaker in Britain typically than they were in the countries that joined the Six. I'm not sure that we can quantify that perfectly, but some of the work I've been doing in the last several years has been trying to put some numbers on that. I'm fairly sure that the price–cost margin story is right – that they are much higher in Britain than in countries like Germany. I'm also fairly sure that we can say that as late as 1970, tariff protection for the British economy is about as high as it was in 1930. Liberalization came quite late in the day, though we need more research on that.

In hindsight, what was the significance of the Werner Plan?
I don't really know. [*Laughter*] I suppose there is a long sequence of daydreams. I recall teaching a course in the mid-1970s on the EEC, which was roughly when the MacDougall Report [EC Commission, 1977] came out on European Public Finance. It essentially argued that if you wanted to implement some sort of progress towards European monetary union and you were think-ing of something along the lines of the ERM [exchange rate mechanism], then if you took away the devaluation possibility you would need other stabilizers because you couldn't trust labour markets to work very well. You would therefore need an enhanced social safety net and the argument involved looking at the EEC compared with the United States. The US as a federal entity is in a position to generate transfer payments from the centre. Nevertheless, through the 1970s what you got is a situ-ation, after Bretton Woods breaks down, in which broadly speak-ing European countries are very worried about exchange rates floating too much inside. You can see that in all sorts of trivial ways. The difficulties of running the agricultural support systems was one which got flagged up at the time. Floating exchange rates are difficult to operate for countries which have high proportions of trade with their neighbours. So I think Europe is, from the end of Bretton Woods, continuously on the look-out for some sort of model which will allow exchange rates to be pretty stable or indeed ultimately completely fixed within Europe. There is then an issue as to exactly how irrevocable that is going to be made. Also there are issues at what point could we create a European central bank. The long-run desire for relatively fixed exchange rates inside the EU seems to me to be very pow-erful from an early stage.

You have produced papers (e.g., Crafts, 1996; Broadberry and Crafts, 1996), which look at, inter alia, *the relationship between UK growth and the policy choices made by British governments since 1945. Is there any reason to think that some of these choices might have been better ones had the UK participated more fully and consistently in the European monetary integration project?*

Let me say first of all that, generally speaking, the conduct of UK macroeconomic policy has been quite poor, at least until the 1990s. You could ask: when was there something potentially on offer, which might have looked a bit better? The issue came to a head in the 1980s as European countries joined the ERM. They tried to instil more discipline into their macroeconomic policy by an arrangement whereby, in effect, they let the Bundesbank stabilize things for them. From the 1970s, through to the early 1980s, Britain does seem to have had a very volatile environment. It doesn't succeed in generating a settled macroeconomic policy arrangement as we go through the MTFS [Medium-Term Financial Strategy], shadowing the Deutschmark, the ERM and the Ken and Eddie show.[8] Broadly speaking quite a lot of us thought at the time that supply-side reforms, which had at last been made in the Thatcher period, had less impact on things like investment than they might because macroeconomic policy had been run badly. I wrote a little pamphlet [Crafts, 1998] on the Conservative government's record when they lost office which did in effect say that macroeconomic policy had been their Achilles' heel. What I wonder about now is whether that story is oversold. Under the current arrangements – with an independent central bank and inflation targeting – the economy has probably been more stable than its peer group both in terms of volatility of GDP and in living memory. Despite this we haven't seen any big revival in business investment. The business investment fraction has broadly speaking looked a bit disappointing. Of course there are some big technical issues about what has been happening to the price of capital goods. Nevertheless, after 10 years of this independent central bank experiment, if anything the evidence is pushing a bit towards the view that macroeconomic stability is not quite as important for investment and long-run growth as has sometimes been portrayed. Now if that is right then alternative macroeconomic arrangements earlier in the postwar period would have made less difference.

---

[8] Kenneth Clarke was the Chancellor of the Exchequer and Eddie George was Governor of the Bank of England.

What I would also have to think quite hard about is whether
Britain was actually a particularly good potential member of what
was on offer in the 1980s. That would be the other line of argument.
As it turned out, when we did eventually start to become a quasi-
member of the ERM in 1986/1987 we found we had difficulties.
Arguably we chose the wrong exchange rate and we found ourselves in a situation where German interest rates didn't necessarily always suit us. In the context of Thatcher's reforms it did seem
to me to be slightly odd that in his Mais Lecture, around 1984,
Nigel Lawson effectively said that what we need is to use fiscal
policy for the supply side and monetary policy for macro demand
management, because to start shadowing the ERM means that you
are going to revert more to fiscal policy as your stabilization tool.
My bottom line is that I prefer a separate currency with an independent bank – our present arrangement – to any of the things that
were on offer before. But I have increasingly started to doubt that
the difference between the amount of instability we saw in the past
and the relative stability recently experienced necessarily makes a
huge lot of difference to developing productive potential.

In other words macroeconomic stability is a necessary but not a
sufficient condition for achieving high and sustained economic growth.
Sure.

Do you think a common money has the potential to improve the policy
choices – or limit the policy mistakes – of all eurozone members?
A common currency is clearly one way of acquiring macroeconomic discipline, provided that you establish an appropriate
framework for the central bank to operate within. We are hopeful
that we know more about that than we used to in the context of
an inflation-targeting regime. Having said that, there are clearly
difficulties at the European level of integrating monetary and
fiscal policy. The Stability and Growth Pact has clearly not
worked as some of its proponents had originally hoped it would.
It remains a bit unclear to me what exactly might supersede it in
the medium to long run. There are good reasons to think that
inflation targeting run by an independent central bank has got
quite a lot going for it. But at the European level there are some
difficulties in implementing that well. It's fairly clear if we go
back 15 or 20 years that a number of countries had very weak
central banks and were quite bad at controlling inflation. If you
think about other things that go with the common currency I

suppose the most obvious thing – aside from macroeconomic discipline – is the potential for enhanced trade. I guess that has various potential welfare gains associated with it and maybe that potential is quite large. In so far as things strengthen the single market, broadly speaking, they are reducing on balance somewhat the scope for governments to screw up supply-side policy. There are some small gains there.

The Single Internal Market programme was conceived in the early 1980s when European growth was relatively poor compared to the United States and Japan. How do you account for Europe's comparatively weak performance at that time?
I would take slight issue with part of your question. While I would agree that Europe's performance was weak relative to Japan, I am not sure it was that weak relative to the US. Perhaps my memory is deceiving me. Having said that I do tend to work on longer time blocks. So if we were looking at 1973–95, which is a conventional break-off period, Europe is still growing as quickly as the US. I am certainly inclined to say that the single market was encouraged by the notion that there had been gains in economic performance from the earlier liberalizations, in terms of the original move towards free trade in manufactures within Europe. There were, however, a number of gaps in that liberalization process and reason to believe that liberalizing along the lines of a single market could produce income gains. You could also say that quite a big part of the story is that with larger markets you would eventually move to larger-scale production. There were productivity gains to be had from rationalization and realization of economies of scale, by removing various non-tariff barriers to trade. That was, in the end, quite well quantified in the context of the Cecchini Report [1988]. Reading between the lines of the Report it seems clear they were imagining that the biggest gains would come from the exit of a lot of existing producers. I remember an Economist Intelligence Report at the time on pharmaceuticals which said 10 of the 12 countries were producing pharmaceuticals, but that if the internal market worked effectively at the most there would be two.

How important has the Single Internal Market programme been in raising economic growth in the EU?
I think its effect has probably been quite modest. The European Commission's assessment suggests that the will wasn't there to

fully implement it in terms of allowing full rationalization to take place and in terms of the rapid introduction of policies compliant with the single market. If we believe the Cecchini Report's original guess that the level of GDP might be raised by 6–7 per cent and then look at what the European Commission thought afterwards might have been achieved, we are talking half of that, or thereabouts. Over a 10-year period, if you translate that into growth rates, it's modest.

Are further market or microeconomic reforms in the EU necessary if the potential benefits of the euro are to be fully realized?
There is clearly scope for considerably more supply-side reforms, and if that were to take place whatever gains there are from the euro in creating a stronger single market would tend to be larger rather than smaller. In other words the evidence suggests that these things are complementary, they are not substitutes for one another. So if we work along the lines that they are complements I guess one could think of quite a number of supply-side reforms which one would like to take place. One very obvious one would be to take protection away from agriculture or at least substantially reform the CAP [Common Agricultural Policy]. It is fairly clear that we could do with many member governments pursuing further labour market reform, though much of that is handled on a subsidiarity basis as it stands. One of the weaknesses of the European integration process is that it is not at all easy to try to pull together product and labour market reforms. It is also very clear from the research that various people have done that there is considerable scope for further reform in services and that the potential gains from liberalization and greater competition in services are potentially quite large. The biggest successes of European integration, in terms of producing a genuinely single market, have been in manufacturing. Yet our economies are now relatively heavily service-sector orientated, and that is where reforms need to take place.

Can a single market of more than 30 European economies function effectively?
I think there are different ways of conceptualizing that question. If you are asking, do I think that 30 countries represent something like an optimum currency area, then the answer is no. If I am right on that proposition and the EU is not an optimum currency area then that limits the gains from integration. It is still unclear how

big the trade gains are from a currency union. I doubt that anyone still believes the original results that Andrew Rose [2000] came up with seven or eight years ago. Nevertheless, some of the results cited in the literature are still quite big, if they turn out to be right. If you think about other propositions I guess the issue then turns on how much harder it is to make reforms, which would strengthen the single market process, in a union of 30 countries. That remains to be seen.

It is clear that, like many other people, you are far from convinced that the EU is close to being an optimal currency area. Do you see the benefits of EMU [economic and monetary union] more in terms of strengthening the single market programme?
If some of the research, post Andrew Rose, which still claims quite big gains is correct, then perhaps the most important aspect of EMU is that it strengthens trade within the member countries of the European community. I do think that there is evidence to suggest that borders in Europe – particularly borders between say the original 15 and the accession countries who joined three years ago – matter. The international trade story of border effects being there, and being perceptible in gravity models, are quite clear in the estimates for the early twenty-first century. Despite having moved ostensibly to a very free trade arrangement with those countries, trade still seems to be inhibited by borders. That does suggest that there are some potential gains there, as noted by the guys who emphasize currency union as trade promoting. That remains a strong possibility.

What policy lessons, for the accession economies in terms of catch-up, can we learn from economic historians' research on West Europe's growth experience?
I think we can generally argue that West Europe's growth was facilitated by having, what in standard World Bank speak are, good institutions. The accession process has on the whole produced institutional reforms which, if they are genuine, would look like they are favourable to becoming more like their West European peer group. If we look at standard ways of summarizing that, we start to see scores for things like adherence to the rule of law increasing, scores for corruption improving, and so on. In a sense what you would like is for the typical Central or East European country to look more like the characterization of Northern Italy compared to Southern Italy. The accession process

has to an extent been a working form of conditionality. Quite an important lesson was perhaps learned that such a process should have been applied to Greece before it joined the Community. Greece is the one country of all whose growth performance following accession is extremely poor for at least 15 years until the late 1990s. The West European story is broadly speaking that institutions need to be okay; also that trade integration on average is favourable. This is something that European accession countries should continue to follow.

The thing which is slightly unsure is the extent we would see across Europe as a whole the experience of European integration entirely being one of convergence, as opposed to a combination of some areas which do converge to the levels of prosperity at the centre and others which seem to be left behind. There are worries for some areas in Europe of it being a divergent rather than a convergent process. In that context, some countries would be well advised to look at how Ireland made a success of this project. If you think back 20 or 30 years I can remember reading lots of things about Ireland being a peripheral, disadvantaged country, far from the golden crescent in Europe. In the Irish case it would seem that some combination of quite good policy reforms and membership of the EU have turned out actually to be highly growth promoting. The slightly questionable aspect of that is the issue of how easy it is to replicate. Ireland happened upon a particular good selection of industries which it attracted with FDI [foreign direct investment]. It is very close to the United States and that may have helped this process of establishing American FDI in Ireland. Ireland was also very aggressive with its corporate taxes. Whether the Irish route remains open to others remains to be seen.

What is your view of the functioning of the European labour market, in comparison, say, to that of the United States?
If we look at European countries on average then it seems pretty clear that they have higher unemployment than in the US. They have higher NAIRUs [non-accelerating inflation rates of unemployment]; they have more long-term unemployment and more, what used to be referred to as, structural unemployment. That's not true of every country in the EU. People like Steve Nickell keep reminding us that the European unemployment problem is at its most severe in a few big European countries. In other countries, labour markets seem to work rather better. Those labour market

problems are relatively recent and have occurred over the last 25 years – this is recent to an economic historian [*Laughter*] – but it certainly wasn't the case in the 'golden age'. If you look at the catch-up process, Western Europe on average in the early 1970s, relative to the US, is roughly where it is now in terms of GDP per person. Since then we have narrowed the gap on average by quite a lot in terms of GDP per hour worked, but fewer hours are worked. Some of that is about holidays and some of it is about unemployment or lower labour force participation. I think we have some worries about the European labour market, especially unemployment. If you are to make a success of the EU in the context of greater globalization then almost certainly that is going to involve not only sectoral but also spatial adjustments. That gets us to ask how mobile European workers are and all the evidence suggests that they are less mobile within the EU than American workers are in the US. We need to worry about long-term unemployment and that maps down into some areas where we have very high regional unemployment as well. That suggests to me that labour market flexibility falls quite a long way short of what would be ideal for an optimum currency area.

Do you think that one market requires one money? For example, the UK is committed to the single market, but not as yet to the euro.
Although you can have a substantial amount of market integration with separate currencies, I do think that the degree of market integration is greater with one money. With separate currencies the evidence still seems to be that there are things like border effects which are there and which matter. So the answer has to be that the degree of integration is less with separate currencies.

The UK, Denmark and Sweden are all 'advanced' EU economies that have, so far, chosen to remain outside the eurozone. Do you think this is a good decision for these economies?
For the UK – which is the only economy I am really qualified to answer your question – the pressure to join the euro from an economic, as opposed to a political point of view, was clearly significantly reduced by the innovation of the MPC [Monetary Policy Committee] and the independence of the Bank of England, in the sense that there was now an alternative game in town. By that I mean that there was something that did look like a relatively plausible and credible way of controlling inflation. Indeed macroeconomic management, in the way the MPC has operated

through inflation targeting, has broadly speaking not added to
the instability of aggregate demand.

Rather, there has been an element of favourable aggregate
demand management about their interest decisions, and overall
their framework hasn't interfered with counter-cyclical policy. In
one way or another the UK experience has been relatively benign
under the alternative arrangement. That isn't intended to imply
that the ECB [European Central Bank] has been managing things
badly. The UK has had from the macroeconomic management
point of view what looks like, to the moment, a viable alternative.
If you then start to ask what would be the losses from being out,
my guess is that they do turn on these trade arrangements. The
thing that did strike me on reading HM Treasury's assessment is
that HM Treasury actually does seem to sign up to this view. I do
think that if you were to seriously believe that evidence then it
would be quite hard to think that you shouldn't join. There was
quite a good IMF [International Monetary Fund] working paper
about three years ago that two guys did which sets this out as a
kind of cost–benefit calculation [Cottarelli and Escolano, 2004].
The logic of that paper does seem quite compelling if you think
that the empirics, which the Treasury seems to believe, are
correct. Despite the fact that the macroeconomic argument has to
some extent gone away, the integration argument may still be
there and it may be the relatively powerful one.

*Has the development of institutions been important to achieving the
agenda of greater European economic and political integration?*
Undoubtedly. The rules of the game, as established by various
European treaties, have in effect pointed to greater European
integration and reduced member governments' discretion. I am
thinking essentially along policy lines linked to competition
policy, state aids and the implementation of greater trade flows
within Europe. A lot of the stuff there seems to me to be very
helpful in that it gets much closer to tying member governments'
hands. In terms of institutions which are more to do with macroeconomic policy, the design of the EMU project as a whole
worries me a bit, especially in the context of what we should do
about fiscal policy in this framework. I suppose it is an interesting experiment to have a single central bank but with still quite a
lot of really strong fiscal authorities around Europe. There are
worries there in the end about how fiscal and monetary policy
might interact. I think there are some questions about how

successful the design of the single currency arrangements has been. That said I don't think at this stage you could say anything that has transpired has been in any way particularly damaging to European growth. I would myself worry about a Europe in which the public sector became enormously large.

What threats and opportunities are posed for the eurozone by its possible further enlargement?
I guess the bigger it is the harder it is to believe that one size fits all in terms of interest rates. There are clearly worries about – for relatively fast-growing accession economies, which might be amongst the more obvious of the next members of the eurozone – how a common currency arrangement would really suit them. It is not obvious, for example, that it has suited Ireland particularly well. Ireland has probably had more inflation than it would have had outside the eurozone. That might also be the experience for some of the new members. Of course, membership of the eurozone may be about other sorts of signals being given. But if you restrict it simply to the question of whether it is likely to give better macroeconomic performance for new members who are likely to join, I am not entirely sure that it will. Does it make things a lot better or worse for existing members? Well, it's adding to integration so we are back to trade gains. The thing I would focus on most is whether it is likely to be good for the new countries who join and I think that is questionable. Some could join too soon and could find that it makes things more difficult.

Taking the long view, what has been the key driver in the history of European integration – is it best explained by the need for European economic and political reform, or by the contingent appearance of people like Schuman, Monnet, and Delors? Is it structure or agency, or both?
In the long view it has to be structure. I'd be inclined to think that those individuals were probably quite important catalysts in that they affected the timing over a short period. If we go back to some of the things we talked about earlier in terms of the desire for a peaceful Europe and the desire for a much better standard of living through economic integration, those are the things which have tended to drive the process of integration forward. What one has tended to see is that as the project rolls along a phase takes place and it seems to create the opportunity and/or need for a further phase. So we get a phase of trade liberalization that doesn't include services. The service sector then starts to become

a much more important part of the European economy overall and it seems sensible to start to try and reform there. We realize that we can strengthen a single market by having a single currency. We recognize that as we integrate there are more externalities, more spillovers, that we need to deal with. That starts to create pressures for institutions which will operate at a somewhat different level of governance than previously. I would be looking for those kinds of thrusts over several decades, rather than particularly highlighting individuals like Jacques Delors. Individuals may have affected the speed at which things happen, but I doubt that they have affected hugely the long-run trajectory.

What is your view of the overall significance of the euro? Can it make a potentially important contribution to the future prosperity of Europe, or, on the other hand, are its weaknesses too pronounced?
I'd be inclined to think that it can potentially contribute. I'd be keen to believe that it does strengthen European integration and that it gives rise to stronger trade, which is likely to be welfare increasing for Europe as a whole. I have mentioned some worries I have about the design of some of the euro arrangements. Nevertheless, I think that for the moment it is reasonable to hope that even though those flaws are there, they are not so profound to cause serious macroeconomic instability. My guess is that macroeconomic management through the ECB will work well enough that it doesn't get seriously in the way of realizing those gains from greater trade.

2. Before the euro: the first steps in the process of monetary integration

2.1 INTRODUCTION

Although the euro – launched on 1 January 1999 – represents a new phase in European monetary cooperation, the economic and political ideas behind the single currency in Europe have a lengthy history. The Werner Report (1970),[9] adopted by the then original six European Economic Community (EEC) members in 1971, and named after Pierre Werner, the president and finance minister of Luxembourg who led the group that produced it, outlined a strategy to achieve monetary integration in Europe either through a single currency or irrevocably locked separate national currencies by 1980 – two decades before the birth of the euro. Although monetary union did not occur *then*, an examination of the Werner Report, its subsequent derailment, and the course of monetary cooperation in Europe in the interval prior to the birth of the euro is still instructive. The purpose of the present chapter is to outline the somewhat halting process of monetary integration before the euro.

2.2 THE BARRE MEMORANDUM

The economic rationale behind the Werner Report was to provide a monetary means to cement together the markets of the 'Six' participants in the customs union established by the Treaty of Rome (1957). Werner was itself the culmination of a series of reflections on the nature of the relationship between the development of a unified market in Europe and the kind of wider policy framework that would support such a market. The basic concern here

---

[9] 'Report to the Council and the Commission on the Realization by Stages of Economic and Monetary Union in the Community', 8 October 1970.

was that while the Six had been very successful in promoting intra-Community trade and general economic growth, they had not made any great cooperative and complementary steps in the conduct of macroeconomic policy.[10] Was this a problem? As early as 1962 the European Commission had suggested that it might be, but the clearest determination that it actually was – and one that paved the way for Werner – came with the 1969 publication of the Barre Memorandum.[11] This clarified the Commission's positions on 'the need for fuller alignment of economic policies in the Community' and 'the scope for intensifying monetary co-operation'. The central message of the Barre Memorandum was unmistakable: the Community could not stop the integration project at the point it had then reached. The fruits of market integration in faster economic growth and rising European living standards were clear but – and it was a big but – the destabilizing and divergent international macroeconomic forces that were evident by the late 1960s might force the Six apart and thereby undermine all that they had together so far achieved. What precisely were these potentially divisive forces?

To answer this question we need to take in a little international context; in particular we need to know something about the international monetary arrangements prevailing at the time. Today there is no overarching international monetary system governing the world's currencies: thus, for example, the dollar, the yen and the euro float in value against one another in the markets for foreign exchange. Their respective exchange rates – simply the price of one currency expressed in terms of another – are determined, like any other price, by the forces of demand and supply. Driven by such market forces, exchange rates change continuously, minute by minute, hour by hour and day by day. But it was not always so. From the end of the Second World War until its collapse in 1971, international monetary arrangements were governed by the *Bretton Woods system*. Bretton Woods[12] was an agreement by the world's major capitalist economies to intervene in foreign exchange markets to maintain exchange rates at

---

[10] The EU's own estimate is that by 1970 intra-Community trade had grown sixfold since the signing of the Treaty of Rome. The Community's economy, expanding more rapidly than that of the US, had also doubled in size.

[11] 'Commission Memorandum to the Council on the Co-ordination of Economic Policies and Monetary Co-operation Within the Community', submitted 12 February 1969.

[12] The name is taken from the mountain resort in New Hampshire in the US where the system was negotiated.

appropriate levels; so, for example, the price of the dollar in terms of the British pound or the French franc would be steady and highly predictable. The point of this was to promote international trade (trade is more straightforward when the prices of foreign goods are stable) and therefore economic growth. Currency stability was also highly prized as a means of avoiding the kind of economic turbulence experienced in the late 1920s and early 1930s that had culminated in the Great Depression.

The six members of the EEC were also participants in the Bretton Woods system which meant that their currencies were 'fixed' against one another, and against all other currencies inside the system. The Six therefore enjoyed both intra-market openness and mutual exchange rate stability – a winning combination that helped to explain the noted and notable expansions in European trade and economic growth. Unfortunately, however, by the late 1960s the Bretton Woods system was beginning to show signs of considerable strain and this posed a dilemma for the Six. Should the Bretton Woods system fail they would still, courtesy of the Treaty of Rome, have an integrated market but the currencies that underpinned it would no longer be fixed against one another; the clear danger was that currency instability for the Six could threaten the very considerable collective economic progress they had made since 1957. To give a simple example, the growing integration of the French and German economies would be unlikely to proceed so smoothly in the presence of severe and unpredictable oscillations between the franc and the mark.

Why then was the Bretton Woods system in trouble? Its major difficulty centred on the central role assumed in the system by the US dollar. In 1944, when the system was created, the US economy was economically dominant. It accounted for about half the world's GDP and two-thirds of the world's reserves of gold. The Bretton Woods agreement fixed the price of gold at $32 per ounce and all other countries then tied their own currencies to the dollar or gold. The intention behind the gold-backed dollar was to eliminate the possibility that excessive inflation could arise in the system through the irresponsible printing of money by any of the system's members. This arrangement established the dollar as the hinge on which Bretton Woods turned. Initially, this was of little concern given the sheer scale, resources and productive capacity of the US economy. However, by the late 1950s and especially the mid-1960s the US began to accumulate large debts to the rest of the capitalist world as it spent huge sums of money on, for example, the prosecution of the Vietnam war. The Belgian economist Robert Triffin summarized the danger that this growing overseas spending and indebtedness posed in what became known as the *Triffin dilemma*.

The Triffin dilemma was expressed as follows. On the one hand, US spending in the rest of the world was viewed as a positive thing as it provided a pool of dollars outside the US which could be used to finance trade and fuel economic growth the world over; the dollar was the world's key currency and uniquely acceptable everywhere. However, on the other hand, the size of the dollar pool raised questions about the currency's convertibility into gold and suggested a growing confidence problem for the dollar that could only be eased if US spending overseas was dramatically reduced. Thus there was a dollar confidence crisis looming if US spending overseas continued, and a world liquidity crisis likely if US spending was curtailed: a dilemma indeed. In the event, the US continued to spend, prompting feverish speculation against the dollar and other currencies that were perceived to be overvalued. Market sentiment shifted decisively in favour of more robust currencies such as the German mark. In the presence of such disruptive forces, currency stability in Europe was likely to be undermined. For the Six, the crunch came in 1968 and 1969 when, amid wider concerns over the integrity of the system, the Bretton Woods parities established for the French franc and the mark became unsustainable: in the face of destabilizing speculation on the foreign exchange markets, the franc was devalued and the mark revalued. Currency turbulence for the EEC had arrived; this was clearly very unwelcome but what, if anything, could be done about it?[13]

This was the question to which the Barre Memorandum was formulating a preliminary answer. Barre's conclusion was that the weaknesses of the Bretton Woods system and its evident inability to ward off crises in the foreign exchange markets demanded that the EEC pursue a course that would allow it to deepen monetary and widen macroeconomic policy cooperation, and thereby achieve a greater degree of mutual stability than might otherwise be possible. Although this view was couched in language that did

---

[13] Gray (2006) supplies some nice anecdotes that hint at how turbulent matters in Europe had actually become. He reports that the avalanche of speculation in favour of the mark in the first three weeks of November 1968 prompted airports in Germany to limit currency exchanges to a maximum of one hundred francs; while train stations in Zurich refused to accept francs at all.

not assume that Bretton Woods was doomed (it actually collapsed in 1971), it did imply that the EEC thought it prudent to begin to build for itself some alternative economic policy and monetary structure. The Barre Memorandum sketched out the generalities of what this might look like in three parts.

In the first place it proposed that thought be given to the 'concert' of *medium-term economic policies*. This translated into an aspiration that there should be the beginnings of some Community-level awareness of the macroeconomic issues confronting each of the member countries with a view, ultimately, to 'improving the synchronization of the national programmes and strengthening the links between them'. Second, Barre concluded that there needed to be better coordination of *short-term economic policies*, particularly national budget proposals, the implementation of which might affect the short-term economic conditions in *other* member states. Presumably, this was at least in part a reference to the dangers of triggering destabilizing currency speculation. Third and finally, Barre proposed the creation of '*Community machinery for monetary co-operation*'. This was to be a *system* for the provision of mutual short- and medium-term monetary support to Community members in balance-of-payments and currency difficulties. Short-term funds could be used to confront immediate crises and support vulnerable currencies; more extensive medium-term loans would be available to address deeper structural problems. The system would sit alongside and complement the proposed arrangements for the coordination of Community macroeconomic policies.

Barre, then, was an agenda for the development of collective economic policy for the Community in the face of recently experienced exchange rate instability and – given the unresolved Triffin dilemma – the likelihood of more of the same as the Bretton Woods system continued to creak. The Barre proposals were quickly and enthusiastically taken up at a Community Heads of State and Government summit in The Hague in December 1969 which agreed that a plan for economic and monetary union for the Six should be drawn up over the course of the following year. The European Council determined in June 1970 that a timescale for union of the remainder of the decade was appropriate and, when it produced its final report in October 1970, the Werner group judged this objective within reach. With the formal adoption of the Werner Report in March 1971, Europe was on a timetable for monetary union by 1980.

2.3 THE WERNER REPORT

The Werner Report (1970, p. 9) was in no doubt as to the advantages that deeper integration would yield:

> Economic and monetary union will make it possible to realize an area in which goods and services, people and capital will circulate freely and without competitive distortions, without thereby giving rise to structural or regional disequilibrium.
>
> The implementation of such a union will effect a lasting improvement in welfare in the Community and will reinforce the contribution of the Community to economic and monetary equilibrium in the world.

This clearly prefigures the one market–one money argument for the euro, but it is interesting to note that Werner did not actually consider a new *single* currency absolutely necessary. The convertibility of existing currencies with no fluctuations in rates of exchange and the free movement of capital would probably be all that was required – thus the Belgian franc would never again move against the Italian lire, tellers in exchange booths in German airports could no longer be snooty about the French franc (see footnote 13), and so on. However, the Report also accepted that the emergence of a new single currency might well be desirable for psychological and political reasons in that it would symbolize the irreversibility of the project.

Werner recognized that monetary union demanded the centralization of monetary policy in the Community. It would not be feasible to allow, for example, interest rates to vary between member countries as this would make the alignment of currencies at agreed parities impossible to sustain. Higher interest rates in one member country would be likely to increase the demand for its currency on the foreign exchanges and drive up its price; while lower interest rates in another country would reduce the demand for its currency and lower its price: the two currencies would almost inevitably move apart. Werner proposed that a pan-European monetary policy should be conducted through a 'Community system for central banks' – what might be thought of today as a forerunner of the European Central Bank.

The Report also proposed the creation of a 'centre for decision for economic policy'. The ambition was that this body would exert a 'decisive influence over the general economic policy of the Community'; in particular it needed to be able to condition national fiscal policies. As we explain in our discussion of the Stability and Growth Pact in Chapter 4, section 4.2, it is not feasible to conduct monetary policy at a supranational level while allowing national governments in a monetary union *complete* discretion over fiscal policy. One or more irresponsible or profligate governments could generate serious macroeconomic disturbances for the whole union.

The Werner Report also envisaged a *gradual* movement towards monetary union. Thus monetary policy, and in particular the setting of interest rates, would become more uniform over time. Similarly, exchange rate stability inside the Community would be improved by first limiting internal currency fluctuations to margins narrower than those prevailing for Community currencies against the dollar (inside the then still-existing Bretton Woods system), and then by still-narrower internal margins according to circumstances. Ultimately, there would be no further possibility of movement for Community currencies: they would be permanently locked and monetary union would then prevail. To provide the necessary support for interest rate coordination and direct intervention in the foreign exchange markets, the Werner Report – following Barre – proposed the creation of a European Monetary Co-operation Fund: a pool of financial resources on which all members could draw (the Fund was established in 1973).

In summary, then, the Werner Report envisaged a steady almost decade-long movement towards European economic and monetary union. This process would embrace the centralization of monetary policy in a new institutional setting and a new Community-level institution which would decisively condition the fiscal policies of member states. Such arrangements – together with the collective financial resources provided by the new European Monetary Co-operation Fund – would facilitate the gradual alignment of Community exchange rates to the point at which they could be irrevocably locked. This was the economics of the new Europe but Werner was not innocent as to its *political* implications. The Report recognized that economic and monetary union would involve a redistribution of sovereignty away from individual member states and towards collective representation at Community level. This was both inevitable and also, according to Werner (p. 12), desirable:

[O]n the plane of *institutional reforms* the realization of economic and monetary union demands the creation or the transformation of a certain number of Community organs to which powers until then exercised by the national authorities will have to be transferred. These transfers of responsibility represent a process of fundamental political significance which implies the progressive development of political co-operation. Economic and monetary union thus appears as a leaven for the development of political union, which in the long run it cannot do without. (Emphasis in original)

The reader may recall from Chapter 1 that the process of European integration has always been about a better politics and a better economics. In Werner's view, at least, these aspirations ran in a close and mutually supportive parallel.

2.4   WERNER ABANDONED

But history shows that monetary union did not happen by the end of the 1970s. In just a few years the Werner Plan (as the adopted Report became known) fell into disarray as the appearance of high and variable worldwide inflation prompted differing reactions among Community members to this new and disturbing problem.[14] Figure 2.1 depicts inflation for the six original EEC members, plus the three countries that joined in 1973: Denmark, Ireland and the UK. The relatively low and stable inflation rates in the early part of the decade stand in stark contrast to the much more uneven performances from 1973 onwards. Particularly noteworthy are the disparate inflation rates in Germany and France. German inflation remained remarkably low throughout the whole decade, at an average of 4.9 per cent. This, it is widely accepted, was the result of the strict anti-inflationary and constitutionally determined policy stance of the independent German central bank, the Bundesbank. In comparison, the rate of inflation in France was on average much higher at 8.9 per cent. The highest average rates among the nine countries were experienced by Italy (12.4 per cent) and the UK (12.5 per cent), with inflation in the UK reaching close to 25 per cent in 1975.

As noted, one of the cornerstones of Werner had been the increasing coordination of monetary policies – especially interest rates – as a means of securing mutually stable European exchange rates, prior to their eventual locking. Once Community

---

[14] Other factors militating against the ambitions of the Werner Plan included the general economic slowdown that heralded the end of the postwar boom, and the first oil-price shock of 1973–74.

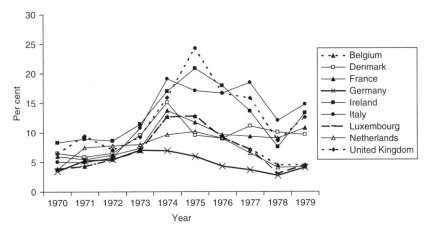

Source: International Monetary Fund.

Figure 2.1   Inflation for the Six, plus Denmark, Ireland and the UK, 1970–79

members began to demonstrate uneven levels of commitment to inflation control – and therefore different forms of monetary policy disposition with *uncoordinated* interest rates – any lasting possibility of the stable alignment of exchange rates melted away. This did not happen all at once as the Six, together with Denmark, Ireland, the UK and Norway, participated unevenly in the 'snake' fixed exchange rate system. In keeping with the aspirations of Werner for the gradual alignment of Community currencies, the snake was launched in 1972 and entailed a set of bilateral bands limiting currency fluctuations between members. However, the system met with difficulties from its inception as, for example, the UK withdrew within a month and Italy within a year. The remaining members of the snake effectively formed two groups of 'hard' and 'soft' participants: the difference between them being a reflection of their uneven commitment to inflation control. As the former group included Germany and the latter France (actually an intermittent snake participant), it became increasingly difficult to envisage monetary union with such deep monetary policy divisions between the two dominant European economies.

The uncertain condition of macroeconomic theory during the 1970s also had an important bearing on the integration process as it developed *after* the broad realization that Werner had ultimately come to very little. The postwar boom had been a period of triumph for Keynesian economics and its preference for the management of aggregate demand as a means to secure high and stable levels of employment and satisfactory rates of economic growth. Unfortunately, not only did the boom seem to be over by the 1970s (and it was not immediately clear why) but, in addition, the new and unwelcome phenomenon of worldwide inflation was something about which Keynesianism had relatively little to say. The next big innovation in macroeconomic thought and policy – monetarism – was as yet still nascent and, in any case, it was doubtful that this would be a doctrine that continental Europe could wholeheartedly embrace. This left the Community in something of a quandary. It had seen its plans for monetary union founder; the snake system could hardly be considered a resounding success; and it, like the rest of the world, was struggling with inflation.

2.5   THE ERM: REVIVING MONETARY COOPERATION IN EUROPE

However, an apparent way forward emerged in 1978 as a result of the personal agency of the German chancellor, Helmut Schmidt, and the French president, Valery Giscard d'Estaing, who together engineered the launch of the European Monetary System and its centrepiece, the exchange rate mechanism (ERM), a fixed system that would supersede the snake (Thygesen, 2004). The ERM became operational in March 1979.

The central economic purpose of the ERM was to create a *'zone of monetary stability'* in Europe. This had two dimensions:

- ERM members' exchange rates would be stabilized against one another.
- This would simultaneously necessitate the maintenance of low and stable inflation rates.

As noted, throughout the 1970s Germany had enjoyed an enviable record of inflation control, particularly in comparison to the other large European economies. The ERM – through its requirement for exchange rate management and monetary discipline – would effectively anchor the monetary policies of participants to that of Europe's staunchest anti-inflationary economy. At the same time, exchange rate stability would continue to underpin intra-European trade and the economic growth prospects of the customs union.[15] In creating the ERM, the European economies were effectively attempting to confront the inflationary problems that had derailed the Werner Plan. While monetary union was, for the moment, no longer the immediate goal, close monetary cooperation would be decisively reasserted after the uncertainties and dissolutions of the snake.

German monetary policy would anchor the ERM in the following way. In joining the system each member was accepting an obligation to maintain its currency within a narrow band ($+/-$ 2.25 per cent) either side of a declared parity with the mark (and with all other currencies in the ERM).[16] Now, given the superior German record on inflation control and the not unrelated typical strength of the mark, partnering in the ERM with Germany would necessitate that members follow the kind of restrictive monetary policy – expressed for many member economies through *un*typically stringent interest rates – favoured by the Bundesbank. Any temptation to use lower interest rates for some other purpose – such as to stimulate demand, output and employment – would have to be resisted simply because this would obviate the basic principle of the system: currency fixity. ERM members could not have it both ways. Either you were in the ERM maintaining agreed parities and therefore anchored to German monetary policy and closing in on its low inflation rate; or you applied a different set of monetary policy priorities, your currency depreciated, inflationary pressures accumulated and you left the ERM. A simple but effective choice for policy makers.

It can be argued that for at least a decade the performance of the ERM was not markedly out of step with the aspirations of its architects. Participants in the system enjoyed greater exchange rate stability with one another than they had managed during the 1970s and there is some evidence that the ERM acted as a force for disinflation around the German anchor after 1983 (see Gros and Thygesen, 1998). This was certainly the view of the British government that elected in 1990 to take up ERM membership as a means of inflation control.

Figure 2.2 illustrates the impact that membership of the ERM had upon members' inflation rates in comparison to the German

---

[15] The notion of a 'zone of monetary stability' is a synonym for the textbook 'anchor' and 'integration' arguments in favour of fixed exchange rates.
[16] The margins for the Italian lire were originally set at $+/-$ 6 per cent.

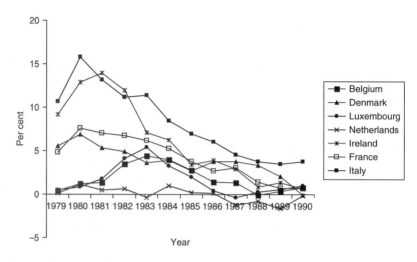

Source: International Monetary Fund.

Figure 2.2   ERM members' inflation differences with Germany, 1979–90

rate between 1979 and 1990.[17] To take one example, it can be seen that the French inflation rate in 1981 was almost 7 per cent higher than the German rate, but the difference is steadily eroded over the 1980s as a whole to the point at which the two rates converge in 1990. The figure also contains some echoes of the 'hard' and 'soft' groupings of the snake. The Netherlands, for example, had long tuned its monetary stance to that of its German neighbour such that its inflation rate closely parallels Germany's throughout the 1980s.

   Figure 2.3 conveys some notion of the kind of exchange rate stability that Community members enjoyed as a result of their participation in both the snake and then the ERM. The figure depicts real effective exchange rates for Germany and France, as compared to those of Japan, the UK and the US for the 1975–89 period.[18] It is evident that the mark and the French franc were relatively stable compared to the currencies of the other three major industrial nations, principally because they had been managed for so long on an intra-European basis (Boughton, 2001).

[17] There were eight members of the ERM at its launch in 1979. The UK was the only Community member that elected not to participate in the new system.
[18] A real effective exchange rate is an index of the purchasing power value of a currency expressed in terms of a basket of other currencies weighted according to the relative importance of their countries' trading relations with the country at issue.

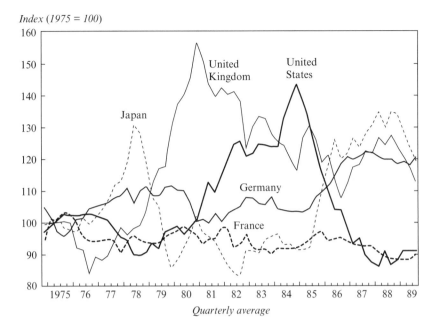

Index (1975 = 100)

Quarterly average

Source: Boughton (2001), Figure 1.7.

Figure 2.3 Real effective exchange rates, selected economies, 1975–89

On the basis of our discussion so far, then, the ERM appears to have been something of a success during the first decade or so of its existence. As a zone of monetary stability it had certainly delivered to its members both lower inflation and relative currency stability. However, there is one further criterion of ERM performance that needs to be considered: the nature and frequency of currency realignments inside the system. Before we get to this, a brief digression is necessary.

Fixed exchange rate systems arise when governments agree, in essence, to *rig* the foreign exchange market. To prevent currencies moving in ways that they consider undesirable, governments can buy or sell them (using other currencies), or increase or decrease interest rates to encourage others to buy or sell. Yet there are limits to this kind of activity. Consider the following example. In the late 1920s the British pound was worth almost $5. In the 80 or so years since then, the pound has depreciated slowly over time – sometimes rallying occasionally – so that now it is worth something around or a little below $2. There really is no way to buck a

market-driven trend such as this. Had successive British governments attempted to fix the pound permanently at $5 they would
have failed, miserably. This is because, in the long run, currency
values are determined by the relative economic performances of
their issuing economies.[19] The pound was the world's dominant
currency in the nineteenth century as Britain was then the
world's most important economy: it produced huge volumes of
goods and services that the rest of the world wanted to buy – pur-
chases that underpinned an equally huge demand for pounds on
the foreign exchange markets. By the beginning of the twentieth
century, British economic dominance was over: eclipsed by the
rise of the United States and continental Europe. This meant that
the steady depreciation of the pound was almost inevitable; as
was the rise of the dollar.

Now, the implication here is that arrangements by which
exchange rates are 'fixed' are *inevitably* transient. Currencies
can be stabilized for a time but they cannot be permanently fixed.
Indeed, to try to do so is actually undesirable and possibly
counter-productive. The corollary here is that currency depreciation and appreciation are positive processes. For economies with
balance-of-payments deficit problems – crudely, a surfeit of
imports over exports in value terms – depreciation, because it
automatically raises the home currency price of imports and
lowers the foreign currency price of exports, actually helps eliminate the deficit. Similarly, for economies with balance-of-
payments surplus problems – again crudely, a surfeit of exports
over imports in value terms – appreciation, because it lowers the
home currency price of imports and increases the foreign currency
price of exports, is also helpful – it tends to eliminate the surplus.

How, then, are we to evaluate a fixed system? Are fixed systems
futile and doomed to failure? The answer to the latter question is
no, so long as the aspiration is to stabilize exchange rates in the
short to medium term rather than set them in aspic. This means
that an additional criterion for judging the performance of the
ERM should be its acceptance of the need for realignments, their
frequency, and the facility with which they are managed. The
ERM's record here is mixed. Up to 1987, ERM participants
engaged in a series of currency realignments of diminishing
frequency and amplitude. This indicates that there was, at least at

---

[19] Admittedly, exchange rate determination is not an exact science. Economists still do not
have a model that can out-predict random guesswork.

first, an acceptance of the need for adjustments in the light of the changing circumstances of particular economies in the system. It also suggests that the system was being effectively managed. Essentially, the frequent currency adjustments of the early 1980s were a learning exercise for the authorities. Finally, the course of the ERM at this stage indicates that participants had heeded some of the important lessons attached to the failure of the Bretton Woods system, where there had been a marked reluctance to revalue and, in particular, devalue. The non-adjustable character of Bretton Woods is widely held to account for its collapse.

So up to 1987 the ERM functioned as a fixed-but-adjustable exchange rate regime, receiving plaudits for doing so from, among others, Robert Triffin. Yet after 1987 there were *no* further realignments until the first ERM crisis in 1992. Such a chronology indicates that, in exchange rate terms at least, the system evinced a growing and even remarkable degree of stability during this period; but there were some serious and potentially fatal dangers lurking here. In September 1987 the ERM was the subject of policy refinement – the Basle–Nyborg agreement – which greatly strengthened the resources that participants could deploy in defence of agreed exchange rate parities. Basle–Nyborg was a direct response to the realignment in January 1987 which ERM participants felt had been forced on them as a result of dollar-centred turmoil in the foreign exchange markets. Speculation against the dollar had resulted in upward pressure on the mark and this had been dissipated by its revaluation against most of the other ERM currencies. The point was that there was nothing in the ERM fundamentals – such as increasingly divergent inflation rates – that demanded such an adjustment at the time. Accordingly, the Basle–Nyborg agreement was intended to forestall any further unwarranted realignments in the future: it was an exercise in Community power *over* the foreign exchange markets.

In parallel with Basle–Nyborg and the positive track record and apparent strengthening of the integrity of the ERM, the EEC also announced ambitious new plans for still deeper economic and monetary integration in Europe. These were embodied in the 1986 Single European Act (SEA) (see Chapter 3, section 3.1.1). The purpose of the SEA was to develop the Community from a customs union into a fully-fledged common market. As noted in Chapter 1, a customs union involves a commitment to free trade between economies, together with common external tariff arrangements with third-party economies. A common market takes the process of integration a stage further by providing for the free internal movement of capital and labour. The SEA also expressed an ambition for the revival of plans for a European single currency: the first such reference since Werner. This marked the beginning of the road to the creation of the euro.

The rationale for the SEA lay in a perception that the European economies were performing less well in economic terms relative to their main competitors than at any time in the recent past. In reaffirming the integrity of Europe as an economic space, the SEA would provide the fillip necessary to confront the problem of so-called 'eurosclerosis', a term denoting the stagnation of the European economy. By 1986 then, in integration terms, the Community was an emboldened collective: resistant to the vagaries of the foreign exchange markets and fixed on a path to a single market and ultimately, though the details had yet to be agreed, a single currency. It was easy to envisage at some time in the future a smooth transition from an increasingly robust ERM to the nirvana of one currency in one European market. Unfortunately, the ERM was soon to rupture along familiar fault-lines leaving plans for the single currency, according to one interested observer, with 'all the quaintness of a rain dance and about the same potency'.[20]

The ERM crisis of 1992, which saw the pound's membership suspended, alongside that of the lira, was prompted by the inflationary implications of German reunification in 1990. The West German government had made huge fiscal commitments to underwrite the reconstruction of East Germany following reunification. The upward pressure this put on German inflation was met with an increase in German interest rates and consequent speculation in favour of the mark. The tightening of German monetary policy posed serious difficulties for other ERM members, especially the UK. Having joined the ERM in 1990 in the midst of recession, the UK was not in a position to raise interest rates in response (to maintain the pound within the agreed band against the mark),[21] nor could it afford to devalue the pound without wrecking its own newly hatched anti-inflationary strategy. With the knowledge that the UK was also carrying a record deficit on the current account of the balance of payments

---

[20] The observer was the then British Prime Minister, John Major.
[21] $+/- 6$ per cent.

(and hence would need to devalue the pound at some stage), the foreign exchange markets viewed sterling as a one-way bet and adverse speculation eventually forced its 'temporary' suspension from the ERM.[22] A year later France found itself in a similar position, mired in deepening recession and unable to cut interest rates given its obligations to maintain the franc's parity with the mark. Again speculators took advantage, but the outcome on this occasion was a widening of all remaining ERM currency fluctuation bands from +/− 2.25 per cent to +/− 15 per cent. The ERM as a zone of monetary stability around the German anchor had effectively ceased to exist.

But despite the apparently moribund ERM,[23] progress towards the creation of what was to become the euro continued to be made. Following the declaration in the SEA that there should be a single currency operating across the common market, the European Union Council of Economics and Finance Ministers (ECOFIN) had mandated a Committee led by the then President of the European Commission, Jacques Delors, to identify how full economic union might be best achieved. The subsequent Delors Report (1989) proposed that a single currency should emerge as a result of three separate but incremental stages. The Delors Report was quickly endorsed by the heads of state of member countries and the first stage of economic and monetary union began on 1 January 1990 (see Chapter 3, section 3.1.2).

In reflecting upon the long drive towards economic and monetary union in Europe, several observations can be made. In the first place, economic imperatives are clearly evident. One consistent theme here has been the need to improve the operation of the European market for goods and services through monetary integration. Under the auspices of the Werner Plan, the snake, and the ERM, the supposition was always that either monetary union or exchange rate stability would help economic agents make better and more efficient microeconomic decisions right across the Community. Another aspect of the integration process has been its macroeconomic payoffs. These have varied between contexts but include, under Werner and the snake, the attempt to insulate the Community from the disturbances expected from the break-up of the Bretton Woods system. The ERM on the other hand was

---

[22] The suspension proved permanent.
[23] The wide-band ERM was re-christened ERM II and still plays a role in the accession of countries wishing to adopt the euro (see Chapter 6).

specifically designed as a collective solution to the inflation problems of the 1970s.

But the integration process in the 1970s and 1980s embraced a political agenda too. The analyses of both Barre and Werner recognized that economic and monetary union would push Europe into areas where national sovereignties would be attenuated by the necessary articulation of authority at the pan-Community level. In the 1970s this proved a step too far as members reacted to the new more problematic economic climate on an individualistic basis, especially in the assertion of national priorities for monetary and fiscal policy. Paradoxically, by the end of the 1970s the Community had come to recognize that to successfully confront the new macroeconomic problem of inflation it *had* to accept that monetary independence should be sacrificed. Unfortunately, as the ERM later fell victim to the same kind of inflexibility that had fractured the Bretton Woods system, several member states were forced to withdraw from this shared arrangement and, ultimately, the ERM evolved into rather a different animal with different purposes. This left the politics of integration delicately poised and Europe with an interesting choice. It could forsake macroeconomic integration and focus merely and in a necessarily limited way upon the microeconomics of the SEA and the single market, or it could push on with deeper monetary integration with all its mutually supportive economic and political connotations. How this choice was exercised is the focus of the next chapter of this book.

We close the present chapter with an interview with the economist and former Belgian politician, Paul De Grauwe.

PAUL DE GRAUWE

Paul De Grauwe is Professor of International Economics at the University of Leuven, Belgium. From 1991 to 2003 he was a member of the Belgian parliament. He is best known for his work on international economics and European monetary union. His many publications in these fields include his widely adopted book, *Economics of Monetary Union* (Oxford University Press, 7th edition, 2007).

We interviewed Professor De Grauwe in his office at the University of Leuven on 7 December 2006.

The Werner Plan was the first considered attempt to introduce monetary integration in Europe, what were the main impulses behind Werner?
I think it was the realization that we wouldn't be able to move further towards integration in Europe unless we stabilized exchange rates. We needed an environment of stable exchange rate relationships because movements in exchange rates – devaluations and revaluations – created trade distortions and tensions within the European Union. That was the major driving force behind Werner. Other people may also have had, at the back of their mind, the thought that the process of monetary unification could be a first step towards greater political unification.

What were the main economic factors behind the derailment of the Werner Plan in the 1970s?
I think that the major problem was that it was a plan – to move towards monetary union by first fixing exchange rates – which did relatively little in terms of coordination of policies. That is why it failed miserably. We learned that it's just not enough to get stable exchange rates. If you don't have the same type of monetary policies, and economic policies in general, then at some point – because of divergences in prices and costs – the structure of fixed exchange rates will not survive and you get speculative crises. That is exactly what happened in the 1970s, especially when the dollar came under pressure. After the collapse of the Bretton Woods system we introduced the snake agreement, fixing exchange rates among ourselves, but this also collapsed. The lesson we learned was that you cannot fix exchange rates without going much further in terms of unifying monetary policies.

To what extent do you think that the problems behind Werner were, in part, also due to the change in the prevailing macroeconomic consensus away from Keynesianism towards monetarism that occurred in the 1970s?

This may have played a role. But I think that this played a much greater role later on in the sense that the move towards monetarism convinced many people that you can't really use monetary policies in an activist way to stabilize the economy. The move towards a supranational European central bank and full monetary union was no longer seen as a great loss because people realized that you can't do anything to stabilize the economy with activist monetary policy. This contrasts with the Keynesian way of thinking where monetary policy is one of the instruments you can use to do certain things by, for example, devaluing your currency. The move away from Keynesianism towards monetarism created the intellectual environment for making full monetary union attractive. But that came later in the 1980s.

Were there any political considerations undermining Werner?

I think this was an episode when politicians started something without really realizing what they were doing. The Plan unravelled because of pressures in the financial and foreign exchange markets. I don't think that there were any important political considerations that undermined Werner.

In retrospect is it fair to say that the Werner Report was ahead of its time?

The idea of moving towards monetary union was certainly ahead of its time. The strategy it had to get there was ill-conceived and was very naive. However, in terms of formulating an objective for Europe, the Report was two decades ahead of its time.

How important was the collapse of the Bretton Woods system of fixed exchange rates to shaping the future direction of monetary integration in Europe?

It was important in the sense that we found out that the financial upheavals in foreign exchange markets following the collapse of the Bretton Woods system created the problem of stabilizing exchange rates within the European Union. This led to the European Monetary System in 1979 as an answer to the turbulence that had existed in the 1970s.

Do you think that the 'Snake' system was significant economically?
No. It was an attempt to save something that could not survive. It looked nice and was great to teach students. [*Laughter*]

Was the introduction of the EMS in 1979 driven more by the macro-economic imperatives of inflation control than by higher aspirations for deeper European integration?
As I said, it was basically an attempt to respond to the turbulence of the 1970s when there had been large exchange rate movements. The main objective behind the EMS was to stabilize exchange rate movements. It was not something that was explicitly aimed at reducing inflation. I don't recall that this was an objective of the founding fathers of the EMS. While it was certainly seen as a step towards union in some form, at the time given the disappointments with Werner there was no real clear objective of using this to move into a monetary union. Some people may have had that at the back of their mind, but politicians certainly didn't. I interpret the introduction of the EMS to be a response to the turbulence of the 1970s. It was understood at the time that the new system couldn't be too ambitious. You couldn't have a Bretton Woods type arrangement, so there were larger bands of fluctuations and also agreement that countries could realign. The idea was that if these realignments were small and the bands were relatively large you could have a system that maintained some form of stability but avoided complete rigidity, which we had learned couldn't be maintained. The ERM evolved into a much more rigid system at the end of the 1980s and that's why it collapsed.

How do you account for the frequent realignments which took place within the ERM during the first half of the 1980s?
They had to do with the fact that countries had very divergent movements in prices and wages, which accumulated over time and required frequent realignments.

Our understanding is that the 1987 Basle–Nyborg agreement was an important turning-point in that, although not its intention, it resulted in the ERM turning into an essentially fixed and non-adjustable system – like Bretton Woods. Why was this mistake allowed to be repeated?
It is a very puzzling episode. I guess the reason why this mistake was made was because there was a period of some years of relative stability, with few currency realignments. This was in part

due to the fact that inflation rates had started to converge so there was less need for currency adjustment. This created the illusion among policy makers that they could, from now on, maintain fixity. That perception was probably not based on good analysis. Another factor was the liberalization of capital movements, which occurred in the second half of the 1980s. That created a big institutional change.

The Single European Act was pivotal in re-establishing the path to the single currency but to what extent was this ambition as much a reflection of ERM countries' confidence that they had the currency markets tamed as it was a complement to the single market? In hindsight, was there a certain monetary hubris or overconfidence on the part of policy makers?
The jury is still out. Was there overconfidence? One can say no because in the end it was successful. The move to a single currency, complete monetary union and one central bank was ultimately realized, so it's difficult to say now that it was overambitious. It may have appeared at that moment in time for many that it was overambitious, but they have been proven wrong. The brute fact is that the single currency exists today and therefore it is difficult to argue that plans for it were overambitious.

To what extent did the recession that occurred in Europe in 1992–93 contribute to the downfall of the ERM?
I think that it was a very important factor. Countries like France and Italy were suddenly in a situation where they were experiencing a severe downturn in economic activity and wanted another kind of monetary policy, yet the Bundesbank was essentially dictating the monetary stance of the entire ERM. The Bundesbank's policy was based on monetary control and low inflation and it did not want to compromise. Countries found that they couldn't implement a monetary policy that was appropriate to their own local conditions. In this respect the ERM acted like a corset as it prevented those countries from stimulating their economies. When speculators realized that the system possessed such tensions they engaged in speculative attacks, which were successful most of the time.

To what extent did ERM II serve a useful purpose before monetary union; does it serve an important function now?
I think the ERM served an important function, but in a negative way. It showed again that in a world of full capital mobility you

cannot maintain fixed exchange rates, except if you go all the way to full monetary union. This comes back to the so-called 'holy trinity' – the inconsistency between capital mobility, monetary policy independence and fixed exchange rates. One of these three has to move. If you want to maintain capital mobility and fixed exchange rates you have to give up monetary independence. If you want to maintain capital mobility and monetary policy independence you have to allow your exchange rate to be flexible. These are the choices. After 1992 Britain chose capital mobility and monetary policy independence and then had to allow a flexible exchange rate. The others decided to move to the other extreme. The ERM made it clear that we would have to make these choices and that we could not compromise. On the continent, given that the degree of trade integration was so advanced, we chose to move to monetary union.

The Maastricht criteria for individual country participation in EMU [economic and monetary union] were macroeconomic in orientation but the criteria conventionally used to judge the viability of an optimum currency area are rooted in microeconomic considerations. How can these alternative approaches be reconciled?
Well it is difficult to reconcile them because basically the Maastricht convergence criteria are irrelevant as a selection mechanism to find out which countries are fit to be in a monetary union and which are not. They really impose only temporary convergence on inflation, public deficits and so on. Once countries are in they can let loose and that's what we observe now. Countries prior to the eurozone managed to converge their inflation rates but since then there has been divergence. The structural factors then play their role. We now observe that wages and prices diverge within the eurozone, creating strong changes in the competitive positions of countries and the need to adjust. The problem is that there is very little possibility of adjustment. What I would say is that the Maastricht criteria were there for reasons other than as fitness criteria to decide which countries would be part of an optimum currency area. In that sense I don't think it is the right approach. We are now confronted with the same problem with euro enlargement.

What is your view of the way in which the Maastricht criteria were ultimately applied in 1997?
It is very clear that half of the eurozone countries did not satisfy one or more of the Maastricht convergence criteria. My own

country Belgium, for example, didn't satisfy the debt criteria. Germany had a debt level above 60 per cent and it was increasing. According to the Maastricht criteria if you have a debt-to-GDP ratio exceeding 60 per cent it should be declining and reach the 60 per cent level at a satisfactory pace. At the time the political will was so strong that these criteria were leniently applied. But now we observe the opposite situation with enlargement. If the criteria aren't strictly met, countries can't enter. That's because the political will to enlarge is very weak. This also illustrates the arbitrary nature of these convergence criteria.

You have suggested (De Grauwe and Schnabl, 2005) that it may be possible for the new accession countries to join the euro area by creatively using the wider ERM II bands. Are there any indications that your suggestion may be taken up by EMU aspirants?
It seems to me that these exchange rate arrangements can be done in a relatively smooth way. One should not forget that this is really a two-year arrangement that you have to fulfil. It's quite clear that at the end of the two years when you enter that these exchange rate arrangements should not be a major stumbling block. The major stumbling block for these countries are the other ones, like inflation and the budget.

In your paper you seem to be arguing that if the new accession countries use the upper band, in particular, in a fairly liberal way that would allow them to achieve the inflation target.
Yes, that was the suggestion we made in our paper, to allow some flexibility within the band. This makes it possible for a currency to appreciate, thereby lowering the inflationary pressure, which is one of the criteria. You don't then get the inconsistency between fixing the exchange rate and achieving the inflation criteria, which may be a problem for some of the countries, especially those with high productivity growth. So technically there is a way to deal with this. If the political will is favourable for these countries to join then mechanisms will be designed which are consistent with the Maastricht Treaty that will make accession easier. Of course if the political conditions are the opposite – which they are right now – things will be designed in such a way that it makes it more difficult for these countries to join the euro area. It all depends on the prevailing political attitude and I'm afraid that the political attitude today is negative.

From the outset, the Stability and Growth Pact has been controversial. To what extent do you think its difficulties are the natural attendants of any attempt at fiscal control?

The major problem I see is that it just doesn't take into account that budgetary matters are almost 100 per cent the prerogative of nation states. It's national governments that decide the level of spending and taxation, and their composition and distribution. That is also where political and democratic legitimacy is tested. Those who make decisions about these matters at the national level face the sanction of voters. We have constructed, top down, a control mechanism by people who do not face this sanctioning process. When the Commission starts a procedure against a particular country these guys don't face the pressure of having to be re-elected. This cannot work. Each time there is a conflict between a national government and a European institution, the European institution will lose. That is the major political weakness of the Pact. In a way it is politically extremely naive to believe that you can have a control system which is top down, while governments face the electorate all the time.

What are your views of the attempts to reform the Pact?

I have mixed feelings about these reforms. In one way you can say that it's a positive trend to introduce more flexibility. It was unrealistic that you could impose a rule, like a budget deficit not higher than 3 per cent of GDP, top down to intelligent people who face the electorate. Take the example of the French prime minister. He faces an election. There is a recession in France and he has to spend more because of rising unemployment and yet he has less revenue from taxes. Then Brussels tells him to reduce spending and raise taxes because there is a holy number three. The prime minister is then expected to say to the French people, sorry I can't help you because number three is there. That doesn't make sense. So it is good to get away from this holy number stuff. There are now many exceptions. But we should have gone further and got completely away from this number madness.

You have argued that, in the absence of optimum currency area endogeneity, the longer-term prospects for the integrity of the euro are not strong unless there is deeper integration that facilitates greater fiscal federalism (De Grauwe, 2006). In the presence of what – in a nice phrase – you call 'integration fatigue' this, presently, seems unlikely. Can it happen? What are the implications if it doesn't?

I think that it will be difficult to move forward towards fiscal federalism, which is part of greater political union. There is indeed integration fatigue. Many people in Europe don't see this as something we should do. On the contrary there is a view that we have gone far enough. If anything there is a move back towards national cocoons. Although this may change, at the moment I don't see any sign of change there. Now what are the implications? There is a serious risk for the future functioning of the eurozone. It seems to me that the absence of political union creates so many divergences given that governments are sovereign when it comes to spending and taxation. Wage and social policies are also purely national affairs. This creates dynamics where countries move in different directions. You then get into a situation, at some point, where you have to adjust again and it's necessary to use fiscal mechanisms to do that. That is the situation we are in today in the eurozone. Some countries like Germany have improved their competitive position dramatically, but mainly at the expense of other countries. What we need now is a mechanism to deal with this problem. The only mechanism we have is deflation in countries that have lost their competitiveness. They will have to go through years of trying to bring down their inflation and that creates a spiral, which is not very attractive economically and is very costly. The root cause of the problem is the idiosyncrasies of all these nation states with their own special policies and institutions. If we don't deal with this problem then in the long run the eurozone will be at risk in the sense that, at some point, some countries may decide that it is not in their national interest to be in a system like this. Of course there are great benefits associated with the euro. But there is also a price to be paid for those countries that are forced into deflation for many years.

Is it fair to say that the longer-term integrity of the euro area will not be firmly established until Europe has experienced and withstood a severe shock?
I don't want to be too pessimistic. There are many possible scenarios, which could lead to a break-up of the system. One is a big shock, such as a war – but let's hope that doesn't happen. Rather than some big shock I think it's more the accumulation of divergences threatening the system that you cannot really correct in a sufficiently harmonious way.

The entry of Greece into the eurozone was a little more difficult than for the 11 founding members. Other 'fringe' economies (we do not intend this term to be pejorative) are committed to joining sooner rather than later. Do you think the eurozone could survive were some of these economies to later leave it? Would it matter if Greece left?

Well economically it wouldn't matter if a small country like Greece were to leave as Greece only represents a few percentage points of the GDP of the eurozone. It would probably not show on the radar screen of the eurozone. However, it may matter far more in a political sense if a country like Greece were to leave. It would create a precedent and result in a loss of credibility in the permanency of the arrangement. Once doubt arises about the permanency of the arrangement you get a very different situation, which can create turbulence.

There have been suggestions, notably from the United States, that in its decades-long focus on monetary reform and innovation, the EU has rather lost sight of its real-economy Lisbon Agenda. To what extent do you think this a fair criticism?

I am quite sceptical about this diagnosis. It is often said that the US is way ahead in terms of technology and innovation. In certain areas that is probably true. But one can easily exaggerate the situation. There are many areas where Europe is up to date technologically and is doing okay. Take the automobile industry. Compared to Europe and Japan the US can't produce a decent car. Although over the last 10 years the US has been growing faster than the eurozone, I believe that an important component of this is just a temporary consumption-driven boom in the US economy. Once this whittles away, comparisons between the USA and Europe will look very different.

Are there any issues around the participation of Belgium in the eurozone that concerned you before 1999? Are there any now?

Belgium has always been an enthusiast of anything European, for obvious reasons. We profit from Brussels as the capital. In Belgium there is a very strong feeling that it is good for us and right from the start there has always been great enthusiasm about the euro. In contrast with other countries, like Germany where there was not much enthusiasm and, in fact, lots of resistance. We were probably the most enthusiastic of the member countries and this has been maintained. We just take it for granted that the euro is good for us.

3. The economics of the euro

Having traced the history of European economic and political integration since the Second World War (Chapter 1), and the long process of European monetary integration prior to the advent of the euro (Chapter 2), we now turn to examine the euro's emergence and the economic principles upon which the new currency rests. We begin by charting in some detail the three main landmark events since the mid-1980s that shaped the transition to economic and monetary union (EMU) in Europe and the launch of the euro in January 1999.

3.1 THE TRANSITION TO EUROPEAN ECONOMIC AND MONETARY UNION

3.1.1 The Single European Act (SEA), 1986

As discussed in Chapter 1, section 1.2, the process of European market unification began when the six founding members of the European Coal and Steel Community signed the Treaty of Rome in 1957. You will recall that the Treaty of Rome established a customs union, the most important features of which included measures designed to eliminate all internal customs duties and trade restrictions between its six member states, and the introduction of a common external tariff on goods from the rest of the world. Although by the end of the 1960s the European Economic Community (EEC) had succeeded in eliminating internal tariffs and quotas on trade between its member countries, there remained various, what we might call 'administrative', barriers to trade which were a drag on the free movement of goods and services. For example, in Europe's car market, trade was discouraged by the imposition of national standards and registration requirements. Significant barriers to the free movement of labour and capital within Europe also remained.

Against this backdrop, and amid concerns that the European economy was failing to match the economic performances achieved by the United States and Japan over the 1970s and early 1980s, in 1985 the European Commission published a White Paper: 'Completing the Internal Market'. This identified nearly 300 legislative measures required to finalize the internal market by proposing the removal of all remaining internal barriers to the free movement of goods, services, labour and capital between member countries. It also envisaged a deadline of the end of 1992 for the attainment of what would then be a European single market. These proposals were embodied in the Single European Act, signed by the 12 member states of the EEC in February 1986. The SEA was the first major amendment to the Treaty of Rome and gave a much-needed impetus to turn the EEC into a truly unified internal market. Let us look more closely at the economic rationale behind the drive to create a single European market within which goods, services, labour and capital can freely circulate.

The main economic argument for the creation of a single European market lies in the potential benefits it can bestow on both firms and households. A single market creates a much larger customer base which enables European firms to realize economies of scale comparable to those achieved by, for example, American firms, given the size of the market in the United States. Firms will also be able to buy intermediate goods in the production process from a wider range of suppliers. Overall, greater competition will lead to efficiency gains as weaker firms are forced to improve their performance or face the risk of going out of business. At the same time, households will benefit from the lower prices and improved quality and service generated by more intensive inter-firm competition. In summary, it is argued that the creation of a single market in Europe will provide a larger consumer base, increase competition, improve productive efficiency, and encourage firms to expand and compete more effectively in both European and global markets. In turn this will enhance growth and prosperity in Europe.

The SEA also expressed an ambition for the revival of plans for a single currency in Europe. For many supporters of the drive for greater European economic and monetary integration, achieving a truly unified single European market required not just the removal of all remaining barriers to the free movement of goods, services, labour and capital between member countries but also a single currency. Completing 'one market' with 'one money' would, it was argued, promote greater intra-European trade through:

- the elimination of the transaction costs associated with currency conversion;
- greater price transparency; and
- the elimination of exchange rate uncertainty and risk between members of the single currency union.

These benefits are discussed more fully in section 3.2.

In 1988 the European Council set up the Delors Committee to consider how economic and monetary union in the European Community (EC) could best be achieved. The brief given to the Committee was 'to study and propose concrete stages leading towards economic and monetary union'. The Committee, chaired by Jacques Delors, the President of the European Commission, was composed of the 12 EC national central bank governors and three independent experts: Alexandre Lamfalussy, the general manager of the Bank for International Settlements (BIS) in Basle; Miguel Boyer, the president of the Banco Exterior de Espana; and Niels Thygesen, Professor of Economics at the University of Copenhagen. At the end of this chapter there is an interview with Niels Thygesen, the sole academic member of the Committee.

3.1.2   The Delors Report (1989)

The Delors Report, which is relatively succinct and very readable, proposed a 'step-by-step approach' towards EMU involving three separate and evolutionary stages. The principal steps in the first stage included: completion of the internal market, accompanied by a strengthening of competition policy within the EC; the removal of obstacles to financial integration; and closer coordination of national economic and monetary policies in order to achieve greater convergence in economic performance. Closer coordination of monetary policies across the Community was to be achieved through increased cooperation between the central banks via the Committee of Governors of the Central Banks of the member states, with the aim of achieving price stability.

The principal steps in the proposed second stage of EMU included: the establishment of the European System of Central Banks (ESCB), whose key task during this stage would be 'to begin the transition from the coordination of national monetary policies by the Committee of Central Bank Governors in stage one to the formulation and implementation of a common monetary policy by the ESCB itself scheduled to take place in the final stage'; and, given progress in achieving greater convergence of economic performance, a narrowing of margins of fluctuations within the ERM (see Chapter 2, section 2.5) in preparation for the final stage of monetary union when they would be reduced to zero.

The third and final stage of EMU would begin with the irrevocable fixing of exchange rates between national currencies (thereby creating a monetary union) and proceed with their eventual replacement by a single European currency. At stage three the ESCB would assume responsibility for the formulation and implementation of a *single* monetary policy in the currency area, the most visible expression of which would be one interest rate as a replacement for multiple separate national interest rates. The Report proposed that the ESCB would be committed to the objective of achieving price stability and would operate independently of national governments and Community authorities.[24] While it would have independent status, the ESCB would be accountable to the European Parliament and the European Council. Fearing that divergent budgetary policies could undermine monetary stability, the final stage included constraints on members' national budgets. The Delors Report also recognized the need to strengthen Community structural and regional policies.

The European Council adopted the proposals contained in the Delors Report when it met in Madrid in June 1989 and the first stage of EMU began on 1 July 1990. During this first stage (1 July 1990 to 31 December 1993) the Committee of Central Bank Governors promoted the coordination of the monetary policies of member states. However, the proposals to establish the ESCB (stage 2) and extend its responsibilities (stage 3), and to irrevocably fix exchange rates between national currencies and eventually replace them with a single currency (stage 3), required changes to the Treaty of Rome. In December 1989 the European Council decided to convene an intergovernmental conference to begin the process of Treaty modification. This intergovernmental conference, which was held in 1991 in parallel with an intergovernmental conference on political union, culminated in the Maastricht Treaty. As we shall now discuss, the Maastricht

[24] This proposal used the German Bundesbank as a model of mandate for the ESCB – see Chapter 2, section 2.5.

Treaty established EMU as a formal objective and set out the timetable and criteria for member states to participate in the project.

3.1.3   The Maastricht Treaty (1992)

The Treaty on European Union (TEU) – more familiarly known as the Maastricht Treaty – was agreed in December 1991 and signed by European heads of state or government on 7 February 1992, in the Dutch city of Maastricht. Although the Treaty went beyond purely economic and monetary issues, and opened the way to greater political integration, in what follows we focus on the transition to full monetary union with the irrevocable fixing of exchange rates between national currencies and their subsequent replacement by a single European currency.

The Maastricht Treaty established that the second stage of EMU would begin on 1 January 1994. The start of the second stage was marked by the establishment of the European Monetary Institute (EMI), the forerunner of the European Central Bank (ECB) (see Chapter 4, section 4.1). In line with the proposals contained in the Delors Report, the EMI's main tasks were twofold. First, to strengthen cooperation – and monetary policy coordination – between the national central banks (NCBs). Second, to carry out preparations for the establishment of the ESCB, for the conduct of the single monetary policy and the creation of a single currency in stage three of EMU. During the second stage the NCBs retained responsibility for the conduct of monetary policy in the EU.

The Treaty confirmed that the final stage of EMU would begin *no later than* 1 January 1999 with the launch of the as yet un-named single currency and the establishment of a European central bank.[25] It also identified the 'convergence criteria' to be satisfied before the then-15 individual member states of the EU would become eligible to join the single currency. The criteria identify the economic conditions deemed necessary for the adoption of a single currency and are a reflection of the need for the participating countries to harmonize key aspects of economic performance before they begin to share a new currency – when, most evidently all participants have to accept a uniform monetary policy, that is,

---

[25] The euro was confirmed as the name of the new currency at the European Council meeting in Madrid in 1995.

one interest rate. This makes divergent economies unsuitable candidates for EMU; the only good candidates are demonstrably convergent economies. The Maastricht criteria were designed to separate the good candidates from the bad.

The convergence criteria established that a country would only become eligible to take part in the third stage of EMU and join the single currency if:

- its inflation rate is not more than 1.5 per cent above the average of the three lowest inflation rate countries in the EU;
- its government debt and deficit are not more than 60 per cent and 3 per cent of its GDP, respectively;
- it has joined the exchange rate mechanism (ERM) of the European Monetary System (EMS) and has maintained normal exchange rate fluctuation margins for two years without severe tensions arising; and
- its long-term interest rate is not more than 2.0 per cent above that of the three lowest inflation countries.

Let us look briefly at the rationale behind each of the convergence criteria in turn. Convergence of inflation rates provides evidence that countries who wish to join the single currency are committed to inflation control and accept that low inflation rates are both desirable and necessary. As such the inflation criterion avoids the potential of inflation bias in a currency union. Convergence of debt-to-GDP ratios reduces the risk of surprise inflation. The higher the debt-to-GDP ratio, the greater is the incentive for a government to engineer a 'surprise' inflation in order to reduce the real value of its outstanding debt. Convergence of budget deficits reduces the risk of default. As a government deficit increases, a country faces a higher default risk. To maintain budget discipline after the introduction of the single currency, the 'Stability and Growth Pact' was subsequently adopted by the European Council in 1997. The Pact effectively rolls forward the debt and deficit criterion of participating countries in order to ensure continuing fiscal prudence among the countries that adopt the single European currency. As we shall discuss in Chapter 4, section 4.2, any country that allows its annual budget deficit to exceed 3 per cent of its GDP may face penalties by the European Council, depending on the success of the action it takes to end the deficit. Exchange rate convergence prevents countries, prior to entry, from devaluing their exchange rate in order to improve their competitive position. Finally, convergence of long-term interest rates both guards against disruption in national capital markets when a country enters the final stage of EMU, and ensures that entrants are able to initially 'live with' the single interest rate set for the whole euro area by the ECB.

Two particular aspects of the Maastricht convergence criteria are worthy of note. First, the convergence criteria were designed as a package in an attempt to scrutinize the EMU candidature of countries and ensure monetary and budgetary discipline. As such the criteria are concerned with *macroeconomic* conditions in potential EMU countries. However, as we shall discuss in section 3.3 below, optimum currency area theory – which indicates whether or not a group of countries will benefit in the long term from adopting a shared currency – stresses *microeconomic* rather than macroeconomic conditions. Second, while the Maastricht Treaty established that *all* criteria would have to be met before a country was entitled to proceed to the final stage of EMU, developments after 1991, not least the successive crises of the ERM, prompted the emergence of more flexible interpretations. You will recall from Chapter 2, section 2.5, that in August 1993 the European Union Council of Economics and Finance Ministers (ECOFIN) decided to widen the band of exchange rate fluctuation in the ERM from $+/- 2.25$ per cent, to $+/- 15$ per cent. This decision effectively transformed the ERM from a fixed, but adjustable, exchange rate regime (with a maximum range of exchange rate fluctuation of 4.5 per cent for the majority of participating countries), to a quasi-flexible exchange rate regime (with a maximum range of exchange rate fluctuation of 30 per cent). As the exchange rate criterion was, in principle, ultimately based on the post-1993 version of the ERM, the stringency of the exchange rate fluctuation margins conceived at Maastricht were dramatically reduced. A number of countries also faced difficulties in meeting the 60 per cent debt-to-GDP ratio criterion. In 1997, nine of the 11 countries that elected in the following year to proceed EMU and join the single currency failed to meet this criterion. However, in the Maastricht Treaty the criterion was deemed to have been met where the debt-to-GDP ratio was declining substantially and was approaching the reference value of 60 per cent at a satisfactory pace. In the event, all nine economies were determined to be sufficiently on course towards the 60 per cent reference value and were therefore able to adopt the euro. These two examples suggest a degree of latitude in the way that certain eligibility judgements were made and are testament to the *political* determination in the EU that economic and monetary union would proceed at the earliest opportunity for the majority of the EU member states.

3.1.4   The Launch of the Euro

In May 1998, of the EU countries deemed to have met the Maastricht convergence criteria, 11 countries (Austria, Belgium, Finland, France, Germany, Ireland, Italy, Luxembourg, the Netherlands, Portugal and Spain) elected to proceed to the third and final stage of EMU. On 1 January 1999 exchange rates between their national currencies were irrevocably fixed and the euro was officially launched. However, during the period from 1 January 1999 to 31 December 2001, the euro did not actually exist in physical form, it existed as a virtual currency. National currencies continued to circulate, while national coins and banknotes were booked in the balance sheets of NCBs in euros. Euro coins and banknotes were first introduced in physical form for circulation in participating member states on 1 January 2002. Between 1 January 2002 and the end of February 2002, national currencies were taken out of circulation and were replaced by the euro, which became the sole currency for participating member states.

Of the remaining four EU member states, Greece – which initially failed to meet the Maastricht criteria – adopted the euro on 1 January 2002. Denmark, Sweden and the UK still retain their national currencies (see Chapter 5). On 1 May 2004, 10 new member states (Cyprus, the Czech Republic, Estonia, Hungary, Latvia, Lithuania, Malta, Poland, the Slovak Republic and Slovenia) joined the EU, as did Romania and Bulgaria in January 2007. As soon as these countries meet the convergence criteria they will have to adopt the euro (see Chapter 6); unlike Denmark and the United Kingdom, they have not been granted opt-out clauses. Having met all the convergence criteria, Slovenia adopted the euro on 1 January 2007, as did Cyprus and Malta on 1 January 2008.

We next analyse the main 'economic' benefits and costs of adopting a common currency within a geographical area. This leads to a discussion of when it becomes optimal for a group of countries to adopt a common currency and to the question of whether or not Europe is an optimum currency area. We begin by considering the economic benefits of adopting a common currency.

3.2   ECONOMIC BENEFITS OF ADOPTING A
COMMON CURRENCY

There are a number of benefits that accrue when a group of countries relinquish their national currencies and adopt a common currency. In what follows we outline the three main benefits of adopting a common currency for members of a currency union. These are:

- the elimination of the transaction costs associated with currency conversion;
- greater price transparency; and
- the elimination of exchange rate uncertainty and risk.

3.2.1   Elimination of the Transaction Costs Associated with Currency Conversion

The most obvious, direct, benefit of adopting a common currency is the elimination of the transaction costs of converting currency between members of a currency union. For example, prior to the introduction of the euro, if a German firm wanted to buy goods from a French firm it would have to pay a commission to a bank to convert German marks into French francs, so that it could pay the French firm in its own currency. When Germany and France adopted the euro these transaction costs were eliminated. Although the banking sector has lost out on the commission it previously received for executing national currency conversions between euro-area members, the elimination of transaction costs represents a net gain to society. However, such gains are small, especially compared to the potential gains from greater transparency in prices.

3.2.2   Greater Price Transparency

A second, indirect, benefit of adopting a common currency is that it results in greater price transparency. When goods are priced in the same currency, direct price comparisons for goods are made easier. In principle, this should increase competition and benefit consumers who can shop around more easily and buy goods from the cheapest supplier. Although the adoption of a common currency results in greater price transparency, it is important to note that price discrimination is unlikely to be entirely eliminated across euro-area countries. Indeed, the European Commission has produced evidence which suggests that there are significant price differentials for the same goods between European Union (EU) countries. This implies that trade is to some extent inhibited by national borders and that border effects can, in part, explain the existence of price differentials. Furthermore, having a single currency is unlikely to lead to much greater price convergence across countries for certain goods, such as groceries from supermarkets, because transaction costs are high (especially consumer travel costs) as a percentage of the price of such goods.

3.2.3 Elimination of Exchange Rate Uncertainty and Risk

A third main benefit that accrues to countries that relinquish their national currencies in favour of a common currency is the elimination of exchange rate uncertainty and risk. Prior to the advent of the euro, if a German firm placed an order to buy goods from a French firm in six months' time it would not know what the future cost of the goods would be in marks. For example, if the exchange rate was 1 mark = 2.50 francs at the time when the order was placed for the French goods priced at 5000 francs, then the total cost of the goods in marks would be 2000 marks. If, however, in the interim six-month period between placing the order and delivery of the goods, the exchange rate were to fall to 1 mark = 2.25 francs (that is, the mark was worth less in terms of francs) then the total cost of the goods in marks would rise to 2222 marks. As such, exchange rate uncertainty is likely to act as a deterrent to trade. *Within* the euro area there is no longer any exchange rate risk, which may in turn lead to greater trade between euro-area countries.

Uncertainty about future exchange rate movements not only results in uncertainty about the future costs of goods and services, which may deter trade, it may also adversely affect investment and economic growth. Elimination of exchange rate uncertainty and risk between euro-area countries may also lead to a reduction in the real cost of raising capital, which may in turn increase investment and stimulate economic growth.

What light has empirical work been able to shed on the effects of exchange rate variability, and common currencies, on trade? Studies undertaken in the 1980s and 1990s provided mixed results. Reviewing the evidence, Bacchetta and van Wincoop (2000, p. 1093) suggest that despite the widespread view that one of the main benefits of adopting a single European currency is increased trade, 'the substantial empirical literature examining the link between exchange-rate uncertainty and trade has not found a consistent relationship'. However, over more recent years, a series of econometric studies initiated by Andrew Rose, Professor of International Business at the University of California, Berkeley, has provided strong support for the hypothesis that currency unions significantly promote trade. In a pioneering piece of work Rose (2000) estimated the *separate effects* on trade of exchange rate volatility and common currencies. He found that while lower exchange rate volatility increases trade, the effect of common currencies on trade is much larger than that of 'reducing moderate exchange rate volatility to zero but retaining separate currencies' (p. 31). With respect to the effect of common currencies on trade he estimated that two countries with a common currency trade more than three times as much as they would with separate currencies. Rose has since undertaken collaborative work with a number of leading researchers in the field, including Eric van Wincoop (Federal Reserve Bank of New York) and Jeffrey Frankel (Harvard University). Two examples will suffice. First, Rose and van Wincoop (2001, p. 386) concluded that a national currency appears to be a significant barrier to trade and estimated that 'EMU will cause European trade to rise by over 50 per cent' and that 'the benefits of trade created by currency union may swamp any costs of foregoing independent monetary policy'. Second, using data for over 200 countries, Frankel and Rose (2002) studied the effect of common currencies on trade and income. They estimated that belonging to a currency union 'triples trade with the partners in question' and that over a 20-year period 'every 1 percent increase in total trade (relative to GDP) raises income per capita by at least one-third of a per cent' (p. 461). Interestingly Frankel and Rose also concluded that 'a country like Poland, which conducts half its trade with the euro zone could eventually boost income per capita by a fifth by joining EMU' (p. 461).

At this point a word of caution is appropriate. Although there is widespread agreement that the adoption of the euro will lead to an increase in intra-euro-area trade, some economists question whether the effects are as large as the above studies suggest. In a recent ECB working paper on the euro's trade effects, Baldwin (2006) has suggested that the consensus view is that the euro has already boosted intra-euro-area trade by 5–10 per cent.

Having outlined the mains benefits of a common currency we now turn to consider its costs.

3.3   ECONOMIC COSTS OF ADOPTING A COMMON CURRENCY

The main cost to a nation of relinquishing its currency and joining a common currency area is that it gives up its freedom to set its own national monetary policy – essentially its interest rate. This also means that *within* the group of countries that *irrevocably* fix their exchange rates between one another, adjustment to the macroeconomic consequences of a shock or disturbance is no longer possible through changes in the value of the exchange rate. In order to illustrate how the loss of independent monetary policy and exchange rate adjustment may be problematic, consider the following scenario.

Suppose that within the EU, consumers *permanently* shift their preferences away from German goods and services to French goods and services. What impact will the shift in consumer preferences have on output, employment and the price level in the two countries? In Germany, the decrease in aggregate demand for its goods will lead to a fall in output, an increase in unemployment and a fall in the price level. In contrast, in France, output will rise, unemployment fall and the price level will rise. However, in principle, as long as wages are flexible in Germany and France both economies will automatically adjust to a new equilibrium at their full employment or natural levels of output and employment.

How does wage flexibility ensure automatic adjustment? In Germany, as output falls and unemployment increases, wages will begin to fall. As firms' wage costs are reduced, aggregate supply will increase and lower prices lead to an extension of aggregate demand until a new equilibrium is established with output and employment in Germany returning to the level attained before the shift in consumer preferences. In contrast, in France, as output rises and unemployment falls, wages will start to rise. Increased wage costs lead to a decrease in aggregate supply and higher prices lead to a contraction of aggregate demand until a new equilibrium is established, with output and employment in France returning to their previous levels.

Automatic adjustment to a new equilibrium will be reinforced by the fall in German wages and prices, which will make French goods less competitive, resulting in a decrease in aggregate demand for French goods, while wage and price increases in France will make German goods more competitive, resulting in an increase in aggregate demand for German goods.

In principle there is another mechanism which would allow both economies to automatically adjust to a new equilibrium in the face of positive or negative shocks. This mechanism requires a high degree of labour mobility between the two countries concerned. Suppose workers in Germany having lost their jobs following the shift in consumer preferences away from German goods were to migrate to France where there is an excess demand for labour. In this case, unemployment need not rise in Germany and the potential for inflationary wage pressures in France will be curtailed as new (German) workers join the French labour market.

To recap, in principle, as long as wages are flexible and/or there is a high degree of labour mobility between Germany and France, then the two countries can automatically adjust to an *asymmetric* aggregate demand shock, that is, one that is uneven in its impact on the two economies. If, however, wages are inflexible and/or the degree of labour mobility is limited, adjustment is likely to be both long and painful. During a prolonged period of adjustment, Germany would experience sustained unemployment and France rising inflation, which would create tensions within the currency union. In these circumstances, policy makers in Germany would favour a cut in interest rates to boost aggregate demand and reduce unemployment, while their counterparts in France would favour a rise in interest rates to dampen inflationary pressures. However, having adopted a common currency neither country would be free to set its own individual monetary policy. As a result, interest rates, which are set in the euro area by the ECB, are likely to be higher than Germany would like and lower than France would like. While income transfers to Germany from elsewhere in the EU might help to alleviate some of the pain caused by the negative demand shock, it is important to note that it would not provide a solution to the adjustment problem.[26]

---

[26] Such transfers are available under the EU's cohesion policy programmes. However, cohesion policy budgets are relatively small, amounting to the equivalent of only 0.37 per cent of the gross national income of the EU27 for the 2007–13 period.

We next consider whether events would have been different if Germany and France had not been in a currency union and had instead retained their own currencies. In this situation, adjustment to the macroeconomic consequences of the asymmetric demand shock could, in principle, have been achieved through movements in the exchange rate. Suppose, for example, that the two countries concerned were operating within a flexible exchange rate regime. In this case, both countries would be free to set their own domestic interest rate as an instrument of their national monetary policy. In an attempt to stimulate aggregate demand and reverse the rise in unemployment, Germany could lower its interest rate, while France – worried about rising wages and prices – could raise its interest rate in order to reduce the French demand for goods and services. Movements in the exchange rate would also tend to boost the aggregate demand for German goods and reduce the demand for French goods. *Ceteris paribus*, following the fall in German interest rates and the fall in demand for German goods (and therefore German marks) the price of the German mark would depreciate, while the rise in French interest rates and the increase in demand for French goods (and therefore the demand for French francs) would lead to an appreciation of the French franc. As French goods sold in Germany become more expensive and German goods sold in France become cheaper, French net exports would fall, resulting in a fall in aggregate demand in France, and German net exports would rise, boosting aggregate demand in Germany.

Alternatively, suppose that Germany and France had retained their own currencies but instead of operating within a flexible exchange rate regime had chosen to fix or peg their exchange rate against *another* currency, such as the dollar. In this situation, both countries would be free to devalue or revalue their exchange rates. In other words, they would be able to change the external price of their currency as an instrument of monetary policy. For example, Germany could choose to devalue the price of the mark against the French franc in order to boost aggregate demand in Germany. Following a devaluation of the mark, German goods sold in France would become cheaper and French goods sold in Germany would become more expensive, boosting aggregate demand for German goods. When a country joins a common currency area it loses its ability to devalue or revalue its exchange rate as an instrument of policy.

At this stage it would be helpful to summarize the main points analysed above. We have seen that when a group of countries join a monetary union they irrevocably fix exchange rates between their national currencies. In consequence, each country sacrifices its ability to change its exchange rate as an instrument of economic policy. While monetary union does *not necessarily* require a single currency, EMU entails a European currency union in which a single currency circulates. The adoption of a single currency, the euro, means that *each* EMU country gives up the freedom it had to set its own national monetary policy and, in addition, forfeits its ability to use exchange rate policy as an instrument of national policy. In these circumstances each country faces the so-called 'one size fits all problem' as it is the ECB that is now responsible for conducting a *single* monetary policy for the euro area (see Chapter 4, section 4.1).

Having discussed the main 'economic' benefits and costs of adopting a common currency we now turn to consider the issue of when it becomes optimal for a group of countries to adopt a common currency.

3.4 COMPARING THE BENEFITS AND COSTS OF ADOPTING A COMMON CURRENCY

Trying to assess whether or not it is advantageous for a group of countries to relinquish their monetary sovereignty in favour of a common currency requires a comparison of the benefits and costs involved. Such an exercise is closely linked to the concept of an optimum currency area (OCA) first developed by Robert Mundell (Professor of Economics at Columbia University). In 1999, Mundell won a Nobel Memorial Prize in Economics partly for this work. An OCA is an area over which it is better to have a single or common currency, rather than separate national currencies. In his analysis, Mundell found an OCA to be a set of regions within which the degree of labour mobility is high enough to ensure full employment when one particular region experiences a disturbance. Mundell's (1961) pioneering work on OCAs has spawned a vast literature on the subject, much of which has been concerned with identifying the key criteria used to determine membership of an OCA. Among the most important relationships between member countries of a potential OCA are: (i) the degree of trade integration; (ii) the degree of symmetry in economic shocks and business cycles; and (iii) the degree of labour market flexibility.

As we shall now discuss, the same criteria that have been used to assess whether a particular group of countries can be considered to be an OCA can be used to judge the suitability of different European countries participating in EMU. Let us examine more closely the factors noted above and see how they affect the benefits and costs of adopting a common currency.

The benefits of adopting a common currency depend, to a large extent, on the amount of trade that takes place between member countries of a currency union. The more *intra* 'currency union' trade undertaken, the greater will be the benefit in terms of both the elimination of transaction costs and the advantages arising from enhanced price transparency. Similarly, the benefit that accrues to a group of countries that relinquish their national currencies and adopt a common currency, in terms of eliminating exchange rate uncertainty and risk, will be greater, the greater is the amount of trade that takes place between them. Furthermore, to the extent that common currencies themselves stimulate greater trade (remember Andrew Rose's estimates we discussed earlier) these benefits are likely to increase over time for countries belonging to a currency union. Table 3.1 quantifies the share of inter-regional trade flows for the world's major regions in 2005. The table shows that Europe undertakes more intra-regional trade than any other region, with almost three-quarters of exports from European countries going to other European countries. The next highest intra-regional trade shares are for North America (55.8 per cent) and Asia (51.2 per cent). This evidence suggests that Europe is indeed the world's primary candidate for common-currency integration.

The costs of adopting a common currency – arising from the loss of national monetary policy autonomy and exchange rate policy autonomy – depend on the degree of labour market flexibility and the degree of symmetry of economic shocks and business cycles, between the countries concerned. As we discussed in section 3.3, following an asymmetric aggregate demand shock, adjustment is likely to be relatively short-lived and painless only if there is a high degree of wage flexibility and/or labour mobility in the common currency area. Where labour market inflexibility prevails, the 'one size fits all' monetary policy problem is likely to create severe tensions among the countries that make up the currency union. This difficulty will be eased where countries

Table 3.1   Share of inter-regional trade flows in each region's total merchandise exports, 2005

Destination→ / Origin↓	North America	South and Central America	Europe	Commonwealth of Independent States (CIS)	Africa	Middle East	Asia	World
North America	**55.8**	5.9	16.1	0.5	1.2	2.3	18.3	100.0
South and Central America	33.2	**24.3**	19.1	1.6	2.7	1.8	13.4	100.0
Europe	9.1	1.3	**73.2**	2.5	2.6	2.8	7.6	100.0
Commonwealth of Independent States (CIS)	5.7	2.0	52.3	**18.1**	1.4	3.1	11.8	100.0
Africa	20.2	2.8	42.9	0.3	**8.9**	1.7	16.3	100.0
Middle East	12.3	0.6	16.1	0.6	2.9	**10.1**	52.2	100.0
Asia	21.9	1.9	17.9	1.3	1.9	3.2	**51.2**	100.0
World	20.6	3.0	43.3	2.2	2.4	3.2	24.0	100.0

Source: World Trade Organization.

in the currency union are subject to symmetric economic shocks and where business cycles among member countries are highly correlated. If, for example, aggregate demand increased in all countries simultaneously, triggering a synchronized upturn in economic activity across all economies, then all countries in the currency union would support a policy of increasing interest rates in order to dampen inflationary pressures. Interestingly, Frankel and Rose (1998) have argued that EMU may not only 'provide a substantial impetus for trade expansion' (p. 1024), but also as a result business cycles may become more synchronized across countries because of currency union. This finding led them to conclude that a 'country is more likely to satisfy the criteria for entry into a currency union *ex post* than *ex ante*' (p. 1024).

What should be apparent from our discussion is that it is a challenging task to assess whether or not the benefits of adopting a common currency outweigh the costs involved for the individual countries concerned. Not only will the benefits and costs vary from one country to another, but they may also be endogenous – meaning that the benefits may increase and the costs decrease over time. What economists have sought to do is identify those 'economic' factors, which can inform *judgements* regarding the suitability of different European countries to participate in EMU. The greater the overall degree of economic integration (both in terms of product and factor markets) between a country and members of an existing currency union, the more likely it is that a country will benefit from joining a common currency.

3.5   IS EUROPE AN OPTIMUM CURRENCY AREA?

While it is not possible to provide a definitive, universally accepted answer to this question, many economists argue that Europe is not yet an OCA. What our discussion has highlighted is the importance of such factors as the extent of trade integration and the degree of labour market flexibility. Many European countries are heavily engaged in intra-EU trade, which is likely to intensify over time as a result of the more widespread adoption of the euro. Against this, the degree of labour market flexibility in Europe is generally quite low (certainly compared to the United States), which makes Europe as an OCA a more distant prospect. Labour mobility, one form of flexibility, between European countries is, for example, particularly low. Leaving aside labour movements across Europe from a number of the new EU member states (for example, Poland), differences in language and culture appear to impede labour mobility between the 15 (pre-2004) EU countries.

Let us conclude our discussion with a quote from Robert Mundell, whom you will recall introduced the concept of an OCA, and who many regard as the father of the euro. At first it might seem somewhat perplexing that given Europe's relatively inflexible labour market, Mundell has been such a strong supporter of EMU; in the late 1960s/early 1970s he put forward the first plan for a single European currency (see Mundell, 1973). However, in conversation with the present authors he pointed out:

> [T]he optimum currency argument has been used both for and against the creation of the euro. People who object to the euro point to labour immobility in Europe. But in fact Europe has just as much labour mobility as it wants. The European Commission sends money to depressed regions so labour won't have to emigrate. The fact is there are strong arguments for making currency areas large and these dominate the case for making them small. (Vane and Mulhearn, 2006, p. 98)

In the next chapter we shall consider the euro's architecture, most notably the European Central Bank and the Stability and Growth Pact. Before turning to Chapter 4, however, be sure to read the interview with Niels Thygesen, which provides some fascinating insights into many of the issues addressed in this chapter.

NIELS THYGESEN

Niels Thygesen is Emeritus Professor of International Economics at the University of Copenhagen, Denmark and is currently Chairman of the Economic and Development Review Committee at the Organization for Economic Cooperation and Development (OECD) in Paris, France. Professor Thygesen was the sole academic member of the Delors Committee for the *Study of Economic and Monetary Union*. He is best known for his work on international macroeconomics and finance, and the international monetary system. His many publications in these fields include his renowned book, *European Monetary Integration: From the European Monetary System Towards Monetary Union* (with Daniel Gros) (Longman, 1992; 2nd edition, 1998).

We interviewed Professor Thygesen in his office at the OECD in Paris on 21 November 2006.

In 1985, the new European Commission led by Jacques Delors under the auspices of the Single Internal Market programme revived the prospect of EMU. What were the main political and economic impulses behind the Single Internal Market programme?
I think the programme was conceived in 1983/84, when Europe was doing relatively poorly compared to the United States. At that time the fragmentation of Europe, in particular with respect to product markets, was a major impediment to growth, the development of Europe-wide firms and trade in Europe. So industry, with some understanding from large parts of the political spectrum, started to work in favour of a single market. That is why I think the drive for a single market came up at that particular time. Although European economies were beginning to recover by 1984 their performance was still not very satisfactory. The idea of a single market also had the advantage of embracing all European economies including the UK under Mrs Thatcher's government which, as you know, was not particularly favourable to European integration.

The Single European Act (1986) contained a reference to the objective of EMU, the first since Werner. Can you say anything about how this came about? Was it primarily through the agency of Jacques Delors, or a more widely shared aspiration? We seem to recall Mrs Thatcher complaining later that no-one had told her that this objective had been included, the inference being that it had been smuggled in.

There is no doubt that Jacques Delors played a vital role in this question – maybe more so than in the single market programme, which was not his initiative. When the idea of a single market developed he thought initially of tagging on tighter monetary integration to the single market. He made proposals to that effect, with the support of a couple of governments in Europe, most notably Belgium. But he was told firmly by the Germans and others that there was no question of this intergovernmental conference also handling monetary affairs – that would have to be the subject of another, later, intergovernmental conference. However, the Germans were not averse to mentioning it as a long-term objective of the European Union. So that was how it got into the Treaty text, as a repetition of an objective of the Werner debates of the early 1970s.

Do you accept that the 1987 Basle–Nyborg Agreement and the evolution of the ERM into an apparently fixed and non-adjustable system led inexorably to the crises of 1992 and 1993?
No, I would say that statement is too strong. The Basle–Nyborg Agreement basically exhausted the possibility of having more coordination of policies without a treaty change. It was seen as not quite enough. Not because people at the time were focused on underlying divergence within Europe that would make it impossible to maintain an increasing degree of exchange rate stability, but more because, in particular, the last realignment inside the ERM in January 1987 was seen as being unjustified subsequently. That realignment didn't really have an economic foundation and was due to tensions with the dollar. Markets perceived different currencies in a different light and that created tensions between the mark and the franc at the time. There was a small adjustment to take the heat out of the markets. But both countries realized subsequently that it wasn't really necessary. So no, I don't accept that the Basle–Nyborg Agreement, which was hatched up later that year, led to tensions that could not be contained. Indeed one shouldn't overlook that nearly all the countries that were at that time in the ERM and who went through the 1992/93 crises came back to the same parities that were established in January 1987. Insufficient underpinnings and management were the reasons that led, soon after the Basle–Nyborg Agreement had been concluded, to the start of negotiations on full monetary union.

If that was the case, how can you account for the fact that the pre-1987 period was one marked by frequent realignments inside the ERM, whereas after 1987 until 1992 the ERM effectively functioned as a non-realignable system?

In the course of the 1980s there was a considerable convergence of inflation rates inside Europe. The French, Italians and the Belgians who had well above German inflation rates came much closer to German inflation levels. This allowed the system to be managed with much smaller and infrequent realignments than in the past. Besides, I think that the experience of having frequent realignments up until 1983 led to a feeling that it would be far better to avoid them. The misalignments inside the system were not, by any means, obvious over the period 1987–90. Then of course with Spain, the UK and Portugal joining the system in the late 1980s–early 1990s that created new tensions. I think it is correct to say that the system did become overly rigid given the presence of, in particular, the three Mediterranean countries in the system. If you look at the UK and subsequent exchange rate experience, one could not really say that the UK was clearly out of line, except in a cyclical sense, but not in a longer-term perspective.

The European Council established the Delors Committee on EMU in 1988, shortly after the ECOFIN decision to abolish all capital controls in the EMS by 1990. This was clearly a period in which governments felt confident about their ability to progressively shape European monetary arrangements. We are interested in your recollections of the leaders and laggards in this process, in terms of both national governments and their political and industrial constituencies. Who and what were the main drivers behind capital liberalization and European monetary union at the time?

The Germans and the Dutch had for several years been teasing the other European countries, saying that they were not prepared to expose their currencies to the judgement of the markets, given that they were still maintaining various restrictions on capital flows – a sign that they were not ready for any further steps towards monetary integration. Maybe to the surprise of Herr [Gerhard] Stoltenberg, the German finance minister at the time, the French, Italians and others came round to the view that it would be to their advantage to liberalize capital flows. Once it became clear that a clear majority was developing in favour of removing residual capital controls, the Germans lost a major argument. Indeed in 1988 they admitted that there was now a case for reconsidering joint monetary management which was, in a sense, counterpart to full monetary integration. Many economists were sceptical and thought there would be an extremely difficult transition phase, which proved to be the case. I think the change of attitude came before the Delors Committee was set up.

In 1988 you were chosen as one of three independent experts, who together with the-then 12 national central bank governors, and two members of the European Commission, comprised the Delors Committee. Did your nomination come as a surprise? On reflection why do you think you were chosen?

Well at the time not that many academics had written a lot about monetary union. I had the advantage, relative to some of my academic colleagues, of having one foot in the central-banking world. I had been an advisor to the Governor of the Bank of Denmark. I had followed the start of the EMS very carefully and had written quite a bit on how it would still be an unstable mechanism. In 1985 I, together with my subsequent co-author Daniel Gros, obtained a substantial funding grant from several of the central banks including the German Bundesbank. In September 1985 I went to the Bundesbank with a couple of other people and we presented the Governor, Mr [Karl Otto] Pöhl, with the argument that once other European countries approached German performance with respect to inflation then the present system would have to be revised in some way. Those countries would want a share in monetary governance in Europe. Pöhl was sufficiently open to that idea and thought that it would be valuable to study the issue. In the group we had a mixture of officials and academics, including Paul De Grauwe. The Bundesbank sent us one of their most conservative members, a president of one of their regional banks, who was a critic of monetary integration. That prepared me quite well for this kind of assignment as I had a practical view of the objections to monetary union, both from the traditional Keynesian view and from the more conservative German view. Nevertheless it was still a surprise when I was nominated to be a member of the Delors Committee. For a long time the idea that it should be a committee strictly of central bank governors seemed to gain ground. That view was certainly favoured by the central bank governors themselves who didn't want outsiders included. They particularly objected to the idea of Jacques Delors taking the chair of the committee. But in the end a compromise was reached. As well as the central bank governors in a personal capacity, and Mr Delors and Mr [Frans] Andriessen of the Commission, it was decided that there would be three independent experts of which Mr [Alexandre] Lamfalussy, the Bank of International Settlements general manager, was an obvious choice. The Spanish former finance minister, Miguel Boyer, was also a natural choice because the report would be delivered during the Spanish presidency. The third person chosen was myself, an academic. I was fortunate and privileged to be chosen. One comment I remember that appeared in the French press suggested that: 'all we can say is that Thygesen has not been chosen to slow the process down'. [*Laughter*]

The brief the Committee was given was to address the question of how European monetary union could be achieved by 'proposing concrete stages leading towards economic and monetary union'. Were you surprised that, as a Committee, you were not asked to express an opinion on whether you thought European monetary union was desirable?
No, I wasn't really surprised. I must say that I think it was very clever to formulate the question in terms of how European monetary union could be achieved. It would have been extremely difficult to get anywhere if the question had been whether monetary union was desirable. Several of the European central banks would not have committed themselves to say whether they thought it was a good or bad idea. They liked and appreciated the formulation of asking the question in terms of – assuming we are going to have monetary union – how could we do it and how could we get there? They were definitely more comfortable with this particular mandate.

Can you give us a flavour of your experiences on the Delors Committee?
It was a committee which worked to a very short timetable. We had eight or nine meetings between September 1988 and April 1989. One reflection is that the governors saw their role somewhat differently. Some of them really took it very seriously that they were there in their individual capacity as experts – they didn't seek advice from colleagues at home. That applied, for example, to Karl Otto Pöhl. Of course, he knew perfectly well what the attitude of his colleagues in the bank was, but he didn't brief them at any time during the proceedings. He only consulted one or two people in the Bundesbank to discuss certain technical issues. A couple of the other governors also behaved like that. Then there were some, such as the UK governor, who were

possibly obliged to seek very careful briefings about everything that could come up. They arrived at the meetings with very full dossiers to cover anything that might be pushed on the agenda. They were always searching their papers to look for good arguments. [*Laughter*]

Much of the actual work was done by the Chairman and, not least, by the two secretaries to the Committee, Tommaso Padoa-Schioppa, now finance minister in Italy and Gunter Baer, who recently retired from the BIS. It was an excellent team because they balanced each other very well. Padoa-Schioppa is one of the intellectual fathers of the whole process of European integration, and monetary union in particular, and a keen Federalist. Baer was a German variety of a good central bank economist. The fact that they had to produce some joint drafts meant that many potential problems were ironed out. So we had a good balanced document to work from. Members also produced a number of background papers as individual contributions to the debate. Our method of working was surprisingly smooth given the difficulty of the assignment. Jacques Delors spent a lot of time during this period reading up on monetary union. He had some background in central banking having been a fairly lowly functionary initially in his career in the Banque de France. In a way, from my point of view, he was too respectful of the governors of the central banks. He never tried to impose himself. Instead he tried to persuade and was very patient. By nature he is not a very patient man so he was taxed heavily in the Committee by some of the reactions he got from members, particularly towards the end when the final text had to be written up and also when the Committee had to decide whether it would push to continue its work beyond delivering its report. Delors's idea was that the Committee would also do a draft of the Central Bank Statute, which was then only produced subsequently two years later by the Committee of the Central Bank Governors themselves. One advantage of central bank cooperation in Europe is that the governors are in office for long periods of time. They know each other well and there is a lot of mutual trust, understanding and respect. This extends to the difficulties that each of them faces relative to their authorities. The other governors understood that the Bank of England governor had to be negative and question a number of issues. It was clear also that some of the central bank governors were uncomfortable about the project. In a sense they said to themselves, we know what we've got and, while it may not be perfect, if we go all the way to monetary union it may complicate our relations with our domestic governments.

The Delors Committee recommended price stability and central bank independence as the cornerstones of monetary policy in EMU. Was this simply a case of using the Bundesbank as the model of mandate, or were there other considerations here?
Well, as you mention, the Bundesbank had become the anchor of the existing monetary cooperation scheme and several countries had explicitly allied themselves to the German view and, for that matter, to the German currency. They liked importing stability from Germany. That was a practical consideration. But, in addition, several countries were also strongly influenced by recent trends in economic thinking, in particular the notions of credibility and commitment which had come up in the preceding decade in the work of Kydland and Prescott [1977], and Barro and Gordon [1983]. Both factors played a role.

Is it a fair assessment that the unanimity and adroitness with which the Delors Committee mastered its brief generated additional political momentum for EMU?
I don't know how much of a surprise it was. The surprise to some in the UK was that Mr Pöhl also signed up. But why shouldn't he? He had won important points in getting the German central bank as a model. The new institution would carry the legacy of the Bundesbank. That was more important to him than the long-term effect of the Bundesbank losing relative influence in Europe. Signing up also removed, once and for all, the Germans from the constant bilateral pressure from the French.

On reflection what do you consider to be the main strengths and weaknesses of the Delors Report?
The Report was pretty good in outlining the main features of the final stage of EMU – the two premises of price stability, as the primary objective, and independence of the central bank. The implications of that and some of the institutional mechanisms required were spelt out. That was probably the strongest point. The weaker point was the other part of the mandate, describing the stages. Some of us were very worried, when the Committee gave its report, we would never get there. This was partly because the Germans and the Dutch, and maybe a couple of others, strongly resisted any experimentation in the joint

management of the transition period. The French, and in particular the Italians were keen on that. In the end the clarity of the
final objective was sufficiently strong to pull the project along.
This outweighed the fragmented transition you had to go
through to get there.

*How was the Report received when it was published? Were you sur-
prised by the speed at which the proposals gained political momentum?*
Yes. I was keen for EMU to happen, but I didn't anticipate the
momentum it would gain. At first the finance ministers, who had
been kept in the dark by several of their central bank governors,
had to look at the Report. Then it had to go to the heads of governments in Madrid, who gave strong impetus to it. However,
the finance ministers came back and said that they wanted to
look at the Report very carefully and technically. They set up a
committee of European finance officials headed by Elizabeth
Guigou, the French minister, and the Committee reported within
a few weeks that they were in agreement. The UK resistance to
the project wasn't mobilized early enough to derail the project.
The British came up with the idea of a hard ECU [European
Currency Unit] as a parallel currency, as an alternative, some
would say, not only in the transition stage but also as a longer-
term solution, but only on the day when the Guigou Report
was published. There was still the question of when the next
intergovernmental conference should be called and that's when
some extraneous political events – the fall of the Berlin Wall –
speeded the process up. In contrast to some political scientists I
don't attribute a completely decisive role to political factors.
Chancellor [Helmut] Kohl from then on had to concentrate more
on the German unification project. He didn't devote all that
much attention to monetary union from the winter of 1989/90.
So it was a product of several circumstances. The Maastricht
Treaty conference was called for December 1990 and the
Germans agreed as a concession that there would be two parallel conferences – one on economic and monetary union, and one
on political union, although it was never very clearly specified
what that meant. At the time when the Delors Committee
reported, nobody anticipated the dramatic events that would
take place in Eastern Europe. Nor did they when the Madrid
Council met in June of that year. If you had told them that
Eastern Europe would experience political turmoil three to four
months later, no one would have believed it.

What were the implications of the fall of the Berlin Wall in 1990 for the EMU project?

Well, as I said, it did I think advance the timing of the intergovernmental conference. It also diverted Chancellor Kohl's attention, understandably, away from monetary union. Chancellor Kohl was subsequently reproached by people in Germany that he had been too casual and neglectful in insisting on German interests in negotiations on monetary union.

At the time how did you interpret the implications of the crises of the ERM in 1992 and 1993 for EMU? What did you think of the British Prime Minister John Major's view that the difficulties of the ERM gave plans for the EMU the appearance of a rain dance with about the same potency?

I can see the point that if you cannot maintain a fairly loose arrangement like the ERM then how can you expect to live up to a commitment to full monetary union. That argument was also advanced in Denmark where my government was a bit more favourable to monetary union than the British government, but still not ready for it. However, I think that in some countries it had the opposite effect because people said to themselves: 'we thought we had a good stable system but it didn't turn out that way'. To have an agreement where you can still change currencies by significant amounts from day to day is not reassuring and the markets will push you into a situation where it becomes untenable. Some thought we had to go beyond that and so the crises were for them an illustration of the need for monetary union. Obviously there was a transitional phase where one had to accept ever-looser rules in the ERM, as happened from the summer of 1993. That again was taken by some – Mr Major and my own Prime Minister – as a signal that plans for monetary union couldn't possibly be put together again. In 1994 and early 1995 there were significant movements of currencies inside the ERM. For example, both Spain and Portugal devalued. But on the whole the system proved robust and it gained the additional point that it had some credibility in markets as it was no longer underpinned by very firm rules and lots of intervention by central banks. So maybe it was a healthy experience for the system, although it did not look like that at the very beginning.

To what extent did you, and other informed commentators, anticipate the pressures that would come to beset the ERM, resulting in the crises of 1992/93?

It was becoming apparent that there was a lot of desynchroniza-
tion inside Europe. After the German unification that began in
1990, German public finances were showing massive deficits.
The Germans were going through a considerable boom, particularly in construction, but also in demand in general as public
spending in the former East Germany rose sharply. In order to
have only a moderate hike in inflation the Bundesbank felt that
they had to raise interest rates considerably. This increase was
much more than most of the rest of the ERM participants found
useful from their own point of view. Nevertheless most of them
stuck to the Deutschmark. The widening of the bands in 1993
was also a response to possible still larger instability in the
Deutschmark than we had seen in the past. There was some
analysis in various newspapers in 1991 that tensions within the
system were building up. In our book, Gros and myself pointed
out that the Spanish and Italian currencies had become somewhat suspect by that time, as was the pound sterling. In the case
of the UK this was more the result of cyclical reasons: the UK had
been through a boom already and was cooling off, needing lower
interest rates. The personal antagonism between officials in the
UK and Germany was in itself an argument for saying that the
exchange rates couldn't hold. Mr [Norman] Lamont, the UK
Chancellor of the Exchequer, and the Bundesbank didn't see eye
to eye at all.

*The Maastricht criteria for individual country participation in EMU
were macroeconomic in orientation but the criteria conventionally
used to judge the viability of an optimum currency area are rooted in
microeconomic considerations. How can these alternative approaches be
reconciled?*
That's a profound question and one that I don't really know the
answer to. Much discussion right now relates to this issue, especially as we are in the process of taking a few more members into
EMU by means of the same, largely, nominal criteria. That doesn't
prevent the ECB from looking at some of the underlying problems
of potential new entrants, which are embodied in the traditional
optimum currency area criteria. The Maastricht criteria were formulated at a time when nobody was aware that we would have
very different members in the future. In my view it is unfortunate
that these criteria have survived into the present when they are
clearly less appropriate than they were in the 1990s. Having said
that I don't regard them as being totally inappropriate. They ini-

tially turned out to be quite easy to fulfil, since 11 members met the criteria on the basis of their performance in 1997.

What is your view of the way in which the Maastricht criteria were actually applied (we are thinking here in particular of the 'creative accounting' which allowed the larger countries to meet their deficit obligations)?
Well the effort was not quite as massive as might have been expected a priori because Italy, Spain and Portugal started from very high rates of interest and the fact that they were able to converge towards the much lower rates in Germany simply through declaring that they were now getting ready for monetary union saved them several percentage points in terms of their budget deficits – in the Italian case by as much as 5–6 per cent of GDP simply through lower interest rates; and then there was the considerable stimulus of lower rates to the domestic economy which made it easier for countries to maintain good growth while consolidating the public finances. So there was a package solution for these countries which was not unattractive. It is true it did lead to questions over accounting – particularly of one-off measures. Italy had a tax for one year – the so-called euro tax. We've seen subsequently of course other examples – the Greeks were called into question for what they did two years later when they were approaching monetary union. These experiences do show, however, that monitoring through a common rules system has advantages in itself. It brings out into the open the kind of accounting tricks that go on in all countries. Now, finally, Eurostat and the monitoring mechanisms are getting to grips with these irregular practices. That's another argument for having these fiscal rules, quite apart from the fact that in the long run it would endanger monetary union if you had countries that were operating at substantial levels of deficit, with relatively high debt. That would create automatic lobbying for low interest rates so as not to make their burden worse. It would be difficult to operate a European central bank where a number of countries were in that position. I think this is a valid argument which remains topical. Only, there has been a reshuffle so that those who were, in the 1990s, in favour of tight monetary policies are now among those who want the lowest possible interest rates – Germany, for example.

A number of commentators have been highly critical of the seemingly arbitrary 3 per cent and 60 per cent limits chosen for the government budget deficit and debt as percentages of GDP. Some have even

suggested they resemble some form of voodoo economics. What is your
view on these norms?
I think that they can be justified. The 3 per cent rule was not
chosen in a completely arbitrary way. By the end of the 1980s in
France, for example, a ceiling of 3 per cent was already widely
accepted. The figure of 60 per cent was more or less the average
debt level in the whole European Union at the time when these
criteria were negotiated. So that didn't seem too outrageous
either. In a sense it was a crude device to pick this figure as some
countries were well above it, while others were well below 60 per
cent. There was also a link between the two figures, which made
them hang together. If you assume that the normal situation is one
in which you have 2 per cent inflation and 3 per cent real growth
annually, giving 5 per cent nominal growth, then a 3 per cent
government budget deficit will in the long run produce a 60 per
cent debt-to-GDP ratio. The two figures seemed to fit together. I'm
not so critical of the numbers. They have since been refined in a
number of ways with the Stability and Growth Pact. For example,
we now have differentiation by country. As a result we now have
a fairly complete and detailed negotiating framework.

The Maastricht Treaty closely followed the main proposals contained in
the Delors Report. How important to its successful transition was the
stipulation of a final starting date of 1 January 1999 for full European
monetary union, rather than leaving the date open ended?
I think it was absolutely vital. That date came in only at the very
last stage of the Maastricht negotiations. Until then the process
was seen as one of waiting until there was a majority of countries
ready for monetary union. Only then would the process start. The
push by the Italians and the French, which Chancellor Kohl
accepted – apparently much to the disappointment of his country-
men – was to say that we would have an ultimate date of 1 January
1999 when the project would start, regardless of the number of participants who were ready. That created an opposite dynamic, in
that countries that were not too far from being able to meet that
date wanted to be sure to be in the first group. That was what drove
the three Mediterranean countries, and maybe others too who
were on the borderline, to make the deadline of 1 January 1999. If
we had not had that final date I think it is quite possible that there
would have only been four or five countries ready by then. Then
you would have evaluated the situation again two years later in
line with the formula originally envisaged. It is possible that

we could never have got there. With the fairly unstable situation around 2000, one can imagine a scenario when it wouldn't have taken off two years later either and the whole project might then have evaporated into thin air. The deadline date was absolutely essential and it came in the last week or so of the Maastricht conference. The Dutch had produced a treaty draft, which did not contain a final starting date. It was only when the Italians precisely formulated the idea, got the support of the French, and then persuaded Chancellor Kohl to accept, that it appeared. It came as a great surprise to the UK and Denmark. I think the UK had already made up its mind to stay out. Denmark was not quite ready for the automaticity which was implied by this formulation. We thought we would qualify by meeting the criteria without too many problems, but then we found that we would be forced to go in automatically whenever that happened.

What is your view of the argument that structural inflexibility in the European labour market may cause problems for the economic and political coherence of the euro area in the presence of asymmetric shocks? Is it fair to argue that the long-term integrity of the euro area will be difficult to verify until the euro area has suffered a serious shock?
The answer to your second question is probably yes. We haven't had a serious asymmetric shock yet. I have always been somewhat sceptical about the notion of asymmetrical shocks. If you look back in history most of the shocks classified as asymmetric have had a strong common element for European economies. Oil-price change and movements in the dollar were the two main ones in the past. There are some specific instances of shocks, of an asymmetric form, that were particularly unfavourable to particular countries. But you can perfectly well have divergence with much smaller shocks because of endogenous movements through rigidities in labour markets, which perpetuate disequilibria for some time. The rigidity of European labour markets is a problem. It doesn't show up so much in differences in inflation or in wage rates. In fact wage moderation on the whole has been quite good. Of course we've not exactly had a booming economy so that has yet to be tested against a stronger upswing than we've seen to date. What we can see is that labour market inflexibility sometimes leads to unemployment and other difficulties. Germany supposedly has a rigid labour market. It has tried to introduce several reforms, but it has not got very far except in the important sense that wages have proved to be quite flexible.

Germany has regained the competitiveness it temporarily lost at the time of the formation of EMU. Obviously the flexibility of the labour market is, in the long term, a very important criterion for the success of EMU. Many economists pointed this out when the idea of European monetary union first came on the table. One somewhat superficial philosophy was to say that when monetary union occurs there will be more focus on structural issues with, on balance, some beneficial effect on the speed of labour market reforms. That expectation has not been borne out so far. Indeed some commentators appear to have shown that if anything the pace of reforms, particularly in labour markets, has slowed down after EMU relative to the period up to its start. However, it is not something that immediately threatens monetary union. It would take a long time for these tensions to build up to such an unacceptable level that they would blow up the whole system.

Arguably, because of the euro, the countries in which the currency circulates have fewer concerns over the exchange rate as a generator of general and particular macroeconomic shocks. What is your view of this attribute of EMU? Are there any lessons here for non-euro EU countries?

I think that this is sometimes overlooked in the rather critical tone that the debate about the euro area has taken on in the recent period. If we had not had the euro a lot of attention would today be focused on differential performance between EU countries. In Italy and Spain, for example, we would now be asking whether their currencies were overvalued or whether a stronger adjustment of interest rates in these countries was needed. Much of the attention, which today is focused on longer-term issues, would still have been focused on averting a crisis in the short term. I'm assuming that complete floating is not really on the cards given integration with the single market. So I think we've saved ourselves from a lot of fruitless conflicts that would have arisen out of a fractured system. And this is an important lesson that's not so evident because it's always difficult to envisage counterfactual scenarios, just as it was hard to imagine in the 1990s what a complete monetary union would be like. Here, of course, there are implications for countries that are outside the euro area. The Eastern European countries are obliged to formally seek membership sooner or later and they don't want to delay for too long because of the advantages EMU will bring. It has lesser implications for the UK, Denmark and Sweden. Take my own country, for example. In Denmark we have aligned ourselves very closely to the euro and our policy closely follows that of the ECB. Sweden and the UK are a bit different in that they have different monetary regimes and they allow some flexibility in the exchange rate. But even in these two countries the exchange rate has stabilized quite a bit and their inflation objectives are about the same as those pursued in the euro area. I would say that the eurozone has attractions for those who are not in it. They are not massive ones and while they shouldn't be oversold, they are still there.

The case for the euro has always been the one-market, one-money argument. The currency is now firmly established. To what extent do you think the argument underpinning it has been validated?
Some academic colleagues of mine used to say that one market requires one money. We have now got one money, but do we have one market? [*Laughter*] There is much painful discussion about the more protectionist attitude that has come up in countries such as France. Some of this discussion has been quite demeaning – particularly discussion about the single market in services and integrating the new countries into the system. Now the process is working the other way around. It reminds me of the way we discussed the issue in the Delors Committee. Padoa-Schioppa and others took the strong philosophical view that it was like a spiralling process and that you couldn't do everything in parallel in terms of market integration and monetary integration. You must have times when one runs ahead of the other. The debate at the time of the Delors Committee was that market integration was running ahead of monetary integration and that in order to sustain the achievements of market integration one needed monetary union. Now that we've done monetary union we discover that there are still things that need to be done on the single market side. We can now say that monetary integration has not only caught up with market integration but has overtaken it significantly. I think there is a strong intellectual argument that it is difficult to sustain a really well-functioning internal market without having a very high degree of exchange rate stability and indeed a single currency.

The main costs of monetary union concerns the problem, for participating countries, of dealing with shocks without the use of independent monetary policy. How important has this been in practice?

It depends crucially on the size of country you are looking at. For the smaller countries the ability to use monetary policy in a more or less independent way was not very attractive, even before the 1990s when this discussion really began. You can discuss whether, in some cases, exchange rate fluctuations have performed a useful buffer function. In the UK you have had good growth performance despite an appreciation of the exchange rate around 2000 and subsequent fluctuations. My own guess is that you could probably have at least as good performance with a stable exchange rate. I believe that the advantages of having an independent monetary policy even for a country of some considerable size such as the UK, are questionable. It is always a balance between the exchange rate being a useful buffer and adjustment mechanism, and it being a source of instability. For most countries in continental Europe the instability that arises from currency markets has now been put to one side.

There have been suggestions, notably from the United States, that in its decades-long focus on monetary reform and innovation, the EU has rather lost sight of its real-economy Lisbon Agenda. To what extent do you think this a fair criticism?
Well it's certainly true that many of the most serious problems of Europe have not been addressed. The problem is that there has never been any clear prospect of a community policy on certain issues, despite the rhetoric. It's basically a national responsibility to improve the innovation initiatives, to spend more on research and development etc. The Lisbon philosophy was that there should be more focus on competing within this more stable framework. It is sad that it hasn't worked that way. I accept the argument that attention on monetary union may have diverted some political energy away from other issues, but there are limitations as to what you can do through a European effort to address most of these issues.

Although the ECB controls monetary policy in the euro area, exchange rate policy is formally conditioned by governments, through the European Council, given the discretion they potentially enjoy in respect of 'general orientations' for the euro. To what extent are these contradictory arrangements? What might be their longer-term implications in a world in which global monetary reform might one day be on the agenda?

That's a wide-ranging question. [*Laughter*] Quite frankly, I think that the influence of governments on the exchange rate system is not very great. The European Central Bank has the central role and on a day-to-day basis is in charge through the way it conducts monetary policy. We have yet to see 'general orientations' being issued. If we ever moved to a new international monetary agreement, with fixed rates or target zones for currencies, then governments would come in. But that is not foreseeable in the near future.

Do you believe that the euro will become a key currency to rival the dollar and, if so, what benefits could you see arising from this?
The euro has gained quite a lot of ground in international capital markets, particularly in the bond market. It has also been important in the financial development of Europe. We cannot yet say that it is a serious rival to the dollar. While the trend is in that direction it will probably take another decade or so before you could use that language accurately. It is happening slowly. For example, there is some movement towards the euro in official international reserves. As for the benefits, there is some seigniorage from having the ability to finance imbalances in your own currency. However, this shouldn't be exaggerated because most of this is done today at market interest rates.

The Werner Plan, the ERM and the euro all have economic bases, but are the primary drivers behind the European integration project economic or political?
I don't deny that they may well be political. But I would say that unless there was a good economic case it wouldn't have got on the tracks. Some colleagues, particularly political scientists, say it was really a political project from the Werner days. Although they cite the Kohl–Mitterrand alliance it is a fact that is sometimes overlooked that Kohl could not have moved in the direction of monetary union without the support of a considerable part of German opinion, including the labour unions and internationally orientated exporting firms who liked exchange rate stability *vis-à-vis* the main trading partners.

One final question. Like the UK, Denmark has not yet adopted the euro. Do you think it will and do you think it should?
I think it should. There would be some marginal economic benefits, as well as simply taking part in the decision-making

process, which shapes our framework. The fact that we have become marginalized is a real cost, but not one that interests the electorate very much. While I think that Denmark should adopt the euro I frankly doubt that we will, having had a couple of referenda where the public have expressed a negative view. The trouble with a referendum is that it is a terrible mechanism for discussing a question like EMU. People often use the opportunity to express their dissatisfaction with the government on other issues. And once you've rejected something by a referendum it is hard to accept it without having another referendum. That will keep our politicians from announcing another one for quite a long time. [*Laughter*]

4. The euro's architecture

Having discussed the development of the euro and its underlying economic principles in the previous chapter we now turn to consider the euro's architecture, in particular the European Central Bank (ECB) its principal institution and the Stability and Growth Pact (SGP). We begin by considering monetary policy in the euro area.

4.1 MONETARY POLICY IN THE EURO AREA

4.1.1 The ECB's Decision-making Bodies

You will recall from our discussion in Chapter 3, section 3.1.3, that the Maastricht Treaty established that the second stage of economic and monetary union (EMU) would begin on 1 January 1994 with the creation of the European Monetary Institute (EMI). The EMI, a temporary body, was superseded by the European System of Central Banks (ESCB) and the ECB, both of which were established on 1 June 1998 by the 'Statute of the European System of Central Banks and of the European Central Bank'. The Statute is a protocol, which is attached to the Maastricht Treaty. In Chapter 3, section 3.1.4 we also discussed how the third and final stage of EMU began on 1 January 1999 when exchange rates were irrevocably fixed for the former national currencies of the then-11 participating member countries of the euro area. When the euro was officially launched responsibility for monetary policy in the euro area was transferred from the national central banks (NCBs) of euro-area member countries to the ECB.

The ECB,[27] with headquarters in Frankfurt am Main in Germany, has two *main* decision-making bodies: the Governing Council and the Executive Board:

---

[27] The ECB lies at the core of both the ESCB and what is officially referred to as the Eurosystem. The ESCB comprises the ECB and the NCBs of *all* European Union (EU) member states, regardless of whether or not they have adopted the euro; whereas the

- The Governing Council is the *supreme* decision-making body of the ECB and is responsible for formulating monetary policy for the euro area. It comprises the governors of the NCB countries within the euro area and all (six) members of the Executive Board of the ECB. Members of the ECB's Governing Council are 'collectively responsible' for making monetary policy decisions, most importantly setting interest rates for the euro area.
- The Executive Board is the operational decision-making body of the ECB. As such it is responsible for the implementation of monetary policy in the euro area, in line with the Governing Council's policy decisions. It comprises the president and vice-president of the ECB, and four other members who are appointed by the heads of state or government of countries that have adopted the euro, on the basis of their professional standing and experience in monetary and banking matters. The Executive Board conveys the necessary instructions to the NCBs of the euro-area member countries to carry out the General Council's monetary policy decisions. It also draws up the agenda for the meetings of the Governing Council, prepares the necessary documents for the Governing Council's deliberation, and makes proposals for decisions taken by the Governing Council. As a result it has a *strategic* role in the decision-making process.

In addition to the Governing Council and the Executive Board (which are chaired by the president of the ECB) the ECB has a third (temporary) decision-making body, namely the General Council. The General Council comprises the president and vice-president of the ECB and the governors of *all* EU NCBs. In contrast to the ECB's Governing Council, which sets interest rates for the euro area as a whole, the General Council has no responsibility for monetary policy decisions in the euro area. Having inherited the tasks formerly undertaken by the EMI, its main responsibility is to give advice on the preparations that are necessary to join the euro area. If and when all EU member states adopt the euro it will be

(cont.)
Eurosystem comprises the ECB and the NCBs of only those countries that have adopted the euro. This means that while NCBs in EU member states which have not yet adopted the euro belong to the ESCB, they are not part of the Eurosystem. In consequence, although they are responsible for their own national monetary policies, they take no part in formulating and implementing the *single* monetary policy of the euro area.

BOX 4.1   THE COMPOSITION OF THE ECB's
DECISION-MAKING BODIES

(a)   *Governing Council*
- NCB governors of euro-area member countries
- Members of the Executive Board
(b)   *Executive Board*
- President and vice-president of the ECB
- Four other members
(c)   *General Council*
- President and vice-president of the ECB
- Governors of all EU national central banks

---

dissolved. Box 4.1 provides a convenient summary of the composition of the ECB's three decision-making bodies.

4.1.2   The ECB's Monetary Policy Strategy

The Maastricht Treaty's blueprint for the ECB established that its *primary* objective would be to maintain price stability in the euro area. However, the Treaty (Article 105) did not define what was meant by 'price stability'. In October 1998 the ECB's Governing Council announced that it regarded price stability to be 'a year-on-year increase in the Harmonized Index of Consumer Prices (HICP) for the euro area of below 2%', and added that this objective 'was to be maintained over the medium term'. Subsequently in May 2003, following an evaluation of its monetary policy strategy, the Governing Council declared that 'in the pursuit of price stability it aims to maintain inflation rates below but close to 2% over the medium term'.

At this point in our discussion four observations are worthy of note. First, the Maastricht Treaty stipulates that 'without prejudice to the objective of price stability' the ECB will also 'support the general economic policies in the Community with a view to contributing to the achievement of the objectives of the Community'. As noted in Article 2 of the Treaty, these objectives include a 'high level of employment' and 'sustainable and non-inflationary growth'. Although the Governing Council of the ECB has a mandate to *support* the general economic policies in the euro area, the Treaty does not give it *direct* responsibility for achieving any other objective other than price stability. This reflects the widely-held view that in the short run monetary policy can only influence real variables, such as output and employment, and that it cannot exert any lasting influence on real variables. Second, underlying the primacy given to the objective of price stability is the now widely-accepted view that price stability is a *necessary pre-condition* for sustainable growth of output and employment. For example, price stability helps economic agents make better-informed decisions on whether to borrow, save, spend or invest. It also prevents arbitrary and unplanned changes in the distribution of income and wealth. Third, the announcement of a quantitative definition of price stability provides a *yardstick* against which the ECB's performance can be assessed. Over time, success in achieving its primary objective is likely to increase the ECB's 'legitimacy by result'. Fourth, reference to inflation rates *below*, but *close to* 2 per cent in the *medium term* reflects a consensus view that it is also important to avoid deflation (a situation where the general price level falls over time) and that monetary policy cannot completely eliminate (some inevitable) short-term variation in inflation.

Having noted that the primary objective of the ECB is to maintain price stability, we next consider the analyses it uses to inform its monetary policy strategy. The Governing Council of the ECB bases its monetary policy decisions on a 'two-pillar' approach to the risks to price stability, involving a monetary and an economic analysis. The ECB's *monetary analysis* (originally described as the first pillar of monetary policy) entails an assessment of the rate of growth of a broad monetary aggregate (M3), in relation to a reference value of 4.5 per cent per annum, that is deemed to be compatible with price stability over the medium term (given assumptions regarding real income growth and the velocity of circulation of money). The money growth pillar reflects the consensus view that inflation is a monetary phenomenon, and that over the *long run* the rate of growth of the money supply and inflation are closely related. A substantial body of evidence exists which suggests that periods of high and prolonged inflation tend to be associated with high and sustained monetary growth. As such, a significant and sustained rise in the rate of monetary growth over and above its reference value would signal a medium- to long-term risk to price stability. One of the main problems with the ECB's monetary analysis is that the growth rate of M3 is generally considered to be a poor indicator of short- to medium-term inflationary pressure within the euro area. However, as Dominguez (2006, p. 77) has acknowledged 'to its credit, there is little evidence that the ECB has, in fact, put much weight on monetary aggregates in its monetary policy decisions'.

The second pillar of monetary policy entails an *economic analysis* that focuses on prevailing economic and financial conditions in the euro area. The analysis involves monitoring a range of indicators (including output, wage and price indices, asset prices, business confidence, the balance of payments and the exchange rate), which are deemed relevant for assessing the short- to medium-term risks to price stability. The two-pillar approach, which provides a cross-check of the risks to price stability from the longer-term monetary analysis and the shorter-term economic analysis, is used to inform monetary policy decisions enabling the ECB's Governing Council to set interest rates with the primary objective of maintaining price stability in the euro area.

Although the ECB has exclusive responsibility for formulating the single monetary policy for the euro area, it is important to remember that monetary policy is generally implemented through the NCBs of euro-area member countries in line with the decisions made by the Governing Council of the ECB. The NCBs, acting as agents of the ECB, carry out most of the operational tasks associated with the implementation of monetary policy in the euro area. In addition, based on the principle of home country control, the responsibility for maintaining the stability of the banking system is entrusted to the NCBs. Indeed, as some critics have pointed out, the Maastricht Treaty failed to include any role for the ECB to act as lender of last resort in the case of a banking crisis. While some commentators have called for a 'single' central bank to be established for the whole of the euro area, it is very unlikely that such an approach would ever be politically acceptable. For a full discussion of the ECB's monetary policy strategy and implementation of monetary policy in the euro area, the interested reader is referred to chapters 3 and 4 of European Central Bank (2004).

Finally, it is interesting to note that while the ECB is wholly responsible for monetary policy in the euro area, the ECB 'officially' shares responsibility with the European Union Council of Economics and Finance Ministers (ECOFIN) for the euro area's *external* exchange rate policy. According to the

Maastricht Treaty (Article 109), ECOFIN has the authority to: (i) conclude formal agreements on an exchange rate system for the euro with non-Community currencies and (ii) formulate 'general orientations for exchange-rate policy' of the euro area (in exceptional circumstances, such as the case of a clear misalignment), as long as such arrangements do not impede the ECB's primary objective of maintaining price stability.

4.1.3 Issues Relating to the ECB's Definition of Price Stability, Independence, Lack of Accountability and Perceived Lack of Transparency

Among the main criticisms levied against the ECB are those relating to its adopted definition of price stability, the degree of independence it enjoys, its lack of accountability and perceived lack of transparency. We start by considering criticism of the ECB's definition of price stability.

Criticism has been voiced that the ECB's definition of price stability – maintaining inflation rates below but close to 2 per cent over the medium term – could result in a deflationary bias. Given the *asymmetric* definition it has adopted, critics point out that while the ECB may find an inflation rate of 1.8 per cent (over the medium term) acceptable – though we do not know precisely what 'close to' means – it would presumably judge a rate of 2.2 per cent unacceptable, as it is outside the upper boundary of the definition. This problem would be overcome if the objective for price stability were to be redefined with a symmetric range. In point of fact since 2000, inflation in the euro area has more often than not exceeded 2 per cent (see Figure 7.3) leading some commentators to suggest that 'in practice, the ECB has behaved as if 2 per cent were the midpoint of its inflation range, not the ceiling' (Dominguez, 2006, p. 77).

Let us now turn to issues relating to the ECB's independence, lack of accountability and perceived lack of transparency. The foundation of monetary policy in the euro area is the independence of the ECB, and that of the NCBs, from political influence. Evidence from a number of studies (for example, Alesina and Summers, 1993) shows that, for advanced industrial countries, there is a striking inverse relationship between central bank independence and inflation performance. In other words more central bank independence is strongly associated with lower and more stable inflation. No doubt with this in mind, and given the fact that the ECB is modelled on the political independence given to the German Bundesbank (see Chapter 2, section 2.5), the Maastricht Treaty (Article 107) established that:

> when exercising their powers and carrying out their tasks and duties, neither the ECB, nor a national central bank, nor any member of their decision-making bodies shall seek or take instructions from Community institutions or bodies, from any government of a Member State or from any other body.

Furthermore the Treaty states that:

> Community institutions and bodies, and governments of Member States have undertaken to respect this principle and not to seek to influence the members of the decision-making bodies of the ECB or of the national central banks in the performance of their tasks.

Such institutional independence is designed to shield the ECB from political interference that might impede it from achieving its primary objective of maintaining price stability. In addition to institutional independence, the personal independence of members of the ECB's decision-making bodies is enhanced by relatively long fixed terms of office. For example, NCB governors have a minimum 'renewable' term of office of five years, while members of the Executive Board have a 'non-renewable' term of office of eight years. Although it is widely accepted that the independence of the ECB is essential if it is to achieve its primary objective, some critics have suggested that the ECB enjoys an excessive degree of independence. For example, as we shall discuss below, meaningful changes in its operations can only be imposed following an amendment to the Maastricht Treaty.

Two other criticisms frequently levied against the ECB concern its lack of accountability and perceived lack of transparency. Critics have suggested that the ECB's democratic accountability is limited. For example, the European Parliament is not involved in the appointment of NCB governors, who dominate the composition of the ECB's Governing Council, and it has no power of veto over appointments to the ECB's Executive Board. Somewhat ironically, given that they are appointed by their national governments, NCB governors are not accountable to their national parliaments for any tasks they collectively perform regarding monetary policy for the euro area. Most significantly, the European Parliament has no power to alter the Statute of the ECB. Any alteration to the ECB's Statute would require an amendment

to the Maastricht Treaty ratified by the national parliaments of
every member country belonging to the EU, that is, including
those that have not yet adopted the euro.

As noted, the ECB's Governing Council is responsible for
making monetary policy decisions for the euro area which are
then implemented through the activities of the ECB's Executive
Board and the NCBs of euro-area member countries. One of the
most important communication channels used by the ECB to
provide information about its policy decisions is the monthly
press conference held by the president and vice-president of the
ECB immediately after the first Governing Council meeting of
each month. A number of criticisms have been made regarding
the lack of transparency in this process. For example, despite
requests from the European Parliament, the ECB does not publish
minutes of the Governing Council meetings. Nor does the ECB
publish details of the voting record of Governing Council
members. The main rationale for the non-disclosure of the voting
record is that confidentiality protects the independence of individual members and shields them from any pressure to vote in
line with their national interests. At the time of writing, all
members of the Governing Council have the right to vote. In
anticipation of the problems that could arise in the decision-
making process with the enlargement of the euro area, in March
2003 the European Council approved an amendment to the
Statute of the ESCB and of the ECB to allow for the introduction
of a 'tiered' rotating voting system. When there are more than 15
euro-area member countries, all NCB governors will continue to
participate in all meetings of the ECB's Governing Council but
the number holding a right to vote in the Governing Council will
be restricted to 15. While the six members of the Executive Board
will maintain their *permanent* voting rights, NCB governors will
exercise their right to vote according to a tiered rotation system.
For example, when there are between 16 and 21 euro-area
member countries, the rotation system will be based on two
groups and NCB governors' voting frequencies will depend on
the relative size of their countries' economies. However, most
commentators agree that the Governing Council is already too
large and that decision making will become even more problematic when the rotating voting system is introduced, especially
given inevitably diverse economic conditions in the euro area.

Having discussed a number of issues relating to monetary
policy we next turn to consider fiscal policy in the euro area and,

in particular, the rules-based fiscal policy framework provided by the 'Stability and Growth Pact'.

4.2 FISCAL POLICY IN THE EURO AREA

You will recall from our discussion in Chapter 3, section 3.1.3 that the Maastricht Treaty identified four convergence criteria that have to be satisfied before a country becomes eligible to take part in the third stage of EMU. One of the criteria – that deficits and debt are not more than 3 per cent and 60 per cent of GDP, respectively – is specifically intended to ensure fiscal discipline. You will also recall that the third stage of EMU began on 1 January 1999 when exchange rates between 11 EU member states deemed to have met the Maastricht convergence criteria were irrevocably fixed and the euro was officially launched. In order to maintain fiscal discipline *after* the introduction of the single currency the European Council in 1997 adopted the Stability and Growth Pact (SGP).

At the outset it is important to stress that, having adopted the euro, national fiscal policy is the only instrument of policy that euro-area member countries are left with to stabilize fluctuations in output in their economies. As we have seen, euro-area members have already given up their ability to pursue independent monetary policy and they cannot use the exchange rate as an instrument of national policy. While member countries retain autonomy over their national fiscal policies, the need for some rules to maintain fiscal discipline in the euro area is widely accepted. Before examining the 'rules-based' fiscal policy framework provided by the SGP, we first examine the rationale for fiscal rules.

4.2.1 The Rationale for Fiscal Rules

The main argument for fiscal rules, which limit the degree of fiscal policy discretion that a government can exercise, is the fact that democratically elected governments appear to be subject to a so-called 'deficit bias'. In other words, evidence has shown that governments tend to spend more than they raise in taxation and pass on the burden of debt to future governments and later generations of taxpayers.

There are three main reasons why high deficit and debt levels are a cause for concern. First – if unchecked – high deficits and rising debt levels can have a detrimental effect on economic growth if the need to finance the debt results in higher interest rates which 'crowd out' private sector investment. Second, a commonly voiced concern is that debts may rise to levels where they are no longer sustainable and default becomes unavoidable. To guard against the risk of free riding, and ensure that the responsibility for repaying debt remains at the national level, the Maastricht Treaty has a 'no bail-out clause'. Article 103 of the Treaty states:

> [T]he Community shall not be liable for or assume the commitments of central governments, regional, local or other public authorities, other bodies governed by public law, or public undertakings of any Member State . . . A Member State shall not be liable for or assume the commitments of central governments, regional, local or other public authorities, other bodies governed by public law, or public undertakings of another Member State.

In short, the clause prohibits the bailing out of any member state in financial difficulty by either EU institutions or other EU member states. Indeed, it was concern for achieving fiscal outcomes that are *sustainable* in EMU that led to the budgetary rules contained in the Maastricht Treaty, which were subsequently incorporated into the SGP. The Maastricht Treaty specified sustainable debt levels to be no more than 60 per cent of GDP. Such debt levels are consistent with annual budget deficits of not more than 3 per cent of GDP. How are these two figures linked? If we assume that nominal GDP grows at an annual rate of 5 per cent, then debt can grow at the same rate and still be sustainable. Given a debt *level* of 60 per cent of GDP, debt can increase annually by 5 per cent of 60 per cent (that is, $0.05 \times 0.60 = 0.03$), or 3 per cent of GDP per year, while keeping the 60 per cent debt-to-GDP ratio constant. In other words governments can run annual budget deficits of 3 per cent of GDP, as they are consistent with sustainable debt levels of 60 per cent of GDP. On the assumption that nominal GDP grows at 5 per cent a year, deficits in excess of 3 per cent of GDP will lead to increasing debt levels.

The third main reason why high deficits and increasing levels of debt are a cause for concern is that they can lead to pressure being exerted on a country's central bank to finance the debt directly, thereby fuelling inflation through money creation. As noted in section 4.1.3, to shield the ECB from political interference that might impede the attainment of its primary objective of price stability, the ECB has been given a high degree of independence.

In addition, to guard against the risk of spillover effects from national fiscal policies to monetary policy, the Maastricht Treaty prohibits the monetary financing of budget deficits by the ECB and the NCBs. According to Article 104 of the Treaty:

> [O]verdraft facilities or any other type of credit facility with the ECB or with the national central banks of the Member States in favour of Community institutions or bodies, central governments, regional, local or other public authorities . . . shall be prohibited, as shall the purchase directly from them by the ECB or the national central banks of debt instruments.

4.2.2 The 'Original' SGP

The SGP, which is based on 'the objective of sound government finances as a means of strengthening the conditions for price stability and for strong sustainable growth conducive to employment creation' (Council Regulations 1466 and 1467/97, 7 July 1997) aims to avoid the occurrence of excessive budgetary deficits in the euro area. The Pact comprises a European Council resolution which provides member states, the Council and the European Commission with 'firm policy guidelines for the implementation of the SGP' and two Council regulations (one on the surveillance of budgetary positions and the coordination of economic policies; the other on the implementation of the excessive deficit procedure), which lay down the detailed technical arrangements. As we shall discuss in section 4.2.4, below, the two Council regulations were subsequently amended in June 2005.

The SGP consists of a rules-based framework for fiscal policy involving two arms, a 'preventive' and a 'corrective' arm. The *preventive* arm of the Pact urges member states to keep to 'the medium term objective of budgetary positions of close to balance or in surplus'. The rationale behind achieving a close-to-balance or in-surplus budget position over the medium term is twofold. First, it seeks to achieve fiscal outcomes that are *sustainable*. Second, it aims to give enough flexibility for automatic (anti-cyclical) fiscal stabilization, for example, by allowing a budget deficit of *up to* 3 per cent during a recession when tax receipts fall and government spending on unemployment benefits rises. Within a framework of multilateral surveillance, member states submit an annual stability programme to the Commission and the Council setting out their fiscal objectives for the coming years (member states who have not yet adopted the euro submit an annual convergence programme). The Council examines and monitors the stability programmes (taking into account the Commission's recommendations) and under an early warning system alerts member states to take the necessary corrective action to prevent any deficits from becoming excessive.

The *corrective* arm of the Pact seeks to ensure that countries that break the limits on deficits and debt laid down by the Maastricht Treaty take the necessary corrective action. A deficit greater than 3 per cent of GDP triggers the excessive deficit procedure (EDP), as long as the excess is not considered to be 'exceptional' or 'temporary'. The EDP is also triggered when government debt exceeds 60 per cent of GDP, unless the level of debt is 'sufficiently diminishing and approaching the reference value at a satisfactory pace'. In preparing an initial report under the EDP, the Commission takes into account 'whether the government deficit exceeds government investment expenditure' and also 'other relevant factors, including the medium-term economic and budgetary position of the Member State'. A deficit in excess of 3 per cent is not considered excessive in 'exceptional circumstances', namely when it results from: (i) 'an unusual event outside the control of the Member State concerned and which has a major impact on the financial position of the general government' or (ii) 'a severe economic downturn'.

A deficit in excess of the reference value of 3 per cent, which results from a severe economic downturn, is considered by the Commission to be exceptional only if there is an annual fall of real GDP of *at least* 2 per cent. Although it is the Commission that assesses the situation, it is the Council (ECOFIN) that decides whether or not an excessive deficit exists. The Council can, for example, decide that an annual fall of real GDP of less than 2 per cent is exceptional where member states provide supporting evidence that the excess resulted from a 'severe recession' with an 'annual fall in real GDP of at least 0.75 per cent'.

When ECOFIN decides that an excessive deficit exists, it makes recommendations to the member state concerned on the appropriate measures to reduce the deficit. Under the Pact, member states agree to correct excessive deficits as quickly as possible and within a year following their identification, unless there are 'special circumstances'. If a member state fails to take effective action to correct an excessive deficit situation the Council can impose sanctions on the member state. The sanctions initially take the form of a non-interest-bearing deposit (not exceeding an upper limit of 0.5 per cent of GDP), but these sanctions can be intensified by conversion of the deposit into a (non-reimbursable) fine if the excessive deficit has not been corrected within two years.

4.2.3 The Main Criticisms of the 'Original' SGP

Less than five years after it first came into force the SGP fell into disarray, seemingly confirming the criticisms of many commentators that the Pact was ill-designed and that it would inevitably fail in its aim to avoid the occurrence of excessive budgetary deficits in the euro area. As we shall now discuss, most of the criticisms were concerned with the *design* and *implementation* of the rules of the original Pact.

In raising questions over whether its rules were sufficiently flexible, critics highlighted a number of faults in the Pact's design. Here we note four of the main faults commonly voiced at the time. First, criticisms were raised that by having a *common* medium-term budgetary objective for *all* member states (close to balance or in surplus) the Pact failed to take into account country-specific circumstances, including structural reform. Second, concerns were raised about the use of the budget deficit as a measure of fiscal discipline. Critics pointed out that not only is the budget balance influenced by the business cycle itself – that is, during an economic downturn (upturn) changes in the budget position *automatically* occur as tax receipts fall (rise) and spending on unemployment benefits increases (decreases) – but it also tends to worsen in circumstances where expansionary fiscal policy is called for, that is, in an economic downturn. Third, criticisms were voiced that the definition of what constitutes a 'severe' economic downturn was far too strict. Economic downturns of the severity defined in the Pact – an annual fall of real GDP of at least 2 per cent; or an annual fall of real GDP of at least 0.75 per cent, subject to qualifying supporting evidence – are, in practice, exceptionally rare. Fourth, critics pointed to the asymmetric nature of the Pact. In periods of slow growth, when budget positions automatically deteriorate, the Pact forced countries to tighten their belts even further to ensure that their deficits remained below 3 per cent of GDP. In contrast, in periods of faster growth, when budget positions automatically improve, countries were not under the same commitment to adjust, with the risk that their fiscal policies would turn out to be expansionary and pro-cyclical, thereby exacerbating economic instability. With regard to this point, a UK HM Treasury (2004, p. 17) discussion paper on the SGP has acknowledged that 'perversely countries can end up cutting spending or raising taxes at the wrong stage of the cycle, at the expense of stability and growth, in an attempt to make up the lost ground that should have been made up when the economy was stronger'. Indeed Annett (2006, p. 13) has argued that 'a key failing of the SGP in its early years was its inability to prompt countries to adjust during periods of high growth'.

To what extent has the SGP achieved its objective of exerting fiscal discipline? Before seeking to answer this question it is worth stressing that, not withstanding its faults, the Pact plays an important role in enhancing the credibility of euro member countries' commitment to fiscal discipline after they enter EMU. Some commentators contend that while, on the whole, the Pact has helped to exert fiscal discipline in the euro-area member countries, its record has been mixed. For example, Annett (2006, p. 26) concluded that 'despite frequent criticism the SGP (especially through its preventive arm) has been quite successful in contributing to fiscal discipline in countries like Austria, Belgium, Finland, Ireland, the Netherlands, and Spain'. However, post-2001 a number of countries failed to keep their annual deficits below the 3 per cent of GDP limit. Portugal was the first country to breach the limit on deficits in 2001, followed by France and Germany (two of the largest member countries) in 2002. Having failed to achieve budget surpluses during the early years (1999–2000) of the SGP when economic growth was relatively high, the post-2001 economic slowdown (see Figures 4.1 and 4.2) resulted in rising deficits in these (and a number of other member) countries and led them to breach the 3 per cent limit. This situation placed a lot of strain on the implementation of the Pact. In November 2003, against the European Commission's recommendation that both France and Germany had not taken effective action to reduce their deficits, ECOFIN decided to hold the excessive deficit procedures for both countries in abeyance. This action prompted a dispute between the Council and the Commission, which was subsequently referred to the European Court of Justice. Ultimately the problem of enforcement proved to be the straw that broke the original Pact's back. With the Pact seemingly falling apart, the European Commission was charged with the responsibility of developing a set of reform proposals for ECOFIN. In March 2005, ECOFIN accepted most of the

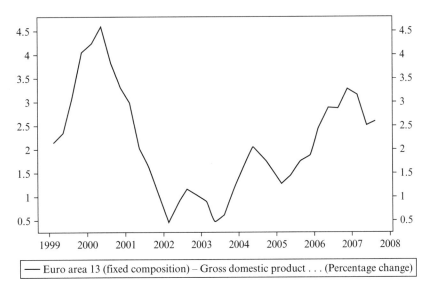

Source: European Central Bank.

Figure 4.1   Economic growth in the euro area (GDP in previous year's prices)

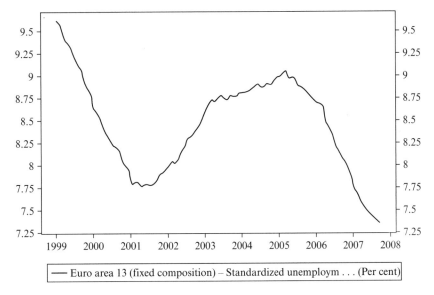

Source: European Central Bank.

Figure 4.2   Unemployment in the euro area (% of labour force)

Commission's proposals for reform and in June 2005 the two Council regulations – on the surveillance of budgetary positions and the implementation of the excessive deficit procedure – were amended to form part of a revised SGP. As we shall now discuss, the revised Pact retains its essential elements – most notably the 3 per cent and 60 per cent reference values for deficit and debt levels remain unchanged – but has incorporated a number of rule changes designed to increase its flexibility.

4.2.4   The 'Revised' SGP

In the light of the experience with the original SGP, a number of reforms were introduced into a revised Pact that came into force in July 2005. The main reforms relate to the two arms of the Pact. With respect to the preventive arm, the revised Pact requires that *each* member state has its own 'country-specific' medium-term budgetary objective. This change is intended to increase the degree of budgetary flexibility by allowing the economic and budgetary circumstances (including public investment requirements and structural reform) of each member state to be taken into account. Medium-term objectives now *differ* between member states and can be revised when a member state undertakes a major structural reform. Having country-specific medium-term objectives contrasts with the original Pact's common medium-term objective for all member states to have their budgetary positions close to balance or in surplus. Furthermore, to address the problem that the budget balance is, in part, endogenously determined the budgetary balances are now measured in cyclically adjusted terms.

With respect to the corrective arm, three main changes came into force in July 2005. First, under the revised Pact the definition of what constitutes a severe economic downturn has been made less stringent. A severe economic downturn, which results in a deficit in excess of the reference value of 3 per cent of GDP, is now defined as a period of 'negative annual GDP growth' or 'a cumulative fall in production over a prolonged period of very low annual growth'. Second, unlike the original Pact, which referred to unspecified 'other relevant factors', the revised Pact provides an explicit list of 'other relevant factors' which the Commission must take into account when assessing whether or not a deficit greater than 3 per cent of GDP is excessive. The relevant factors include, for example, potential growth, 'prevailing cyclical conditions' and major structural reforms such as 'reform of retirement pension schemes'. Third, the revised Pact incorporates changes to the special circumstances that define, and the deadlines for correcting, excessive deficits. Excessive deficits still have to be corrected within a year following their identification, unless there are 'special circumstances'. However, in contrast to the original Pact where special circumstances were undefined, in the revised Pact the list of 'other relevant factors' serves as a basis for deciding whether or not there are special circumstances. In addition in the revised Pact, member states have to adhere to a *minimum* improvement of *at least* 0.5 per cent of GDP per annum. Finally, in the revised Pact the initial deadline for correcting an excessive deficit can be revised and extended where member states have taken effective action, in line with the Council's recommendations, but fiscal targets have subsequently not been met because of 'unexpected adverse economic events with major unfavourable consequences for government finances'.

How far these reforms will overcome the main problems that beset the original Pact is open to debate. The spectrum of opinion ranges from those who argue that the changes have greatly strengthened the Pact, to those who contend that the changes have fatally undermined the Pact's ability to deliver fiscal discipline and will lead to higher deficit and debt levels. What most commentators agree upon is that fiscal discipline in the euro area relies to a large extent on peer pressure and the desire to maintain national prestige. No country wants to be singled out as profligate, running excessive deficits and debts that are fiscally unsound.

Having considered key aspects of monetary and fiscal policy in the euro area, and in particular the part played by the ECB and the SGP, we next discuss enlargement issues for the eurozone. Before turning to Chapters 5 and 6 you should first read the interview with Charles Wyplosz. Both as a specialist in the field of study and as a member of the Shadow Committee of the ECB's Governing Council, Professor Wyplosz is in an ideal position to shed light on many of the issues addressed in this chapter.

CHARLES WYPLOSZ

Charles Wyplosz is Professor of International Economics at the Graduate Institute of International Studies, Geneva, Switzerland, where he is Director of the International Centre for Monetary and Banking Studies. He is best known for his work on international financial flows and their impact on the macro economy, and macroeconomic policy. In addition to his many publications in these two broad fields he is co-author of two leading textbooks: *Macroeconomics: A European Text* (Oxford University Press, 1993, 1997, 2001; 4th edition, 2005) (with Michael Burda) and *The Economics of European Integration* (McGraw-Hill, 2004; 2nd edition, 2006) (with Richard Baldwin).

We interviewed Professor Wyplosz in his office at the Graduate Institute of International Studies in Geneva on 13 March 2007.

The European Central Bank's model of mandate was the Bundesbank. To what extent do you think that the Bundesbank provided a good template for the design of the key institution of the eurozone?
That's a good question. The Bundesbank was considered then to be one of the most successful central banks in the world, so it was natural to use it as a model. At that time it wasn't clear exactly what particular features made the Bundesbank successful. Independence was one of the explanations; another was quantitative money growth targets; and a third explanation was the federal aspect – it was a bank that catered not to a centralized nation, but a federal nation, which was good for European monetary union as the EU is not one nation. All these ideas were taken on board indiscriminately. As a result we are now stuck with this money targeting problem which was the first pillar, but has now become the second pillar of monetary policy. We now understand that this was not the crucial part of the Bundesbank's success. Even worse, by then there were early signals that the Bundesbank was messing up the money growth target. But the rest – the idea that central bank independence is key and how to think about federal arrangements – were ideas that were taken on board and that have served us well.

What are your views of the ECB's twin-pillar approach to the conduct of monetary policy? In particular, to what extent is the monetary pillar a useful indicator of likely future inflationary pressures in the eurozone?
Let me start with the second part of your question. We are getting more and more evidence that money growth is a very poor

indicator of inflationary pressures. Now, we all teach our students that money growth and inflation are eventually the same and that's probably true. But when we live in a very low inflation world – with financial innovation round the corner and with money circulating all over the world, we don't even know what the money supply of the euro is within the euro area – money growth is a bad indicator of inflationary pressures. The problem is the perception, especially in Germany, that the Bundesbank's success depended on quantitative money growth rules. Many people think that if the euro is not run by a modern-day version of the Bundesbank we are going to be in trouble. Hence we now have this mythical view of the money growth target as a pillar of monetary policy and this is becoming more and more of a problem. Of course there are two ways of thinking about what the ECB is doing. One is to say that they are using the money growth target and that is going to lead them to make mistakes. The other, more cynical, way of thinking about what the ECB is doing – which I believe is closer to the truth – is to suggest that while they make all the right noises about the money growth target to please German public opinion, in reality they don't give a damn about it. The problem with the latter approach is that it makes communication, transparency and understanding about what the ECB is doing pretty cumbersome. I am still worried that some people in the policy-making committee may be making a principle of upholding the money growth rule and that for political reasons we may end up making silly decisions. While I don't think that it has happened to date it still bothers me, as it could make the quality of discussion within the committee pretty poor if people are split along ideological lines.

Do you think that the ECB's asymmetric inflation target gives too depressive a twist to monetary policy in the eurozone?
No, I don't think that there is any evidence for that. ECB Governing Council members have been very flexible. They have overshot their supposed 2 per cent ceiling almost all of the time since 1999, which seems to indicate that they are not asymmetrical. They didn't panic at all when they were above the 2 per cent target. It's more a case that they are extremely imprecise about what they are doing.

What did you think of the ECB's 2003 clarification of its inflation target as less than but close to 2 per cent over the medium term?

A cover up. [*Laughter*] They had a silly way of putting it before, so I suppose that it is a little less silly now. They don't want to do what all other central banks do and say what they would like to do and what their margin of error is. It very much derives from the monetary pillar because a segment of the ECB believes that they have to do what the Bundesbank did and the Bundesbank didn't do inflation targeting. They think that anything that would resemble inflation targeting would be high treason of that received wisdom. Quantitative money targeting is one of the things that has been picked up from the Bundesbank and its effects are reverberating on a wide range of issues. *De facto* they are inflation targeters and they have kept the inflation rate between 1.5 and 2.5 per cent. Although that is what they are doing, when you tell them that they are inflation targeters and that they are aiming at 2 per cent, plus or minus 0.5 per cent, they get extremely upset.

To what extent are you sympathetic to the view that its lack of account-ability makes the ECB too powerful an institution for the conduct of economic policy in a democratic setting? Might it add to Europe's democratic deficit?
Yes, it adds to the European democratic deficit. We have seen in a number of countries, including France, an enormous amount of misunderstanding of what the ECB is doing. The ECB's legitimacy is suffering as a result. Is it because they are not sufficiently accountable? I think so. They are not accountable like most other central banks are, partly because it is a central bank of several countries, rather than one country. The European Parliament is also reasonably weak in general and, in particular, has only the power to call ECB officials to come and talk. The ECB's limited amount of accountability is a big problem.

The ECB recognizes the importance of good communication of its interest rate decisions – and the means by which these have been reached – to the schooling of economic agents' expectations. What is your view of the ECB's present decision-making process and the limited public scrutiny to which this is subject?
The decision-making process is extremely unclear. The principal decisions are taken by the Governing Council, which now has 19 members. Nobody believes that 19 members can make a complicated decision. The way they cover this up is by saying that there is always a consensus. To me, consensus means that some people control others. If the three of us should start discussing what

should be the right interest rate we would fight. I am on the Shadow Committee set up by the German magazine *Handelsblatt*. Every month we meet one week before the ECB does in order to go through the motions of deciding what the interest rate should be. We are always completely split and the discussion is quite lively! The Shadow Committee consists of 19 economists – bank and academic economists – so I should imagine that it would be even more difficult for 19 central bankers to agree without a vote. So there is a complete cover-up of what's going on. We know that six of them live in Frankfurt and that they talk a lot to each other. The other 13 members are in different parts of the empire. One can infer from that, that most of the groundwork for decision making is made by the six, who officially never meet to discuss monetary matters. The decision-making process is a complete mess in the sense that there is no procedure compared to the way the Maastricht Treaty mandates how it should be done. According to the Treaty, the procedure is that they should vote, but they don't and they are adamant that they don't. The only redeeming feature is that the six people in Frankfurt make the decisions and the others toe the line. So far the six have done a good job, but the process itself is terrible. Even if the decisions arrived at are right, how can you communicate that process? Communication is problematic when we have this press conference each month. I have often thought about writing down the text of the press conference before it happens, or at least a short statement. I am sure that I could get 90 per cent of the words right and in the right order. The text of the press conference is completely pre-programmed and totally uninteresting.

What implications does eurozone enlargement have for the decision-making and public scrutiny issues raised in the last question?
Well, it will make for a bit more of a mess because they are due to let the decision-making group increase to 25 members and then there is a cap and a complex rotating procedure, inspired by the Fed in the US. Nineteen members is already too big, so to go to 25 members will mean that it will be even more of a problem. However, in the end, as a practical matter I don't think it will matter very much. Despite all my misgivings, the monetary decisions they have taken so far have been the right ones. They haven't made any major mistakes. The problem for me has more to do with legitimacy and accountability. I am concerned that monetary union still remains very controversial. The Germans still want the

Deutschmark; the Italians discuss when they will be leaving; the French think that politicians should decide monetary policy and that central bank independence is terrible; and so on. In every country there is a problem and that can be traced to the fact that they haven't earned their legitimacy because they are very poor at public relations and they are not willing to be transparent.

The case for fiscal rectitude in a monetary union is arguably unimpeachable – members cannot be allowed individual free rein to themselves contribute to monetary instability through fiscal profligacy. In this context what are your views of the principles underlying the Stability and Growth Pact?
I would disagree with what you have said in the following sense. You are absolutely right to say that, as a general principle, badly undisciplined fiscal policy is a threat to monetary stability. But the threat is by no means mechanical, automatic or guaranteed, if the central bank is independent and chooses not to underwrite fiscal profligacy. There could be a public debt collapse, but that would not affect money and monetary policy unless there was a currency collapse at the same time. Although one can go from fiscal indiscipline to monetary instability, there are a number of ifs in between. The monetary union has 13 members right now. Suppose when Slovenia joins that the government of Slovenia goes nuts, amasses a huge public debt and defaults. Nobody in Frankfurt will hear about that. If, on the other hand, it's the government of Germany that is running huge deficits and it defaults, that would shake the monetary union and create currency problems, which in the end could hurt the euro. If you have a very independent central bank, which is serious about its monetary policy and is not going to bail out governments, then I'm not at all convinced that there is a serious threat to monetary stability. I'm not even sure that we need the Stability and Growth Pact. My interpretation of the Pact is that it followed from the Maastricht entry conditions. The deficit and debt criterion for joining the monetary union has been violated by almost every member to start with. The criterion was invented by Germany because they were scared of having Italy in the monetary union. They introduced this criterion as they thought that it would keep Italy forever out, because Italy was way beyond the 60 per cent debt limit. The Germans didn't want to share their currency with the Italians. They then thought that if you put that kind of condition for entry, but once you're inside you could ignore it, it makes no

sense. This led to the Stability and Growth Pact. It very much reflects the fear of the Germans at the time not wanting to share their currency with countries they did not trust. In one way that is understandable given their history of hyperinflation. This view reflects both poor thinking about institutions and a poor understanding of economics. I don't deny that it's good to have some collective understanding that you have to abide by fiscal discipline, but in my view the case for a compulsory bureaucratic system like the Stability and Growth Pact is very weak.

What are your views of recent attempts to clarify and improve the Stability and Growth Pact?
Clarify and improve is a nice way of putting it. [*Laughter*] I don't think that they have clarified the Pact. In fact it has become murkier. They have introduced all sorts of provisions and qualifications. For example, if you spend money on a good cause it is alright to have a budget deficit. What is a good cause? They have opened up a huge loophole there. Initially, back in 1997, the Germans wanted it to be a completely automatic procedure with no room for manoeuvre. The revision has instead introduced a lot of room for manoeuvre. For me the Pact is now nearly irrelevant. When we had this crisis in 2002/03 it was clear that although Germany and France were the culprits at the time, they had no intention whatsoever of respecting the Pact. In my view, peer pressure is all that is left. In that sense it is an improvement.

Can you elaborate on your view that the Pact should promote national institutions for fiscal responsibility that deliver better policy outcomes?
That is part of the problem I have with the Pact. Monetary union involves giving up one's currency and sacrificing national monetary policy. It does not involve sacrificing national fiscal policy, which is the only remaining macroeconomic tool. I think that it is extremely important not to hijack the ability to conduct national fiscal policies. As we discussed earlier, I am very concerned that the single currency doesn't have a good legitimacy. People throughout Europe are still attached to the idea of one nation, one currency. Provoking citizens into giving up more than they are willing to give up is very dangerous. Most people did not quite understand the monetary union project. In most countries it would not have been accepted in referenda, certainly not in Germany. So in a way it was an elite group of politicians and

economists who created the monetary union and who hijacked public opinion. As a result, it is not a very sturdy arrangement. When Brussels tells Germany or France that their budgets next year should be 3.2 not 3.5 per cent of GDP, I think that they are doing something which is very dangerous in terms of acceptability of the European project. From that I conclude that fiscal discipline should be a national matter. In addition I don't think that there are serious spillover effects, except if a really big country like Germany of France were to become undisciplined – which is not what we have seen. People are very attached to governments preparing their budgets with their national parliaments. That is very deeply engrained in our democracies, for good reasons. While we need to find better ways of achieving fiscal discipline than we have done in the past, this has to be a strictly national matter.

You have been critical of the appointments process to the Executive Board of the ECB's Governing Council in suggesting that the large countries have, in effect, a reserved seat. Does this presage questions about who runs the ECB and in whose interest?
Let me make just an early statement so that you understand where I was coming from there. An independent central bank is a technocratic body that should be given an inflation objective. Most people, including many politicians, don't understand that it is a technical thing to achieve a 2 per cent inflation rate. You leave it to technicians to fix the inflation rate, just as you do when your car needs fixing. If you bring together a bunch of technicians they will agree, as they have the same frame of reference. Clearly there will be disagreements about judgements, but these will be very circumscribed disagreements. As a profession we have learned a lot and now know pretty much how to run a central bank well. By introducing nationalism one starts taking away what should be a technical matter and making it a symbolically political matter. I would like to see the appointment of the best monetary economists – the Ben Bernankes and the Mervyn Kings from Europe – irrespective of where they are from. This is how it is done in any normal central bank. Having a German seat, a French seat etc. is bad in principle. What makes it worse is that people are not scrutinized for their professional quality. The decision to appoint people is delegated to the country whose seat is at issue. So when it is a German seat the Germans come and say: 'we have chosen so and so'. The others cannot ask: 'is it really the

best person in Europe we can find to fill this position?'. Because it is a political process the average quality of board members in the ECB is not as high as you would find in say the Fed or the Bank of England.

What is your view of the general conduct of monetary policy in the eurozone to date – given the context of what is an immense monetary innovation has it been at least as good as could have reasonably been expected, or is there room for significant improvement?

What really amazes me is that in spite of all the criticisms I have voiced – the wrong monetary policy strategy of using the money growth pillar and a bizarre composition of too many people, which both look like a recipe for disaster – they have done extremely well. It is a puzzle to me. One interpretation is that all my criticisms are wrong and misplaced, and that I just fail to understand the way they operate. I'm prepared to accept that interpretation because I don't understand why they have done so well so far. Another interpretation is that there has been a lot of progress in monetary theory and in our understanding of central banking. In other words if reasonable people apply reasonable principles that are now accepted in central banking circles, then there is not much room for making mistakes. Am I completely wrong or are we collectively wise? My answer is that we are collectively wise.

Is there another possibility, namely that the environment has been benign and that we have not had a shock to date to test the system?

Sure. It might just be a case of 'so far so good' and that when a serious test occurs, if there are serious flaws in the institution they will be revealed. What a serious test could be is another question. A major international disruption? That's hard to see. A big bank failure within the monetary union? That is unlikely, given the huge progress in supervision and regulation. So maybe a test will never happen.

The optimum currency area approach to monetary integration places great stress on the contribution to be made by labour market flexibility. Do you find it at all strange that the institutional framework of the eurozone largely – even completely – abstracts from labour market considerations?

That's a tough question. What is clear is that when the monetary union was created, the optimum currency area principles didn't play any role in the thinking of the officials who designed it. It was very much a politically driven process and also a fear-of-crisis process. Labour market imperfections are a problem now that we are in a monetary union. The European monetary union is not an optimum currency area. As a result there are costs. Take Germany, for example. Germany has had very poor growth performance from the beginning of the monetary union – until last year – which is largely explained by the fact that their labour market did not adjust fast enough to an overvalued currency. The silver lining is that, at least so far, we have had a surprising amount of wage moderation. Why has this been the case? One interpretation is that people in different countries have somehow taken on board the fact that you can't play with wages any more in the good old way. In a monetary union, slippage will have to be clawed back. The other interpretation is that wage moderation has happened because of poor growth. The real question then is whether over the next year or so – as the output gaps are closed and unemployment falls – we are going to see strong wage pressures return and labour market problems resurfacing. That is the next challenge. This is also why I think the central bank is right to err on the side of prudence. The fact that we haven't cleaned up labour markets in the biggest countries is the original sin of the monetary union. On the other side we have seen some labour market reforms since the monetary union and some people hope that monetary union will be the agent of change.

There are suggestions that the euro may, in the medium term, threaten the position of the US dollar as the world's premier currency. Do you think this is likely, and what do you see as the main implications should it happen?
Unless the US makes a huge policy mistake – and there is no reason to suppose that this will happen – I don't see the euro replacing the dollar. What the euro can do is acquire international currency status, alongside the US dollar. The euro is starting to emerge as a competitor, it appears to be as good as the dollar. In the bond market, for example, more and more people around the world recognize euros. Now one can ask what kind of problem will this create? Is it a good or a bad thing? My only concern is a conceptual problem that the ECB right now doesn't understand that euros that circulate outside of Europe are not part of the money supply. This goes back to the quantitative money supply growth target that we discussed earlier. If the ECB wants to worry about money growth

targets, it should focus on euro growth inside, not outside the Euroland. It should worry about domestic euros, not international euros. The seigniorage revenue from that is ridiculously low. It's nice, but it's not even candies for the children at Christmas.

There have been suggestions, notably from the United States, that in its decades-long focus on monetary reform and innovation, the EU has rather lost sight of its real-economy Lisbon Agenda. Is this a fair criticism?

Well, yes and no. It depends on what you call Europe. If you call Europe the European institutions like the ECB, I'd say no. On the other hand if you think about Europe in terms of countries, then I'd say yes, but with a big proviso. The Lisbon Agenda is talking about structural reforms. Like fiscal policy I think that structural reforms ought to be strictly national matters because they entail sacrificing some people for the common good since it implies transfers within a country. I think that the Lisbon Agenda is a really silly undertaking, which is not working. It is a distraction and maybe a pretext not to do things. The big problem is that the three large countries of Euroland – Germany, France and Italy – also Portugal, have not undertaken the reforms that other European countries have, for purely domestic political reasons. Germany has made some progress, but not much. So in that sense the leaders of Germany, France, Italy and Portugal are to be blamed for forgetting about the real side of the economy. That is not a collective failure. You have had very important reforms in several countries, which are part of the monetary union. Some countries have delivered, others have not. I am very worried anytime there is a suggestion that these things should be forced upon individual countries by the centre. Again it is a sure way of undermining legitimacy and political acceptance. It is interference in very deep political affairs because it affects income distribution, with some groups losing and others benefiting. Such big transfers raise very complicated questions and should be left to local politicians.

What is your view of ERM II – is membership a robust criterion against which to partly judge an economy's readiness to join the eurozone?

Again this is a silly legacy of history. The ERM was created before the monetary union came into existence. With hindsight we can see the transitional step in history where a number of countries learned how to collectively manage their bi-lateral exchange rate;

when they realized that it was working, then they decided to go to the next step and completely fix the exchange rate. It was a very useful historical episode. There is no good reason at all why it was decided to make ERM membership a pre-condition for monetary union. Imposing that now, 20 years later – on countries that have a very different situation and come from a very different tradition – at best makes no sense and at worst is counterproductive. We have member countries that are *de facto* in the euro because they have currency boards. Telling other countries that they have to be in this straitjacket when they are undergoing transition and are catching up, creates delicate problems that we can do without. So in that sense it is counter-productive. All of these things are what I sometimes call the European judicial view, namely trying to straitjacket the economy by legal rules that have no economic justification.

A question about the country in which you work: would Switzerland benefit were it able and willing to join the eurozone?
Yes and no. The Swiss have a strong currency, as strong as the euro. They have a long tradition of quality central bank management. The experience of the last few years is that the exchange rate has been very stable. A big chunk of their trade is with the European Union so they need a stable exchange rate *vis-à-vis* the euro. So far the experience has been that there has been enough stability for them to be happy. Should they go the next step? Legally it's impossible. Economically, the Swiss central bank claims that it is happier outside the eurozone because Switzerland has lower interest rates. This low interest advantage is gradually being eroded, though.

One final question. Are there any issues we have not touched upon during the course of our interview on which you would like to express an opinion?
The only thing we haven't covered, or at least only indirectly, is the fact that the ECB is not an innovative central bank. For that matter neither are the US Fed and the Bank of Japan. Surprisingly, the world's three biggest central banks are slow in terms of moving ahead and developing a concept close to where the standards are in the profession. If you take people at the head of the ECB they are not chosen for being creative monetary economists, but rather for being faithful civil servants. There might be exceptions, but they are not innovative people by temperament. Whereas when you

talk about people like Ben Bernanke, Mervyn King and Rick Mishkin, these people have spent all their lives trying to be at the frontier. That is not what you find among the leadership of the ECB. The impression of slow tooling-up is a concern for me.

5. Euro-area enlargement: Denmark, Sweden and the United Kingdom

5.1 INTRODUCTION

In Chapter 3, section 3.1, we charted the three main landmark events since the mid-1980s – the Single European Act, 1986; the Delors Report, 1989; and the Maastricht Treaty, 1992 – that shaped the transition to economic and monetary union (EMU) in Europe and culminated in the launch of the euro. You will recall that the third and final stage of EMU began on 1 January 1999 when exchange rates were irrevocably fixed for the former national currencies of the then-11 original members of the euro area. Of the remaining four EU member states, Greece failed to meet the Maastricht convergence criteria – subsequently adopting the euro on 1 January 2002 – while Denmark, Sweden and the UK elected to retain their national currencies.

The purpose of the present chapter is to consider membership issues for the three 'outsiders' among the 15 (pre-2004) European Union (EU) countries. To understand why Denmark, Sweden and the UK have not, as yet, adopted the euro requires a discussion of the background to some of the main issues around membership for *each* country. Although the economies of all three countries are closely linked to the euro area – for example, all three economies exhibit a high degree of convergence of their business cycles with that of the euro area and also undertake substantial trade with the euro area – there are a number of country-specific issues which inform their individual approaches to EMU. We begin by looking at the case of Denmark, which – with the UK – was granted an EMU opt-out clause as part of the provisions of a Protocol annexed to the Maastricht Treaty.

5.2 DENMARK

To date there have been five Danish referendums on European Community/Union matters which relate specifically to the process of economic and monetary integration.[28] The first of these took place on 2 October 1972 when the Danes voted decisively – 63 per cent to 37 per cent – in favour of joining the European Economic Community (EEC), which had been established by the Treaty of Rome 18 years earlier. As we discussed in Chapter 3, the first major amendment to the Treaty of Rome came when Denmark, along with the then-other 11 members of the EEC, signed the Single European Act in February 1986. Denmark's signature to the Act followed a 'consultative' referendum when the Danes voted by 56 per cent to 44 per cent in favour of approving the Act. However, by the time the Maastricht Treaty was signed in 1992 the balance of Danish public opinion, once seemingly in favour of the European integration project, appeared to have turned a corner. In a referendum the Danes voted by 51 per cent to 49 per cent against approving the Treaty.

The outcome of the referendum on the Maastricht Treaty posed a serious problem to progress towards achieving further European integration since the Treaty had to be ratified by *all* member states before it could come into force. In order to solve the problem, a compromise solution was agreed by heads of state and government at the Edinburgh European Council in December 1992. The resulting so-called Edinburgh Agreement established that Denmark would not automatically proceed to the third stage of EMU, and therefore introduce the single currency, even when it fulfilled the convergence criteria. Given this EMU opt-out cause, and certain other provisions relating *exclusively* to Denmark, in 1993 the Danes voted by 57 per cent to 43 per cent in favour of ratifying the Treaty.[29]

The Maastricht Treaty – which confirmed that the final stage of EMU would begin no later than 1 January 1999 – identified the convergence criteria to be satisfied before the then-15 member states of the EU would become eligible to join the single currency. In May 1998 the 11 countries deemed to have met the convergence

---

[28] The Danish Constitution necessitates that a referendum is held on any legislation which would authorize a transfer of national powers to supranational authorities.

[29] Under the Edinburgh Agreement, Denmark also obtained special arrangements or opt-outs on three other elements of the Treaty relating to: the development of EU defence policy; cooperation in the fields of justice and home affairs; and Union citizenship.

criteria elected to proceed to the third and final stage of EMU. Although Denmark would also almost certainly have been judged to have met the criteria, the Danish government decided against calling an early referendum on the issue of full participation in EMU – no doubt mindful of the outcome of the June 1992 referendum which had voted against approving the Maastricht Treaty.[30] It was not until early March 2000, when support for the euro was deemed to be strong, that the Social Democrat Prime Minister Poul Nyrup Rasmussen finally proposed that a referendum be held on whether to participate in the single currency and replace Denmark's national currency, the krone, with the euro. In the ensuing seven-month period of debate that followed the pro-euro campaign was supported by the ruling government, the main opposition parties, most of Denmark's media and business community, and a majority of trade unions and employers' organizations. Opposition to Denmark's participation in the single currency came mainly from the far left and far right of the political spectrum. As events transpired, the referendum, rather than being a vote on the economic benefits and costs of adopting the euro, turned into a proxy vote on a range of issues. This was, in part, the result of the strategy employed by the 'no' campaigners who focused much of their attention on such emotive issues as: concern for the future of the Danish welfare state; fear of increased immigration from Central and Eastern Europe with the future expansion of the EU; and worries that further European integration would lead to a loss of Danish sovereignty and national identity. The referendum was held on 28 September 2000 and when the results were announced they signalled a clear majority – 53 per cent to 47 per cent – against adopting the euro.[31]

Three aspects of the Danish no-vote are worth highlighting. First, as noted above, the results of the referendum reflected opinion on a far wider range of issues than whether or not, in purely economic terms, it would be advantageous for Denmark to adopt the euro. In a research paper on the referendum, Miller (2000, p. 17) concluded:

> Danish public scepticism about EMU derives not just from a reluctance to give up the krone for the euro, but from the belief that this is the start of a process leading to the eventual loss of Danish sovereignty in a federal

---

[30] In line with its Constitution, before proceeding to full participation in EMU Denmark has to hold a referendum on the issue.

[31] The turnout at the referendum was over 87 per cent.

'United States of Europe'. One of the main fears was the possible weakening of the generous welfare system. For many, the economic arguments for joining were simply not convincing and they saw no significant negative economic consequences from remaining outside the euro-zone while continuing to shadow the euro. There has been a reluctance to trust either the government or the opposition, or the leaders of any of the pro-euro parties. One commentator noted a 'growing frustration at the refusal of domestic politicians to admit that the euro is as much a political project as an economic one'.

Second, notwithstanding the no-vote, Denmark's EMU opt-out clause remains intact. In consequence, the Danish government is free to organize another referendum on Denmark's adoption of the euro at some point in the future. However, before doing so the government will have to be convinced that its electorate will almost certainly vote in favour. Third, one of the main consequences of the no-vote is that, at least in principle, Denmark has retained its autonomy in monetary and exchange rate policy. In practice, however, Danish monetary policy closely shadows the European Central Bank's (ECB) 'single' monetary policy for the euro area. Let us briefly explore why this is the case.

The central element of Denmark's monetary policy is its fixed exchange rate policy *vis-à-vis* the euro, which it undertakes within the formal framework of the EU's exchange rate mechanism (ERM II).[32] As we shall discuss more fully in Chapter 6, ERM II seeks to maintain stable exchange rates between the euro and participating member states' national currencies – currently Denmark (krone), Estonia (kroon), Latvia (lats), Lithuania (litas) and Slovakia (koruna). Within ERM II, the standard band of exchange rate fluctuation is +/− 15 per cent around a central rate. However, due to its high degree of convergence Denmark was able to reach an agreement with the ECB in 1998 on a narrower band of fluctuation of +/− 2.25 per cent. The central rate has been set at kr. 7.46038 per euro, necessitating that the krone can only fluctuate between kr. 7.62824 and kr. 7.29252 per euro. As the Danish Central Bank maintains a *stable* krone rate *close* to the central rate (that is, a fixed exchange rate policy *vis-à-vis* the euro) it has very little freedom to pursue an independent monetary policy. With the krone tied to the euro, Danish monetary policy closely shadows the ECB's monetary policy. Furthermore, to maintain a fixed exchange rate with the euro, Denmark's inflation

---

[32] Prior to its participation in ERM II, Denmark operated a fixed exchange rate policy throughout the 1980s and 1990s where the krone was closely tied to the German mark.

rate must remain in line with that experienced in the euro area. This means that changes in Danish interest rates closely follow those set in the euro area by the ECB. Given this situation it is somewhat ironic that the governor of Denmark's central bank has no say in the deliberations of the ECB's Governing Council which, as discussed in Chapter 4, section 4.1, is responsible for setting interest rates for the euro area as a whole. When it comes to fiscal policy Denmark, along with the euro-area member states, has endorsed the objectives and requirements of the Stability and Growth Pact (SGP) (see Chapter 4, section 4.2), but unlike the members of the euro area cannot be subjected to sanctions if it fails to take effective action to correct an excessive deficit situation, should one arise.

Having looked at the background to some of the main issues around membership for Denmark, we next turn to consider the case of Sweden.

5.3 SWEDEN

Following a referendum held in November 1994 when the Swedes voted – 52 per cent to 47 per cent – in favour of joining the European Union, the Riksdag (the Swedish parliament) formally approved the decision to join and in January 1995 Sweden became a member of the EU.[33] It did so as a state with a derogation from joining the final stage of EMU as it did not fulfil all the necessary conditions for the adoption of the single currency. Unlike Denmark and the UK (see section 5.4, below), Sweden was not granted an EMU opt-out clause. This means that as soon as it meets all the necessary conditions laid down in the Maastricht Treaty it will automatically proceed to the final stage of EMU.

To understand why Sweden has not yet qualified to adopt the euro it is helpful to backtrack to 1997 when the Swedish government declared that the decision on whether Sweden should join the single currency would be taken by the Riksdag following a referendum on the issue. In December 1997, the Riksdag decided that Sweden would not seek to participate in EMU from its inception in 1999 due to a lack of popular support. However, regardless of this political decision, Sweden would not have been able to join

---

[33] Prior to joining the EU, Sweden had been a member of the European Free Trade Association and party to the 1992 treaty establishing a European Economic Area.

the euro from the start as it did not fulfil all the necessary conditions for the adoption of the single currency. While it fulfilled three of the four economic convergence criteria – having achieved a high degree of price stability, a satisfactory budgetary position and convergence of long-term interest rates – it failed to meet the exchange rate criterion as the Swedish krona had not participated in the exchange rate mechanism.[34] In addition, Sweden did not fulfil the criterion on legal convergence as legislation – in particular relating to the Sveriges Riksbank (Sweden's central bank) – was not fully compatible with the rules of the Treaty and the Statutes of the European System of Central Banks (ESCB) and the ECB. European Commission and ECB convergence reports have since reached the same conclusion. The most recent Commission and ECB convergence reports issued in December 2006 both concluded that while Sweden has achieved a high degree of sustainable convergence, having met three of the Maastricht economic criteria, it still has not fulfilled the exchange rate criterion. Furthermore, Sweden still does not have all the necessary national legislation in place to fulfil the criterion on legal convergence.

Let us return to the issue of popular support for the euro. Although, unlike Denmark, Sweden has no constitutional obligation to hold a referendum on the single currency, in line with its declared strategy, in November 2002 the Swedish government announced that a referendum on whether Sweden should adopt the euro would be held in September 2003. The 'yes' campaign received the support of four parliamentary parties (Social Democratic, Moderate, Liberal and the Christian Democratic), the Confederation of Swedish Enterprise, the main trade unions and the majority of Sweden's media. Three parliamentary parties (Left, Centre and Green) were opposed to Sweden adopting the euro as its currency (see Miller et al., 2003). To suggest that political support for, or opposition to, the euro followed distinct party lines would, however, be misleading as there were internal divisions within each party, especially within the four parties whose leaders were all pro-EMU. For example, while the Social Democratic Prime Minister, Goran Persson, actively supported the 'yes' campaign, five of his cabinet ministers failed to toe the party line and openly argued against joining EMU. When the referendum was held, the Swedes voted emphatically – 56 per cent to 42 per cent – against introducing the euro.

---

[34] Since 1992, the exchange rate of the Swedish krona has been allowed to float.

In line with our earlier discussion of the Danish referendum held in September 2000 which also rejected adopting the euro, three aspects of the Swedish no-vote are worth highlighting. First, as with the Danish referendum, the results in Sweden reflected opinion on a range of issues. Shortly afterwards the European Commission President, Romano Prodi, suggested that Sweden's decision had been based on political rather than economic factors, including fear that the Swedish people were losing their national identity. Second, notwithstanding the no-vote, the possibility of Sweden joining the euro at a later date remains, subject to: (i) fulfilment of all necessary conditions; (ii) parliamentary approval; and (iii) a yes-vote in a referendum.[35] Having said this, given the sizeable margin (14 per cent) voting no, and with a high turnout of 81 per cent, it is highly doubtful that the Swedish government will call another referendum in the near future unless opinion polls indicate a sea change in favour of the euro. This in turn is very unlikely to happen without a marked improvement in the relative economic performance of the euro area compared to Sweden (see Tables 5.1–5.3).

The third aspect of the Swedish no-vote we wish to highlight is that Sweden has retained its autonomy in monetary and exchange rate policy. Ever since 1993, the primary objective of monetary policy in Sweden has been the attainment of price stability under a flexible exchange rate regime. In 1995 the Riksbank

Table 5.1   *Economic growth in Denmark, Sweden, the United Kingdom and the euro area (percentage change in real GDP from previous year)*

	1999	2000	2001	2002	2003	2004	2005	2006
Denmark	2.6	3.5	0.7	0.5	0.4	2.1	3.1	3.2
Sweden	4.3	4.4	1.2	2.0	1.8	3.6	2.9	4.7
United Kingdom	3.0	3.8	2.4	2.1	2.7	3.3	1.9	2.8
Euro area	2.9	4.0	1.9	0.9	0.8	1.8	1.5	2.8

Source: OECD Economic Outlook 81 database.

[35] All parliamentary parties have pledged to respect the outcome of any future consultative referendum.

Table 5.2 *Unemployment in Denmark, Sweden, the United Kingdom and the euro area (standardized rates expressed as a per cent of the civilian labour force)*

	1999	2000	2001	2002	2003	2004	2005	2006
Denmark	5.1	4.4	4.5	4.6	5.4	5.5	4.8	3.9
Sweden	6.7	5.6	4.9	5.0	5.6	6.3	7.3	7.0
United Kingdom	5.9	5.4	5.0	5.1	4.9	4.7	4.8	5.3
Euro area	9.1	8.2	7.8	8.2	8.7	8.8	8.6	7.9

Source: OECD Main Economic Indicators.

Table 5.3 *Inflation in Denmark, Sweden, the United Kingdom and the euro area (percentage change in consumer price indices from previous year)*

	1999	2000	2001	2002	2003	2004	2005	2006
Denmark	2.5	2.9	2.4	2.4	2.1	1.2	1.8	1.9
Sweden	0.5	0.9	2.4	2.2	1.9	0.4	0.5	1.4
United Kingdom	1.3	0.8	1.2	1.3	1.4	1.3	2.0	2.3
Euro area	1.1	2.1	2.4	2.3	2.1	2.2	2.2	2.2

Source: OECD Economic Outlook 81 database.

defined this objective as limiting the annual increase in the consumer price index to 2 per cent, with a range of tolerance of $+/-$ 1 per cent around the target. The no-vote means that the Riksbank has retained national control over interest rates to meet its explicit inflation target, alongside a flexible exchange rate policy.

We next turn to consider the case of the United Kingdom, before reflecting on euro themes common to all three countries.

5.4   UNITED KINGDOM

Like Denmark, the UK was granted an EMU opt-out clause as a condition for approving the Maastricht Treaty. This means that the UK is not required to adopt the single currency. The UK government's position, which has remained unchanged since 1997, is that it is committed in principle to joining a successful euro area, subject to five economic tests *and* a referendum.[36] Let us briefly consider the background to this position.

In 1997, the UK government announced that five economic tests must be met before it will consider participating in the final stage of EMU. These assess whether:

1. *convergence* of business cycles and economic structures with the euro area will 'allow the UK to live comfortably with the euro-area interest rates on a permanent basis' (HM Treasury, 2003, p. 5);
2. *flexibility* – in particular in labour markets – is sufficient to allow the UK economy to deal with asymmetric shocks;
3. *investment* will be boosted in the long term;
4. *financial services* will benefit through an improvement in the competitive position of the UK's financial services industry, particularly in London; and
5. *growth, stability and employment* will be promoted by joining EMU.

The Treasury's 1997 assessment of the five economic tests found that the UK was not convergent with the then-prospective euro area and that flexibility was insufficient to facilitate an adequate response to economic shocks. In consequence it concluded that the risks of membership meant that the UK would not be able 'for some time' to reap the potential benefits of EMU in terms of higher investment, growth and employment.

The most recent assessment of the tests by the UK Treasury was undertaken in June 2003. What conclusions did the Treasury reach on each of the five tests?

1. *Convergence.* While the assessment acknowledged that there had been a significant increase in the extent of convergence with the euro area since 1997 – due to insufficient compatibility of UK business cycles with those of the euro area and certain structural differences, for example, relating to the housing market – it concluded that the convergence test had not been met.
2. *Flexibility.* In a similar fashion the assessment acknowledged that there had been a marked improvement in labour market flexibility in the UK since 1997, but concluded that 'at the

---

[36] These tests are in addition to the convergence criteria laid down in the Treaty.

present time, we cannot be confident that UK flexibility, while improved, is sufficient' (HM Treasury, 2003, p. 5).

3. *Investment.* With respect to the third test, the assessment concluded that 'if sustainable and durable convergence is achieved, then we can be confident that the quantity and quality of investment would increase ensuring that the investment test was met' (HM Treasury, 2003, p. 5).
4. *Financial services.* The assessment concluded that the financial services test is met.
5. *Growth, stability and employment.* In line with the investment test, the assessment concluded that 'we can be confident that the growth, stability and employment test would be met once sustainable and durable convergence has been achieved' (HM Treasury, 2003, p. 6).

Overall the 2003 Treasury assessment concluded:

> [S]ince 1997 the UK has made real progress towards meeting the five economic tests. But, on balance, though the potential benefits of increased investment, trade, a boost to financial services, growth and jobs are clear, we cannot at this point in time conclude that there is sustainable and durable convergence or sufficient flexibility to cope with any potential difficulties within the euro area (HM Treasury, 2003, p. 6).

Three aspects of the UK's decision not to participate in the third stage of EMU are worth highlighting. First, if and when the government decides to recommend full participation in EMU, the decision to enter will be subject to a referendum. Second, like Sweden the UK does not currently fulfil all the necessary conditions for entry. Specifically the UK does not meet the exchange rate criterion as the British pound has not participated in ERM II. Third, the UK retains its autonomy in monetary and exchange rate policy. Let us briefly outline the UK's current monetary policy framework.

The objective of monetary policy in the UK is to deliver price stability, as this is seen as a necessary pre-condition for achieving sustainable growth in output and employment. Price stability is currently defined by an inflation target of 2 per cent. The symmetrical target is measured by the annual increase in the consumer price index. In 1997 the Monetary Policy Committee of the Bank of England was given full operational independence to set interest rates to meet the government's inflation target. Alongside this monetary policy framework, following the UK's

departure from the ERM in September 1992, the exchange rate
has been allowed to float.

Having considered some of the main issues around membership for each of the three 'outsiders', we conclude this chapter by
identifying some common themes that help explain why all three
countries have yet to become full members of EMU.

5.5   CONCLUDING REMARKS

In each case, Denmark's, Sweden's and the UK's decision as to
whether to participate in the single currency depends on economic and political considerations.

Participation in the final stage of EMU requires that each
country fulfils all four economic convergence criteria laid down
in the Maastricht Treaty. As we discussed in Chapters 2 and 3, to
achieve a high degree of sustainable convergence requires: a high
degree of price stability; sustainable public finances; exchange
rate stability; and converging long-term interest rates. The
exchange rate criterion stipulates that before a country can
enter the third and final stage of EMU it has to have been a
member of ERM II and maintained normal exchange rate fluctuation margins for *two years* without severe tensions arising. While
Denmark fulfils this criterion, Sweden and the UK do not as they
are not currently members of ERM II. Instead of targeting the
exchange rate, Sweden and the UK use monetary policy to target
inflation and allow their exchange rates to float. In consequence,
unlike Denmark, interest rate changes in their economies do not
necessarily have to automatically follow those set in the euro area
by the ECB. From the standpoint of 'formally' meeting the
requirements of all four economic criteria, Sweden and the UK
will not be able to join the euro area for *at least* two years after any
decision to enter ERM II.[37]

Meeting the Maastricht economic conditions is necessary before
any country can adopt the single currency. For Denmark and the
UK, however, this is not sufficient as in both countries their EMU
opt-out clauses remain intact. In the case of the UK, an additional
hurdle exists in that the government has announced that the

---

[37] Interestingly although participation in ERM II is voluntary for the non-euro-area
member states, member states with a derogation, such as Sweden, are expected to join.
The fact that Sweden has to date not done so suggests that the Swedish government
regards membership of ERM II as voluntary.

decision to participate in the third stage of EMU depends on its five economic tests being met. In Sweden's case, even if it were to fulfil all the necessary economic conditions for the adoption of the euro it still does not meet the criterion on legal convergence.

Furthermore, the governments of *all* three countries have declared that they will not apply for full membership of EMU until their electorates express support for the euro in a referendum – in the case of Denmark its Constitution requires that a referendum has to be held on the issue before it can proceed to take full participation in EMU. This presents an obstacle to euro enlargement involving all three 'pre-2004 outsiders' because, as Niels Thygesen has observed, 'The trouble with a referendum is that it is a terrible mechanism for discussing a question like EMU. People often use the opportunity to express their dissatisfaction with the government on other issues'.[38] The Danish and Swedish referendums demonstrated that in voters' minds the decision to retain their national currencies was influenced not just by an assessment of the economic advantages and disadvantages of full EMU entry but also by a range of wider issues. These wider issues embraced opinions on such matters as sovereignty and national identity.

While the economies of Denmark, Sweden and the UK are all performing relatively well outside the euro area – especially with respect to economic growth and unemployment as reference to Tables 5.1–5.2 clearly reveals – it seems unlikely that the governments of these three countries, and their electorates, will favour exchanging existing policy frameworks for that of the euro area.[39] In these circumstances, euroscepticism is likely to persist. In the case of Sweden and the UK, full EMU membership would result in a marked change in the conduct of their monetary and exchange rate policies with the associated potential risk of deterioration in their relative economic performances. The exchange rate between the Swedish krona, British pound, and the euro would be irrevocably fixed. Furthermore, both countries would lose their autonomy in monetary policy and would be subject to the single interest rate set by the ECB for the euro area as a whole. As noted, Denmark's case is somewhat different as it already ties

---

[38] See interview at the end of Chapter 3.

[39] The latest government convergence programme for the UK, which was submitted in line with the SGP, noted that under its existing policy framework 'UK GDP has now expanded in 57 consecutive quarters . . . the longest ongoing expansion among the OECD [Organization for Economic Cooperation and Develpoment] countries' (HM Treasury, 2006, p. 1).

its currency to the euro and, therefore, follows the monetary policy lead of the ECB.

Given these considerations it is far more likely that enlargement of the euro area will proceed, at least in the foreseeable future, through the accession of a number of the post-2004 EU member states – the subject matter of the next chapter. However, before turning to Chapter 6 you should first read the interviews we undertook in May 2003 with Willem Buiter and Patrick Minford, two leading economists who hold strong views on whether the UK should relinquish the pound in favour of the euro. Using the UK as a case study, these interviews illustrate how individual assessments of the economic pros and cons of EMU membership allow for very different positions to be taken.

WILLEM BUITER

Willem Buiter is Professor of European Political Economy at the European Institute of the London School of Economics and Political Science, UK. From June 1997 to May 2000 he was a member of the Bank of England's Monetary Policy Committee. He is best known for his work on macroeconomic theory and policy, monetary economics and international finance.

We interviewed Professor Buiter in his office – when he was Chief Economist and Special Counsellor to the President – at the European Bank for Reconstruction and Development in London on 7 May 2003.

Economic Benefits

Transaction costs
Would you accept that for the UK the reduction in transaction costs of changing currency are likely to be relatively small?
Well, I don't think they are likely to be any smaller than for the other countries that have joined, like Germany and France. But, yes, the direct resource savings from no longer having to fiddle about with currency exchange are certainly modest.

Would the reduction in transaction costs be offset by the one-off costs of currency conversion?
Your guess is as good as mine. It depends on how strongly you discount the future. The costs are all upfront, whereas the benefits are *ad infinitum*. So, for the farsighted, the net return will be positive, while for the myopic, the short-sighted, the net cost of switching will be negative. I think that the 'vending machine costs' have been greatly exaggerated. Some extra costs occur at the retail level, but this is really something of an order of magnitude that disappears in the margin of error in figures used to put national accounts together. We are dealing with a single currency reform of the kind many South American countries do on a periodic basis. For the UK, it would be rather like decimalization. It really is chicken feed.

Exchange risk
One of the central economic arguments advanced in favour of joining the euro is the elimination of exchange rate risk with eurozone trading partners. How important do you consider this argument?

It depends on your definition of exchange rate risk. I've always felt that short-term volatility is more of a nuisance than a real threat to prosperity. But persistent medium-term misalignments, which are not really a risk but rather a persistent, awkward reality associated with a floating exchange rate under conditions of free international movement of capital, these can be very significant. Of course what matters for trade and growth, and economic performance, is the stability of the *effective* exchange rate, which is not just the euro but includes the non-euro currencies, especially the dollar. So it's that volatility and those misalignments that really matter. The euro is the largest chunk of currency risk for the UK. As many opponents of the EMU have pointed out, it is certainly theoretically possible that the variability of the effective exchange rate, which included the dollar and other currencies could go up, even if the bilateral exchange rate with the euro is fixed. It's a nice point and any student who raised this in response to an exam question in macro 2, would get a good mark. But practically it is completely counterfactual. In reality, the variability of the effective exchange rate would diminish. Much more important, as I said, is the elimination of persistent real exchange rate misalignments due to nominal exchange rate movements that are unwanted, undesired and preventable. Britain has had these since before I joined the Monetary Policy Committee in '97. It's only in the last year or so, and rather spectacularly in the last few months, that the massive overvaluation of the pound has begun to unwind. Not through deliberate policy actions but because the market has, for reasons not patently clear, recently decided that it is going to re-price the euro, the dollar and the pound. I do think that killing off the exchange rate as a mechanism that causes unwarranted, undesirable changes in the relative competitiveness of Britain and the Continent is going to be a major gain for the UK. It is also a major gain from the point of view of firms contemplating investment here and contemplating expanding their operations here. Without the pound locked in place with the euro firmly and credibly, I think Britain will suffer and is already suffering, compared to what it could have been, from staying outside the eurozone.

So you would take at face value the statements by a number of the larger multinational companies that they would think very seriously about the desirability of investing or extending investment in Britain as a location if we do not join the euro?

Absolutely. Why would they say it if it weren't true? They have no incentive, pecuniary or otherwise, for distorting the truth. These are people who have serious money at stake, not ideologues with a political agenda.

Do the benefits with respect to trade in goods and services depend on Britain's share of trade with the eurozone, as compared to other parts of the world? For example, at present roughly 50 per cent of Britain's exports go to the eurozone. Is this the clinching argument in your view?
This is one major argument, yes. There is also a trend: we can anticipate that this share will increase. Remember Europe, in the sense of the EU and also the EMU, is growing. Denmark and Sweden will, I expect, become full EMU participants before too long. The eight East European accession candidates will join the EU in 2004, and I hope the EMU as full players in no more than two years afterwards. So will Cyprus and Malta. This will increase Britain's import and export shares with the eurozone. It is for Britain the key competitive margin. That key competitive margin is determined to a significant extent by financial asset markets that reflect many factors, both fundamental and spurious, that may have nothing to do with underlying costs, competitiveness and productivity positions of the UK and its continental competitors. The relative price of British and competitors' goods, relative cost comparisons, are too serious an issue to be left to the foreign exchange market.

How do you react to the counter-argument that a large volume of Britain's trade is denominated in dollars; in other words while we might gain more security in respect of our eurozone trading partners we would potentially expose ourselves to less certainty in respect of our trade with the dollar area?
As I said earlier, in principle it's certainly possible that there could be increased variability *vis-à-vis* non-euro areas, for instance the dollar area. Theoretically, though not in practice, it could be the case that the volatility of the effective exchange rate of sterling increases. However, it is important not to confuse prices being denominated in dollars – priced in dollars – with prices being rigid or sticky in dollars. The numeraire need not have any behavioural significance. The fact that in Tashkent many hotels price their rooms in dollars doesn't mean that these prices follow US dollar hotel prices. The question of the numeraire is not the same as: 'what is the influence of US

dollar price and cost developments for Britain's external trade position?'.

Empirical studies examining the link between exchange rate stability and trade have provided mixed results. However, a number of recent studies (see, for example, Rose, 2000; Rose and van Wincoop, 2001) of the impact of exchange rate volatility on trade has provided strong support for the hypothesis that monetary unions significantly promote trade. For example in their 2001 AER article, Rose and van Wincoop [2001, p. 386] 'estimate that EMU will cause European trade to rise by over 50 per cent' and that 'the benefits of trade created by currency union may swamp any costs of foregoing independent monetary policy'. How robust are these findings?
I'm a great believer in the desirability of the adoption of the euro by Britain. But these kinds of studies are, let's put it gently, not incredibly robust. Those are wild numbers and I don't believe a word of it. You could divide that estimate by 10 and still get something that maybe looks too large. You never serve a good cause by overstating the case for it. There is a key 'omitted variable' problem in these studies. Countries that belong to a currency union are also likely to have harmonized laws and regulations for cross-border transactions within the union. Non-tariff trade barriers like the abuse of phyto-sanitary standards, health and safety regulations and discrimination between nationals and non-nationals in the application of administrative measures that cause delays in completing transactions, are likely to be weaker for trade within the currency union than for trade across the boundaries of the union. How do you distinguish between the effects of the progressive implementation of the Single European Act and those of adopting the euro?

Take another example. People have looked at what's happened to Britain's share of trade (imports plus exports) in GDP and found that it has lagged behind that of the EMU members between 1999 and 2001. However, the same can be said for Denmark and Sweden, two countries that have remained outside the European Union, and which have also increased their trade-to-GDP ratios. The driving force behind this increase is likely to be found in exchange rate movements. The US dollar started to appreciate against the euro in the last quarter of 1999. The appreciation of the US dollar against the pound sterling was much less strong. The nominal exchange rate appreciation was also an appreciation of the real exchange rate, an increase in the price of traded goods relative to non-traded goods. Even with constant trade volumes, this relative price change would raise the share of trade in GDP. I think most of these tests have to be redone and redone properly. So I do not rely for my advocacy of joining on what I consider to be wild and woolly estimates of the likely impact on trade.

Returning to the issue of foreign direct investment [FDI]. Do you believe that a reduction in foreign exchange risk will help to secure Britain's place as a preferred location for foreign direct investment?
You know Britain has a lot going for it. It has a flexible labour market, reasonably good labour relations and reasonably attractive taxation of profits. This gives Britain an edge for investors. But exchange rate uncertainties, *vis-à-vis* the obvious alternative location for foreign direct investment on the Continent, is a negative. Of course there are other factors affecting FDI choices, which have nothing at all to do with the exchange rate, for which Britain is badly positioned. For example, Britain has the worst infrastructure in the industrial world. Much of its labour force has relatively low skills and educational qualifications compared to those in the advanced continental European countries. These things work against investment in Britain. On balance the elimination of exchange rate uncertainty would be a net plus for Britain and, together with its greater flexibility, help compensate for its human capital weaknesses and inadequate infrastructure.

Increased price transparency
One of the central economic arguments advanced in favour of joining the euro is that by increasing transparency in price comparisons it will promote greater competition between firms and benefit the consumer. What is your view of this argument and, in particular, how much room do you think there is for benefits to producers from economies at scale as a result of the advent of the euro?
The benefits come not so much from economies of scale, but from more effective competition. There are some economies of scale that remain unreaped. But in many industries the main argument for adopting a common currency and enlarging the market is not economies of scale. It's simply that greater price transparency makes it easier for consumers and other customers to arbitrage. Of course you need also the rest of the Single European Act. It's no use having completely transparent pricing and then not being able to trade because of barriers. One of the problems with the studies of Rose and others you referred to earlier is that what they attribute to the common currency is in fact much more likely to

be due to the fact that regions have a common legal structure and a much diminished set of non-tariff barriers to trade and transit. How many countries do you know that have a common currency and not a common judiciary system? There are some. Most of the 50 per cent increase in trade [see Rose and van Wincoop, 2001] attributed to a common currency reflects the authors' inability to discriminate between the positive effect of a common currency and the positive effect of having a single jurisdiction, a single market and the elimination of other barriers to trade and transit. But I think that price transparency does matter. I find it much easier to aggressively search the web for the cheapest place to buy x, y or z when things are priced in a single currency. Of course a single currency is not the end of it. You can have a single currency and still not be able to buy a right-hand-drive car in Belgium because of some other silly administrative, legal or fiscal obstacle in the way. What makes the single market, even more than the single currency, is the Single European Act and its gradual implementation across the existing union.

Do you think that people's aggressive behaviour in markets is increasingly driven by technology – by access to the internet, for example – and that this is more important than whether or not prices are denominated in some common currency?
I think that they all matter. There has been a massive increase in the amount of trade taking place over the internet. It is much easier to get information about alternatives and options over the internet, especially if you use the modern specialized search engines that are available. Nevertheless, the fact that you have to come up with foreign currencies to effect transactions means that you're going to be taken to the cleaners at least twice for every transaction. That's a discouragement to effective international arbitrage and trade. It's not a question of either or. It may well be that the internet matters more, but it's very hard to quantify these things. The fact that there is free lunch there, even if it's a small free lunch, still means that I would take it.

Foreign key currency?
Do you think it is possible or likely that the euro will gain key currency status to rival the dollar and, if so, what kind of benefits could you see arising from this?
I think that it will definitely happen. In fact it's already happening – more slowly than some people anticipated – but it is

happening. The benefits are minor but not negligible. People all over the world – central banks, private individuals, legitimate businesses, criminals – now all hold part of their cash reserves in euros as well as in dollars. That means that there is additional seigniorage revenue for the monetary authorities of the EMU area and since that ultimately gets passed back to the national central banks and thus the national treasuries, it means a small bonus to taxpayers in these countries. The seigniorage gains accrue from the international use of the euro as reserve currency, a vehicle currency and as a favourite refuge currency for people that are either afraid of monetary mismanagement or of the law, or both. While these are minor gains, that aren't going to make or break the issue, they are nice to have. At the moment I think that something like 70 per cent of all US dollar bills are held abroad. Of course the euro is nowhere near in that position but it could certainly rival the dollar in due course. The fact that we have these large denominations for the euro makes it much more attractive for organized and disorganized crime to use it as a store of value. Ken Rogoff, the current chief economist at the IMF [International Monetary Fund], wrote a paper a while ago pointing out that having these very large denominations was a very antisocial act because it is only of interest to those who wish to hold wealth out of sight of the authorities. The largest American bill is 100 dollars. Originally there was going to be a 1000 euro bill, but it stopped at the 500 euro level. I think that it would be civilized behaviour, though not revenue-maximizing behaviour, and cooperative behaviour in the fight against crime and money laundering, to reduce the maximum denomination of the euro to 100, the way the US dollar is. The only people to benefit from the larger denomination are the criminal fraternity.

Economic Costs

Loss of monetary independence
The main potential cost of monetary union concerns the problem, for participants, of dealing with shocks without the use of independent monetary policy. The debate is informed by the literature on what constitutes an optimum currency area (see Mundell, 1961). The US is widely acknowledged to be an optimum currency area, what characteristics of the eurozone might give rise to concerns that it is not an optimum currency area?

I don't think that there are any. I believe that optimal currency
area arguments, of the traditional variety, are largely irrelevant in
the modern world, where the desirability of different exchange
rate regimes are really driven by your judgement about the
efficiency of the foreign exchange market in a world without
capital market restrictions. From a technical, economic, point of
view the only optimum currency area is all those countries and
regions of the world that are linked by unrestricted international
capital mobility. So from that point of view, all of Europe, the
US, Japan, bits of Central and South America, and other bits
that don't have capital controls are an optimal currency area.
Politically of course you can't quite manage that. Independent
monetary policy is part of national sovereignty. It is a constitutional, political, as well as a technical economic issue. Arguments
about asymmetric shocks, about factor mobility, about the
absence of a large federal tax authority capable of redistributing
between regions – all these arguments are basically vacuous,
either on logical a priori grounds or empirically.

I think the strongest argument is the one concerning asymmetric shocks, as it is not immediately obvious why it is wrong.
Nominal rigidities are the only reason why the exchange rate
regime matters. If countries are fundamentally inefficient, if real
wages are growing regardless of productivity developments, if
there is massive structural unemployment, then the exchange
rate will not make a blind bit of difference. So it's nominal rigidities that matter. If, in the presence of such nominal rigidities, there
are asymmetric shocks that require relative price or cost adjustments in order to evoke the right demand and supply responses
then in principle, an ideally managed nominal exchange rate may
be a more effective and less costly instrument for effecting these
relative price or cost changes. Unfortunately the exchange rate
cannot be managed that way in a world where the exchange rate
floats and is determined in a financial market that is driven by
many substantive, fundamental or arbitrary irrational forces.
Britain has had an independent floating currency, more or less,
since it was pushed out of ERM 1 on Black Wednesday. In the
three years that I served on the Monetary Policy Committee
we had a persistently overvalued sterling, and an unbalanced
economy where a sheltered sector was booming ahead. The international exposed sector, especially manufacturing, was being
crippled, squeezed and squashed by the excessive strength of
sterling. What did we do about it? Nothing. The exchange rate

was not an instrument, the exchange rate just happened to us. Each time we predicted, quarter after quarter, that the exchange rate would fall, quarter after quarter it either remained constant or went up. We systematically got the outlook for sterling wrong and we could never treat sterling as an instrument. Britain has been subject, until very recently, to a rather wild run-up in house and real estate prices. Again this was an asymmetric shock: it wasn't happening elsewhere. Could monetary policy be used to address it? No. Monetary policy is otherwise engaged targeting the rate of inflation. So the notion that the exchange rate is there as an instrument to be used flexibly to achieve relative cost or price changes which otherwise have to be achieved in painful ways – by one country inflating less rapidly than another or even being pushed into temporary deflation – is just an illusion. It has not happened here since 1992, and it has not happened elsewhere. The notion that asymmetric shocks make a case for monetary independence is bogus. The monetary authorities in a modern financially open economy cannot use the exchange rate so as to take care effectively of asymmetric shocks. I've been there. We tried and we couldn't.

What about the problem of differences in language and culture, which impede labour market mobility between eurozone countries?
You need to consider what monetary policy buys you, if it works. Ideally, managed exchange rate changes permit you to achieve, more rapidly at less cost, relative cost or price changes that would otherwise occur more slowly and with greater cost. So it has a temporary effect. To achieve the same thing through labour mobility you'd have to have cyclically reversible labour mobility. I am not talking about one region being structurally depressed, like Appalachia or the South of Italy, and another region being structurally booming, with labour migration from one region to another. Exchange rate changes are not a substitute for such secular migration, which involves secular, permanent differentials in productivity levels and productivity growth rates that induce permanent flows. The exchange rate only permits you to mimic what temporary, or more precisely, reversible flows will do. It's not necessary, of course, that individual workers would have to move temporarily. All you require is that the net flows are reversible; you don't just move for a year and then come back, the cost would be far too high. What happens is that more people would move out and fewer

would come back. Very few countries have significant labour mobility at cyclical frequencies. There is more in the US than here, but it is still pretty minor. What this means is that either the US is not an optimal currency area (because even they don't get this kind of high frequency labour mobility between states), or that you can have an optimal currency area without labour mobility and cyclical frequencies. I think that the latter is the case. It would be nice to have greater labour mobility on the Continent for many reasons, especially as it would allow regions to allocate resources more efficiently and grow faster. But exchange rate flexibility is not an effective substitute for not having that kind of labour mobility.

Does the persistence of high unemployment across Europe suggest that labour markets in EMU economies are less flexible than in the UK?
What is interesting about the Continent are the enormous and persistent differences between the performance of individual countries which are hidden by the average. German economic performance is awful and their labour markets are probably the most inefficient on the Continent. At the same time, while there has been a cyclical downturn in the Netherlands, the Netherlands has been running its economy with 3.5 per cent unemployment, even lower than the UK. Ireland of course has had an immensely dynamic and flexible labour market. Spain has moved from having an unbelievably inefficient labour market, 10–15 years ago, to one that is much more efficient today. Likewise Portugal. It's the three biggies, France, Italy and Germany that get the booby prizes for labour market inflexibility. But these are national policy choices that these countries make and can unmake. The nice thing is you can be in the EU, and in the EMU, and not be subject to the average degree of inefficiency in the Union, as many examples from Finland to the Netherlands and Spain have shown. Within the euro area, labour market efficiency is going to depend on domestic structural reform, on legislative, regulatory regimes that remain the prerogative of the domestic authorities. You can mess it up like the Germans do, and the French and the Italians do to a certain extent, or you can make a success of it as the Scandinavians, the Dutch and the Irish have done. If Britain opts for the euro, it wouldn't have to opt for the average labour market practices of the Continent. Britain can choose its own labour market practices. There are some aspects where the British labour market has much greater

flexibility and there are others, including training and appren-
ticeships, where Britain could learn a lot from the Continent,
including Germany.

Would joining EMU be like joining a less forgiving version of the ERM?
No. That is a complete fallacy. The reason the ERM was the disaster it was, is that Britain's membership of the ERM did not represent an irrevocable commitment. That is the key thing and
really the only thing that matters. If there is a chance that joining
EMU would be like an old-fashioned promise to peg an exchange
rate and then stand up and say 'over my dead body only', and
everybody is already calling in the undertakers, then it would be
just that. But it is not the way that the euro cookie is baked. It
is an irrevocable commitment. What you are fixing is not an
exchange rate but a conversion rate. The pound would cease to
exist as an independent currency. It would simply be a non-
decimal denomination of the euro. There is no comparison
between the best of all possible worlds, which is a common
currency, and the worst of all possible worlds, which is a not
fully credible quasi-commitment to some fixed, or quasi-fixed,
exchange rate regime. None of the disasters that struck Britain in
'92 will occur if, and when, Britain joins the euro. The markets
knew that the British political system would not stand a 15
per cent interest rate. The only way that the then-Chancellor,
Mr [Norman] Lamont, could have defended Britain's position in
the ERM would have been to raise interest rates even higher than
that. It was clear that it was a one-way bet and markets are very
good at making one-way bets.

*What is your view of the five tests that the present-Chancellor, Gordon
Brown, has set for British membership?*
Well, I think that they've all been met. I don't think that *convergence*
is a big issue. Even if Britain experiences asymmetric shocks, it is
not something you can compensate for effectively with an independent national monetary policy. That is the monetary stabilization fallacy, the oversell of exchange rate management. To the
extent that convergence between any two regions can be expected,
Britain has converged. The test of *flexibility* is a strange one. It is not
clear in some of the discussions whether the issue is UK flexibility
or eurozone flexibility. The only thing that matters to the UK is
whether the UK has the flexibility and it is obvious that it does. As
regards the *City*, even if the gains from adopting the euro are small,

as I believe they will be, it's clear that there are going to be gains and not loses. As for *FDI*, Britain is already experiencing the fall-out from being lukewarm towards joining the euro. On balance the macroeconomic stability of the British economy will be enhanced in EMU relative to what it would be under independent monetary management. There is a link, although it may be difficult to establish, between overall macroeconomic stability, employment and growth. I therefore believe that the fifth, the summing-up test has been passed already. All in all I'm happy with the way things have turned out these last few years.

Do you have any views as to the appropriate entry rate if we were to join?
With the euro where it is, the UK could join today. The rate has to be negotiated between the UK and its continental partners. I think that they will negotiate a rate, which is not a mile away from where we are today. Certainly one that is quite a bit more competitive than it would have been a year and a half ago.

Other potential costs
Patrick Minford (2002) has highlighted two further potential costs of EMU. One concerning the move to increased harmonization of taxes, and other institutions, which he argues would adversely affect labour competitiveness and thereby damage UK output and employment. The other is the projected state benefit deficits of Germany, France and Italy which he believes would place a heavy burden on UK taxpayers. What is your response to these two concerns?
The last point is the easiest one to respond to. It is not just a *red* herring, it is a scarlet herring. The argument that the British worker bee will have to bail out the improvident butterflies or grasshoppers in France, Germany or Italy, with their large unfounded social security and state retirement pension schemes, is complete baloney. These countries do indeed face a serious problem of provision for old age. The current contribution rates by Italian and German workers are not sufficient, because of demographic and productivity developments, to realize the expectations for state pensions of current and future pensioners. Somebody is going to be disappointed. If the intergenerational conflict is limited to Italian workers and Italian pensioners, either Italian pensioners will have their pensions cut, or Italian workers will have to cough up more, or a combination of these two will happen. If neither the current Italian worker nor the

Italian pensioner gets clobbered, then other beneficiaries of Italian public spending will suffer, or other Italian taxpayers will have to pay if public debt default is to be avoided. If none of this works, there could be public debt default. Holders (domestic and foreign) of Italian public debt would suffer. In Britain most of that clobbering has already occurred. Britain has the lowest replacement ratio of state pension benefits to the average wage, of any rich European country. This has been achieved, to a large extent, by de-linking the state pension from earnings and linking it to prices, which is a very neat trick, if you can get away with it. The consequence of this is that in Britain, since the British public has not increased its saving rate to any significant extent, we are faced with a growing problem of poverty in old age. What is going to happen is that some other item in the budget – state benefits for poverty relief, extra grants to keep granny warm in the winter – will have to be paid out, to make up for the difference between what the state pension affords and what society will tolerate as a minimal acceptable standard of living for its citizens. Another example, the health service in Britain is unfunded and is paid out of current revenue. While health spending in Britain is going to go up steeply we don't expect that the Italians or German taxpayers are going to come in and bail out the British patient. Once more, the British taxpayer financing the continental benefit deficit is a complete nonsense. The Italians and Germans will sort out their own problems. It's an intergenerational conflict that came about because of inconsistent expectations and disappointments on population growth, longevity, the birth rate and productivity growth. Each country is sorting, and will sort the problem out in its own way. The notion that having a common currency would make it more likely that somebody in a stronger position – even if Britain were in that position and I would deny that it is – would bail out a weaker brother is completely ridiculous. I lived in Newhaven, Connecticut for many years, when 20 miles or so up the road Bridgeport went broke. We weren't lying awake in our beds at night in Newhaven trembling with fear that we would have to bail out the improvident Bridgeportonians. What happened was that Bridgeport had control of its finances removed by the State of Connecticut and spending in Bridgeport was slashed and local taxes were raised severely. They went through a very unpleasant and painful adjustment. There was no raid on the kitty of Newhaven. I think that this argument is the worst kind

of cynical manipulation of underlying xenophobia. It is a dis-
honest argument and many of those that make it know that the
argument is untrue.

*What about the concern that harmonization of taxes would adversely
affect labour competitiveness?*
It is an argument that in principle could have merit. Technically
of course there's no link at all between a common currency and
the harmonization of anything, other than interest rates. At the
technical, legal level the argument is completely spurious.
What I think is correct is that joining EMU is not just a technical, economic decision, it is also a political, constitutional
decision. It is another step on the road to a more federal Europe,
which I think is a good thing. Obviously, if you don't like it, it's
a bad thing. To the extent that joining, rather than not joining,
represents the strengthening of the integrationist, federalist
momentum in Europe, it is more likely that some things
that were previously under national jurisdiction would now
become a matter of common concern and joint decision, using
qualified majority voting. Remember that all these areas
that Professor Minford and others put up as evidence for
the prosecution are all areas where unanimity is required.
Unanimity means just that. If one country, even Luxembourg
or soon Malta, votes against it then it won't happen. I actually
believe that in certain areas greater harmonization might
well be desirable. In other areas this is not true. I think tax competition is an efficient way of keeping the Leviathan under
control. I recognize that the growth of state spending is not just
driven by platonic concerns with efficiency and poverty relief.
There's usually a bureaucratic imperative there and also political considerations. To the extent that tax competition helps rein
in the Leviathan it may be a desirable thing. While there
are cases for harmonization, there will have to be unanimity.
Britain will be able to pick and choose what she will, or won't,
harmonize.

Euro institutions
*The Stability and Growth Pact has been subject to some criticism and
there may be an emerging agenda for its reform. What are your views of
the Stability and Growth Pact as it relates to the UK's possible euro entry?*
Remember that Britain is already subject to some key aspects of
the Stability and Growth Pact. In fact the requirement that the

budget, in the medium term, be close to balance or in surplus applies to Britain. It applies to anybody who is in the EU. The Pact is an example of how legitimate concerns and good intentions may still lead to an unfortunate accident. It's inflexible, its numerical criteria are arbitrary and it does not provide the right incentives to achieve fiscal sustainability in the long term, because it does not provide any direct incentives for fiscal tightening during boom periods. This has now been recognized. You don't get the President of the European Commission calling the arrangement stupid and rigid if there aren't widespread views that either constructive reinterpretation, or formal redesign, of the Pact is necessary. The Pact is part of the Treaty and the Treaty can only be changed by unanimity. Formal revision of the Pact may be a long-term exercise. In the short term we are going to see more of the *ad hoc* hand waving and disorganized flexibility that we have seen in the past. This is not a very pretty sight, but I think it is inevitable given the fact that the formal reconsideration of what the Pact should be is institutionally so difficult. When two of the largest countries, Germany and France, are persistently exceeding the key numerical deficit limit and are not falling off the edge of the cliff, the absence of a rationale for these limits becomes clear even to those who are most firmly attached to them. Most people who now defend them, defend them simply because they are there. Giving up on a commitment is bad for credibility, even when the commitment is to something arbitrary The EC [European Community] is in a box. It has the responsibility to enforce observance of a Pact that makes little sense. What do you do? Do you give up on the commitment and lose credibility, even if you construct a more sensible Pact? If you stick to it, you may end losing credibility anyway. I believe that in the end the light will shine even through this particular darkness and the Pact will become a way of leaning on fiscally suspect EU members to ensure that the longer-term sustainability of their public finances is not endangered.

Britain has a macro policy framework based around an inflation target and central bank operational independence for setting interest rates. Joining the euro would mean accepting an alternative framework with the ECB at its centre. What are your views on the desirability of such development? For example, is the UK's model for central bank independence preferable to the eurozone's?

By and large, yes. There are a couple of weaknesses, which I have pointed out many times. The main one is that, in principle, the Chancellor can change the target anytime he or she wants to. That's just too easy. I do believe that the operational target should be set politically, to get legitimacy. But it should be harder to change than it is in the British system where it is possible for a party to get a majority in Parliament with 30 per cent of the vote and to do what it wants. There ought to be some mechanism, which makes it more difficult to change the operational target. Apart from that I think the only thing that could be subject to improvement is that the terms for the external members should be changed: they should be appointed to a single, 5–7-year term rather than to renewable three-year terms. I think this would be better all round for both the substance and the appearance of independence. But these are minor things. Of course both the ECB and Bank of England have their ultimate objectives determined by politicians. The ECB has, in the Treaty, price stability as its objective. The difference of course is that the operational implementation of that objective, in the UK, is done by Gordon Brown and in the EU it's done by the ECB. I would prefer that the ECB's operational target be set politically, but again in such a way that it would not be changed frequently and frivolously. One obvious way to do that would be to have it set by unanimity in the Council. That would make it very hard to change. It would also help if this particular operational target were a bit clearer than the current messy inflation target that dare not speak its name. The ECB doesn't have an inflation target. The inflation rate that the ECB deems consistent with its price stability objective is an inflation rate between zero and 2 per cent. It's too cute. They should have either a 1 or 2 per cent inflation target and make it symmetric so that it's clear that there is no downward bias. As a technical economist I would urge them to drop one of the two pillars for monetary policy. The value of broad monetary aggregates, as indicators of future inflation, is so restrictive and limited because of the noise in the velocity of circulation of the aggregates, that it deserves no more special consideration than a host of other monetary and financial indicators. By all means look at the monetary aggregates, but don't hang your supposed operational monetary policy hat on something which is a will of the wisp. Then there is their unwillingness to reveal the vote, which I think is unfortunate. This means that there is a lack of accountability and transparency. I would also like them to publish edited minutes. Currently a statement is made immediately following the meetings. This timing makes it clear that the statement was ready well before the meeting; it therefore has no value as an indicator of what the main arguments that shaped the discussion were. I also have some trouble – though again it is not a hanging issue – with their predilection for consensus seeking in decision making. You don't need a consensus, you need a majority. Disagreements in wild and woolly subjects like monetary economics are to be expected. This need to present a united front and consensus is part of the high priestly tradition of monetary policy making that is overdue for a clean-out. On the whole I think that the ECB has a structure that can be turned into something that is really quite effective. As it is, they are not doing badly. Inevitably, since they are a very young institution, without any institutional pre-history, they tend to conduct policy by looking in the rear-view mirror. But as they gain self-confidence, and a track record, they will target future anticipated inflation rather than be driven excessively by the recent behaviour of inflation. None of these matters is an insurmountable obstacle to Britain joining. In fact if Britain joins it will accelerate the technical and institutional changes that I consider to be desirable, especially if Britain comes in at the same time as Denmark and Sweden, and before too long a handful of countries from Eastern Europe. Then, of course, you will need to change the voting mechanism. I sympathize with the inevitable mess that the Treaty requirement of one country one vote has left them in. How do you get a decision-making body that makes sense with ultimately, 27 or more countries? You will need an abacus or a small calculator to figure out who votes when under the recent proposals for a three-class voting mechanism for the national central bank governors. The accountability and transparency of the process really suffers. The paradox is that the ECB is meant to be a European institution, where everybody votes without any regard for national conditions, looking only at EU-wide economic developments. Yet at the same time, the vast majority of members of the Council are selected on the basis of nationality. At some point, that will have to go. With a body of, what could be, 33 people, three football teams, you can't have sensible discussion even if you don't all vote. You don't make monetary policy at a cup final and this is what the atmosphere would be like. If they could just get themselves to abandon all nationality requirements, that would be the ideal. But of course we can't get that in a Europe where the nation state is still the bricks and mortar of what goes on.

Politics

The Werner Plan, the ERM and the euro all have economic bases, but are the primary drivers behind the European integration project economic or political?
They're political. They always have been. The EU, right from the days it was the European Coal and Steel Community in the early '50s, from the Treaty of Rome on, has always been a political wolf dressed in economic sheep's clothing. The objectives have always been political, and they still are political. For me that's a good thing. But one has to be clear about that. I think too many proponents of EMU present it as a technical, economic exercise. While it's that too, with important economic aspects to it, the overriding issue is what do we want Europe in the twenty-first century to look like.

Finally

Are there any other issues we have not touched upon in the course of our discussion, which you think are germane to the debate?
None that I can think of. [*Laughter*]

To what extent do you think that joining the EMU is a leap of faith?
Everything is a leap of faith. Staying outside the EMU is a leap of faith. Going in is not a leap of faith in the sense that that would be an enormous risk.

Do you believe it would be a risk not to join?
From the long-term point of view of getting maximum British input into the European decision-making councils, you have to join. Britain is already increasingly on the sidelines of economic decisions. People don't like to admit it, but more and more decisions are being made by the non-officially existent Council of the EMU12 and that will only intensify. In my view it is necessary for Britain to be inside the tent in order to counteract the *dirigiste* tendencies that are part of the continental tradition. However there is also a part of the continental tradition that is much more liberal, like the Dutch, the Danes, and the Belgians. There has never been a better opportunity to change Europe to a more liberal stance than now with new members coming in. The new members

coming in to the EU, especially those who have had backgrounds as economic and political satellites of Russia, are much more likely to be effective allies of Britain and the more liberal wing in the European family. Europe is going to shift away from its *dirigiste* traditions and positions on many issues because the proponents of that will be a distinct minority after 2004. I don't think that people fully realize how much the political equilibrium inside the European Union is going to shift. There's going to be a new voting system. For qualified majority decisions, for instance, Poland is going to have as many votes in the Council (27) as Spain and only two less than Germany, France, Italy and Britain. Collectively, the accession countries only have 5 per cent of the GDP of the existing Union members, but in terms of voting rights they are a third. We are going to see a very different European Union emerge and Britain wants to be there when it starts. It doesn't want to be in its usual position of joining late and reluctantly, and then complaining loudly forever after that things aren't the way they ought to be, or would have been if only we had been there earlier.

PATRICK MINFORD

Patrick Minford is Professor of Applied Economics at the Cardiff
Business School, UK. He is best known for his work on macroeconomic models based on rational expectations, macroeconomic
policy analysis and supply-side economics.

We interviewed Professor Minford in the Crowne Plaza Hotel
in Liverpool on 15 May 2003.

Economic Benefits

Transaction costs
*Would you accept that for the UK the reduction in transaction costs of
changing currency are likely to be small?*
Yes. Estimates from the European Commission (1990) – which are
probably as reasonable as you can get – found them to be around
0.1 per cent of GDP. The reason they gave is that for a country –
like the UK – with an advanced banking system, the vast majority of transactions go through the banking system at zero cost.
Anyone using a hole-in-the-wall machine or a credit card incurs
no transaction costs. This means that you are left with tourists,
who incur costs changing money. The general feeling is that such
costs, if anything, are likely to decline because more and more
people use hole-in-the-wall machines and credit cards. I always
think that the killer argument for transaction costs is that they are
such a small benefit, but in order to get them you've got to change
your money into euros. The House of Commons Trade and
Industry Committee (House of Commons, 2000), which came up
with a huge variety of estimates, said that the best central guess
would be £30 billion. Although this is a guess, it probably is going
to be a substantial sum. So if you set the costs of currency conversion against the present value of the transactions costs, and
allow for some growth, you're probably talking of changeover
costs of a similar order to the benefits you get. So fundamentally
I think that transaction costs are zero and are too trivial to worry
about. What I've found is that most pro-euro people tend to agree
and they don't really want to stress them anymore.

Exchange risk
*One of the central economic arguments advanced in favour of joining
the euro is the elimination of exchange rate risk with eurozone trading
partners. How important do you consider this argument?*

Well this is the big argument. There are two parts to the argument. First, you need to consider how big a barrier to bilateral trade exchange risk is. With the exception of more recent studies by Rose (2000) and McCallum (1995), evidence suggests that it's quite small. For years and years, in my youth, middle age and later on, we had lots of estimates from organizations, like the IMF and the OECD, which couldn't find any effect of currency variability on trade. There are good theoretical reasons to suggest that the costs of this sort of monetary variability are likely to be pretty trivial. For example, the fact that traders will hedge using the financial market facility in order to diversify. Then Rose, using a gravity model of trade, came up with an estimate that the currency union factor gave a tripling of trade. He subsequently [see Rose and van Wincoop, 2001] suggested that it could lead to a 50 per cent increase in trade. But these numbers are riddled with econometric problems, which are well known to people who undertake this type of cross-sectional analysis. The initial Rose study had a lot of small dependent countries with the mother country, this being the main example of currency union. The difficulty is one of selection bias. There could well be some unobservable factor causing these countries both to be tightly linked to the mother country and to choose currency union as part of that general linkage. If you have selection bias you can't unravel the separate effect of being in a currency union because, effectively, a third cause accounts for both the growth in trade and currency union. The third cause is particularly close political relations. When you find countries where you can – in a time series as opposed to a cross-section – locate a point at which the structure changes from being currency union to non-currency union, you should then be able to identify the effect on trade. There are two nice examples of this. One is Singapore, from Malaysia, which I think was in '68. The other is Ireland, from the UK, in '79. Although I'm not aware of any study on Singapore, there is no evidence of a casual sort to suggest that Singapore's trading with Malaysia was affected very much. Thom and Walsh (2002) in their study of the Irish experience couldn't find anything, once they allowed for all the basic trends taking place. So when you look at the time series, where selection bias is absent, you find that Rose's evidence doesn't carry through. I think this is the general consensus among economists regarding Rose's evidence. McCallum in his 1995 study of trade patterns between Canada and the US, found that the border had a huge effect on trade. Contiguous states have much less trade across the border, than contiguous states inside Canada and inside the US. But again, is that due to politics or to currency union? How do you disentangle the two effects? McCallum, to be fair, didn't mention currency union, but his study has been pressed into service by others as evidence in support of currency union. Mostly what determines trade is real factors. It's hard to believe that monetary factors are really important in trade.

The second part to the argument is peculiar to the UK. Suppose currency risk is important. What you will get, in the case of the UK, is trade diversion due to the formation of a preference with other members of the euro area. You will create a barrier against the non-euro area, which is basically the dollar area. Now in Britain's case just over half of our trade, broadly interpreted, is with the non-euro, i.e., dollar, area. Most of the rest of the world is linked, either explicitly or implicitly, to the dollar. What we find is that the euro to dollar rate is incredibly variable. The history of it has been astonishingly variable. Going back to before 1999 you see the terrific variability of the Deutschmark against the dollar. As the Deutschmark is a pivotal currency of the euro area it is reasonable to assume that the same variability would have occurred with the euro before 1999. If we join the euro we close down the currency risk with the euro area, but boost it massively with the dollar area. In the early '80s the Deutschmark–dollar rate moved up 50 per cent and then in the second half of the '80s it dropped 50 per cent. It's done more or less the same in the run-up to the introduction of the euro. When we undertook stochastic simulations [see Minford et al., 2004] allowing for these shocks we found that the currency risk for the UK was slightly greater inside the euro area than outside, because of the greater variability of the euro versus the non-euro currencies. I sometimes use an analogy of a seesaw, with the euro and the dollar at either end of the seesaw. If you join one end of the seesaw you're going to be unstable against the other end. Essentially that is what would happen. Currency risk against the dollar would increase massively. Suppose the currency risk against the dollar rose as much as the currency risk against the euro fell. Although, on average, there would be an equal amount of currency risk, welfare would decrease due to risk aversion. Halving a risk is much less good for you than a doubling of risk. In the case of the euro the actual level of risk would rise because the volatility of the euro against the dollar is so great. Now, what happens outside the euro is that when one of these currencies goes up we sit in the middle of the seesaw. In this way we manage to keep our currency instability down, in spite of the great currency instability of these two big blocs. In brief if Britain joined the euro, we would experience much higher currency risk against the dollar and suffer trade diversion.

Could your argument be used as an example of Friedman's (1953) case for flexible exchange rates? Would retaining the pound and maintaining flexibility against both the dollar and the euro be the best solution for the British economy?
Well, in a world of two major currencies, where the UK is mid-Atlantic in terms of its trade, it makes sense. Roughly half of Britain's trade is with the dollar area and the other half with the euro area. The flexible exchange rate argument is a second-best argument. Suppose we were based in a world in which the euro and the dollar were the same currency. In that situation it would be very hard to make a monetary argument that didn't mean that we were better off in a monetary union: because money is a network good and we would be sharing the same money. Friedman's argument on flexibility of exchange rates is a second-best argument which applies in a world where you have great differences in monetary and other policies that cause exchange rates to fluctuate. In a world like that I think that Friedman's argument goes through and that is essentially the argument that I am using here. In a second-best world, where the euro and the dollar are highly unstable against each other, flexible exchange rates are going to give you less currency risk and more welfare, than if you were to link to one or other of those two currencies.

Do you believe that a reduction in foreign exchange rate risk will help to secure Britain's place as a preferred location for foreign direct investment?
I think of investment as part of trade. I don't think that one can make a different argument for investment than that made for trade. Often investment is an alternative to trade, where you invest in order to replace trade. Essentially the same set of arguments apply to investment as they do to trade. Suppose we take the view that currency risk is a trade barrier although, as I say, I think the evidence is pretty tiny; then it is also an investment barrier. What one would find is that there would be an incentive for investment to locate in the UK in order to take advantage

of the closer links we have with the Continent. However there would also be a disincentive for American or dollar investment to locate in the UK since our links with the dollar area would be less close. You'd expect a directional affect on investment, favouring the euro area and militating against the dollar area.

Increased price transparency

One of the central economic arguments advanced in favour of joining the euro is that by increasing transparency in price comparisons it will promote greater competition and benefit the consumer. How important do you consider this argument?

Transparency is really about price comparisons made by consumers and businesses. When traders are comparing prices they usually have quite a lot of time to do so. Therefore what we can call the costs of using a calculator, or a computer, are pretty low. Transparency has always seemed to me to be a peculiarly weak argument for the UK, or for any situation where we're talking about distance relations. Whether you are a consumer buying through the internet, or a trader or a company dealing with consumers, or an importer or exporter, the business of currency conversion is built into systems as just another part of the natural commercial operation. People often say that it would be tremendously good if Britain were in the euro in order to be able to buy cars in Europe through the internet. Well I can't see that, as the extra computer stroke it takes to give you the price of a car in your own currency is trivial. It's similar to the transaction cost argument when you've got an advanced banking system. Essentially computers or calculators are going to give you price comparisons the whole time. Now, I think where transparency is quite important is where you've got a land border and you're constantly crossing it. Maastricht, in Holland, would be a classic example of a place where if there were two currencies it would be more of an inconvenience to consumers than with one currency. Consumers crossing the border between Holland and Belgium would need to think in Dutch currency and Belgian currency in order to make price comparisons. In Britain we don't have any land borders. The nearest we get to one is Northern Ireland, which is not a very important land border. All these arguments regarding costs and benefits are very country specific. This illustrates the country specificity of price transparency. It just does not seem to be important to the UK for the basic reason that we have no land borders.

To what extent do you think that greater price transparency will enable producers in the eurozone to achieve economies of scale?

I think one has to be a bit cautious when talking about the subject of economies of scale. They seem to be important in both manufacturing and in the service industries. However, the emphasis of an awful lot of our trade with the dollar area is on services. Trade with the European Union is much more based on manufactures. So while the economies of scale argument is important for manufacturing trade, people often neglect economies of scale or scope in the services trade. If currency risk is important you need to balance the trade-diversionary effect on dollar area trade with the trade-creating effect on euro-area trade. It always surprises me that people who get so excited about this argument have never looked at the contractionary effect on dollar-area trade. You're back to the seesaw analogy I used earlier. I'm not terribly impressed by the argument about economies of scale because a similar argument applies in reverse to the dollar-area trade. The most dynamic part of our markets is in services. In any case the structure of our trade activity is likely to alter. Manufacturing trade is likely to decline both as a share of our trade generally and as a share of our trade with the Continent, especially when you think of the way in which emerging markets are taking over manufacturing. I find the emphasis on a declining area of activity puzzling. Currency risk is important and the economies of scale argument probably has some validity, but there seems to be no reason to believe that it won't be offset by the disadvantages to trade and economic activity which is mainly shared with the dollar area

Future key currency?

What are your views on the possibility of the euro becoming a key currency to rival the dollar? What benefits will ensue should this happen?

This is all about seigniorage. Being able to borrow cheaply on world markets by issuing your own currency. If the euro is successful and gets established and doesn't break up, there is clearly going to be some seigniorage. I suppose it would be greater than that enjoyed by the Deutschmark, the French franc and so on. If in fact the euro is seen as a very sound currency and is very widely used in trade, it will encourage its use in reserves. So far there is not much sign of that and there is great uncertainty about the future of the euro. The great difficulty, which most people inside the euro area appreciate, is that as long as there are many different countries with sovereignty sharing this currency you can't exclude the possibility that one of them will decide that it doesn't suit them anymore and they leave. Many currency unions have broken up in the past and this particular currency union may well break up. Therefore the whole argument about seigniorage is fraught with the risk of break-up. No one is going to want to go heavily into the euro until they are absolutely sure that it's going to be there for the long haul. Having said that, suppose it does settle down and it is there for the long haul and that does increase seigniorage. How big is this likely to be in welfare terms? The general assumptions about seigniorage are that it is pretty small. As for the UK joining the euro to share in the seigniorage, I would say that that is a very small argument. If the euro is a success, then by joining the UK would gain a little bit of a share of this seigniorage, which would presumably be greater than the seigniorage it gets from sterling. But I don't think we are talking about anything other than a pretty microscopic number even if all these caveats are satisfied.

Economic Costs

Loss of monetary independence
The main potential cost of monetary union concerns the problem, for participants, of dealing with shocks without the use of independent monetary policy. The debate is informed by the literature on what constitutes an optimum currency area (see Mundell, 1961). What characteristics of the eurozone might give rise to concerns that it is not an optimum currency area?

There was a lot of literature, before the euro was launched, about whether or not the countries that went ahead and joined were part of an optimal currency area. On the whole the consensus was that they weren't. But in one sense we can put this question to one side. The issue for the UK is whether *we* join the euro, given that other countries are willing to put up with the costs of being in a non-optimal currency area and assuming the euro survives. The issue boils down to an empirical matter of how big the costs are of sacrificing your degree of freedom in setting interest rates. Now we know that there will be costs. Whenever you sacrifice an instrument of policy you are bound to lose something in terms of your ability to stabilize your economy in a desired way, whether it's stabilizing inflation or output, or stabilizing some other aspect of the economy that you're concerned about. It is an argument about the variance of the economy. It's not an argument about the average level of output or inflation because it should be possible to get the same average level of output, and the same average level of inflation, inside or outside the euro area. In effect, what would happen inside the euro [area] is that average output would gravitate to the same level as it would outside and the average inflation rate would also be the same, assuming the euro area pursues the same sort of inflation target that we do, which seems a reasonable assumption. So the issue is the volatility of the UK economy inside the euro area, compared to having your own currency and this degree of freedom, namely setting your own interest rate and by implication your own exchange rate. I lump the two together because in order to have an independent monetary policy you have to have your own exchange rate. It is an empirical matter of how much you would lose in terms of extra variability of the economy if Britain were to join. You've got to tackle this question by looking at the economy and effectively modelling it. There isn't any other way that I know of at any rate, of actually assessing how much it would affect the UK economy to be in or out of the euro. We [see Minford et al., 2004] carried out a stochastic simulation study of the UK economy using the Liverpool Model. We used the method of boot strapping and bombarded the economy with the same shocks as have occurred in the last 16 years, quarter by quarter. We simulated a very large number of these scenarios, of repeated shocks, for a period of about 10 years each and came up with some estimates of what would happen to variability in and out of the euro. In short, inflation variability is massively increased. This is exemplified by the case of Ireland and the fact that if you've got a real exchange rate that's moving around between the euro and the dollar, and you trade a lot with the dollar area, your trading prices move around a great deal in terms of the euro. We also found that real interest rate variability was much increased. Again, you can see the Irish example of this: with nominal interest rates being set in Frankfurt, and inflation moving around, you get huge real interest rate variability. Under the Monetary Policy Committee arrangements, inflation variability has been tiny with a standard deviation of inflation of something like half a per cent. The inflation targeting regime is one that keeps inflation variability quite tight, because of great credibility and because everything is subordinated to keeping inflation under control. In a currency union the average inflation for the union can be stabilized in the same way, but inflation in individual countries depends on what happens to this real exchange rate. This is where the euro's volatility against the dollar becomes very important in terms of destabilizing trading prices. We also found that output and unemployment variability increased by a significant percentage, by 30–40 per cent in terms of variance. We took a weighted average of these increased variances, giving a low weight to the nominal ones and the real interest rate, and quite a high rate to the real ones of unemployment and output, and came up with an average worsening of welfare of 75 per cent. Essentially what one can say is that joining the euro would create a lot more variability in the macro economy. The welfare implications of increasing the boom and bust factor, by say 75 per cent, must be considered to be a significant cost in terms of the perceived preferences of the British people who don't like boom and bust. Although the welfare measure of variability is essentially arbitrary and we don't know how to translate it into an equivalent change in average living standards, in terms of what we know about the preferences of voters, that sort of variance increase is likely to be pretty important. That is the major cost of joining.

In the late '80s–early '90s the debate over whether or not Britain should join the ERM was, in part, shaped by the question of whether the UK responds to shocks differently compared to other countries in Europe. Do bi-polarity ERM arguments still carry weight?
You know, an awful lot of the literature looks at things concerned with the euro area as a whole. Yet issues are very much specific to a country. Obviously the UK experiences asymmetric or specific shocks. The question you need to answer is 'how long is a piece of string?'. We sought to answer the question in our stochastic simulation study [see Minford et al., 2004]. You've got to look at what shocks actually hit the UK economy. We took the last 16 years as being a reasonable period to calibrate the shocks that would hit us from the euro area and found that a very large fraction come from the shocks to the euro itself. In other words, there is a serious cost from abandoning your own interest rate, but there is an even bigger cost from being linked to the euro area when that is itself being hit by large real exchange rate shocks *vis-à-vis* the dollar. This was quite an interesting finding. We hadn't realized until then how important the volatility of the euro against the dollar was in actually driving volatility in the UK economy. We discovered in the course of these stochastic simulations that this was a

major factor. It accounted for the finding that our currency risk, which I referred to earlier, was actually a little bit greater on average inside the euro area. A lot of that was because of the shocks of the euro itself on the UK economy. One can see this happening in real time with Ireland. When Ireland joined the euro in 1999, the euro promptly dropped by something like 20 per cent, causing quite big disturbances for the Irish economy. Within three years Ireland had an inflation rate that peaked just below 8 per cent. That was almost directly attributable to the euro dropping, driving up prices in Ireland in terms of euros for dollar trade. Dollar trade is immensely important to Ireland. You saw in real time this effect actually happening in the Irish economy with real interest rates going highly negative, feeding the boom and inflation rising sharply.

What are your views on the five tests which must be met before Britain can adopt the euro? Which, if any, are especially important? Do the tests reduce to the optimum currency area question?

Well, the five tests organize the question in a slightly unusual way from an economist's viewpoint. The first is about convergence, the second about flexibility, the third is about the city, the fourth about investment and jobs, and then there's the last one which is a sort of sweep-all-up test of whether joining would be good for the British economy. One can see that politically it is quite a neat way to pose the question of whether or not we should join the euro. If you're trying to produce something that's going to play in the newspapers, you wouldn't organize it in the way our present discussion is structured. The Treasury has found plenty of scope to cover everything in the tests. Nothing has been left out because of the fifth test. The city test lies slightly oddly in there, because the city is, after all, one sector of the economy. Why don't we have other named sectors, like manufacturing, services or even higher education? As I said, the tests are all-embracing, but they are slightly unusually organized from an economist's viewpoint.

Other costs

In your IEA paper (Minford, 2002) you highlight two further potential costs of EMU. One concerns the move to increased harmonization of taxes, and other institutions, which you argue, would adversely affect labour competitiveness and thereby damage UK output and employment. Won't moves to increase tax harmonization occur regardless of whether or not we join the euro?

To some extent I think that is true. But the point about joining the euro is that we would be joining an extra club, a club within a club. At present we have a veto in quite a lot of areas, like tax for example. Suppose that it is argued inside the euro club, that to make the euro more easy to manage it would be good for countries to harmonize x, y or z. There is no veto inside that club. It's an extra layer of pressure to which we'd be subject. If you join an inner club, of a club that has an outer-level veto, you're taking a risk that in the inner level you would effectively be pressurized into abandoning any veto you can maintain in the outer level. I think it's an extra layer of pressure. Unfortunately, the way in which the euro is envisaged as an instrument of unification politically means that it's likely to be quite a potent sort of pressure, politically. The sort of pressure that would be brought to bear would take the form that Britain is up to its spoiling game again. It has joined the euro but it won't really cooperate in making the euro a success. Britain's being awkward again, not going along. It would be that type of argument that would be used by our neighbours. If we do join the euro we would be implicitly agreeing to abide by whatever the rules are of the euro-running club. We would be admitting ourselves into a club where we're not quite sure how the rules will evolve.

The other concern you raise in your IEA paper is the projected state benefits deficits of Germany, France and Italy, which you argue would place a heavy burden on UK taxpayers. Doesn't the UK have a similar looming state pension crisis?
Not really. The OECD studies [see Roseveare et al., 1996] that I drew on shows the UK as having its state pension benefits more or less in line with contributions. Pretty early on in the Thatcher government era we raised the retirement age of women, indexed the state pension to prices and also reduced the benefits under the state earnings related pension scheme. Those actions substantially reduced the problem. Our demographics are also slightly better and our unemployment rate is lower. There are a number of things which have been quite helpful to the UK in that respect. Recent government actions have increased pension liabilities somewhat, but they have all been done within the context of the government actuaries feeling that things are okay. In contrast, the situation on the Continent is, if anything, getting worse. There have been some attempts at reform, which have altered

the situation since the OECD studies in 1996. But at the same time on the Continent unemployment is much worse than in the UK and growth is much weaker than previously projected. These problems could be solved by cutting benefits, but politically it's very hard to cut benefits. The grey vote is politically very important in these countries, as it is everywhere else. The reason this problem should concern us is because if we were to join the euro we join a club within a club. Again, it's the same answer as I gave earlier. If you join a club within a club, you are subject to all sorts of new pressures. Quite clearly in the context of the Treaty of Rome there's absolutely no way in which we could be called upon to pay for anybody else's pension obligations. But suppose we are inside the euro area and a country was having great financial difficulties and might default on its public debt. One can imagine the discussion inside the euro club – it threatens the currency, it threatens the credibility of our monetary policy, it causes all sorts of problems to us – we members should somehow take avoiding action. Some people have argued that it would clearly show up in the form of pressure on the central bank to inflate away the problems to some degree. I think the problem is bigger than that. In the case of all these things it's about joining a club whose rules we can't control and that introduces political uncertainty. A clearly drawn up treaty obligation controls that uncertainty. It clearly delineates limits to what can happen. These two further potential costs I highlight in the IEA paper are not easily quantifiable because they involve significant uncertainty about how rules might develop in a situation of being a member of a club, where the rules have yet to be made clear. The fact is that the euro is being treated as another step on the road towards political unification. Now, one could imagine a single currency that was run under very different rules, like the gold standard, for which one would have a very different reaction. But the way in which this particular currency has been launched and is likely to evolve politically makes it a project that we have to evaluate in terms of political unification. It's in that spirit that I include those two costs because you cannot close your eyes to the fact that this is what you're letting yourself in for when you join the euro. One could imagine, as I say, a euro mark X that would be a different set-up – much more hands off, much more in a context of a European Union of independent nation states, without this project of unification – but that isn't the animal that we appear to be joining. It's in that context that harmonization and state pension arguments come into play. They are very hard to evaluate but clearly they pose, in principle, potential risks of quite large dimensions. We know that if we were to harmonize totally with the Continent we'd be back to the bad old days of the '70s in terms of unemployment and labour market rigidity. If we were to pay our GDP ratio share of state benefit deficits of these other countries, we would be in for a pretty big bill.

Euro institutions

The Stability and Growth Pact has been subject to some criticism and there may be an emerging agenda for its reform. What are your views of the SGP as it relates to the UK's possible euro entry?

I've always argued against the Stability and Growth Pact. I thought it was a particularly crude way to try to control the bail-out worries of Germany and ironically it has bitten Germany hard. It was a bad Pact because it was so inflexible and crude. It didn't even allow for cyclical adjustment of deficits. It was particularly and transparently crude to ignore the effect of recession on actual deficits. It also ignored the fact that in steady state if you've got debt of say 50 per cent of GDP, and nominal GDP is growing at 5 per cent, you can have a 2.5 per cent of GDP deficit, without raising the debt-to-GDP ratio. It was calibrated crudely and it's collapsed. Now the issue is what will succeed it and the answer might be something worse. What the Commission has come up with is an incredibly intrusive set of investigatory procedures. What they want, for any country that comes into a grey zone where the Stability Pact might conceivably apply to them, is for that country to become the object of a Commission investigation into their spending, their tax, and all their policies. It would be even worse to have the Commission crawling all over your books, with jumped-up reasons that you might be a cause of bail-out to some other country. We know perfectly well that there's no problem with bail-out provided you meet solvency criteria. Solvency is what really matters to bail-out. These rules are all highly artificial. They would take away a lot of parliamentary authority over public spending and taxation, and this is what really defines Parliament's authority. In this country people like Bill Morris, General Secretary of the Transport and General Workers' Union, are outraged that the Pact might stop the Chancellor spending on the NHS [National Health Service]. Personally I wish the Chancellor wouldn't spend so much on the NHS and would open it up much more to market forces and private funding. But the issue is a domestic one, to be decided by us not the Commission! It's another example of a situation where there is a significant source of risk because you are not quite sure what the rules will be and what effect they are likely to have on you.

Britain has a macro policy framework based around an inflation target and central bank operational independence for setting interest rates. Joining the euro would mean accepting an alternative framework with the ECB at its centre. What are your views on the desirability of such a development?
I think that the ECB's framework has problems, which are quite widely recognized by economists. They have a framework that does not appear to generate good interest rate-setting behaviour. It's pretty clear that they've been far too late in reacting to the emerging recession in the euro area and that they have been quite distracted from what one might call pragmatic inflation targeting by the first pillar, the money supply pillar. We know that money supply rules can be very easily distorted and they have not been upfront about the difficulties of that distortion. In the end they were forced to be by the sheer conflict between the inflation target and the first pillar. Another thing is the asymmetric nature of their target: a 2 per cent ceiling on inflation has given a slight deflationary twist to things. Deflation is emerging as a worry quite widely now. This has caused them to move recently to a more symmetric approach; but it is still not as clear as it should be. There is also the problem of non-transparency. We don't really know what goes on inside the ECB Council and that makes it very hard to make plans about future monetary policy. There are rumours of great fights between the Germans and the Italians, represented on the ruling body, but we've no idea of what actually goes on. Interest rate decisions are announced like a bolt from the blue every so often, without much clarification. Most economists, and I'm certainly in this consensus, feel that the system needs quite a lot of overhaul.

Politics
The Werner Plan, the ERM and the euro all have economic bases but are they the primary drivers behind monetary integration in your view?
It's been clearly politics on the Continent. Politics drove the euro. On various occasions I've been invited to participate in debates on the euro with continental economists and politicians. There

has always been complete impatience with economic argument. The euro has always been a political project. In some quarters economic difficulties were welcomed because they would reinforce the drive to political unification in order to deal with economic problems that crop up. It's politics that will have to save the euro on the Continent and preserve its survival. There are enormous problems in the EU due to the differences of the various economies. Germany, for example, is in serious recession with lots of problems and its plight is exacerbated by being tied to the euro. If there were a free vote today on the euro in Germany they would be out tomorrow. It was politics that drove the euro and which has so far preserved its existence. But politics is an impossible argument to play in the UK, which is why we've got the five tests. The one reason we would never join the euro is politics, because we do not want a United States of Europe.

What do you think of the argument that it is important for the UK to participate fully in the whole process in order not to be left behind and maintain a degree of influence both in Europe and on the wider world stage?
I think that the Iraq war has been immensely salutary in clarifying this argument. It's quite clear from the Iraq war that: (a) we have no influence within Europe and that by joining we would have even less and (b) our influence in the wider world is much greater outside than inside Europe, and had we been inside Europe we would have been completely manacled by a very difficult European consensus. Even the Foreign Office, which has always been the great political supporter of European Union because of keeping 'our seat at the top table', must realize now that if we were to be a part of the United Europe in which all these decisions on war and peace were taken by the European consensus we would be dragged along by something which would be extremely uncomfortable. On a whole range of issues we've always been a minority in the European Union because our traditions are all quite different. Our whole way of organizing our economy, our politics and our links historically with the Anglo-Saxon world, are all quite different from traditions inside the Continent.

What are your views on the enlargement process of the European Union and the euro area?
Well clearly, someone like me who wants a Europe of nation states and is not in favour of a United States of Europe, for both political

and economic reasons, welcomes enlargement. Enlargement is a ray of light in the whole process because it seems to me impossible to run an enlarged Europe without much greater flexibility and devolvement of powers than has currently been the model. Enlargement will challenge the Franco/German hegemony. While I welcome enlargement, I am pretty sceptical about how big an effect it will have in the medium term because these countries will be kept at a distance for quite a long time. It's quite clear that the Franco/German project is to try to strengthen the whole of the organization. We've now got this preposterous Constitution for Europe that has just been published, which would be immensely centralizing and socializing, and quite clearly the Franco/German project is to rush ahead with this before these outer Eastern European countries join. The French and the Germans want a Franco/German-led super state.

Finally

Are there any other issues we have not touched upon which you think are germane to this debate?
Well, one thing that people have raised and we've tried to deal with in the stochastic simulations [see Minford et al., 2004] is the what-if issue. What if there was more flexibility, what if we could use fiscal policy more, what if the mortgage market became more fixed interest etc. So there is a bunch of things like that we looked at to see if they would change the stochastic simulations rankings. Another thing that Willem Buiter has raised, in the same spirit, is whether sterling could be more volatile outside the euro. We've looked at those things and basically the answer is that they don't alter the orders of magnitude. You have to have a pretty incredible combination of changes in the environment to change the calculations materially.

Would it be fair to say that the decision to join or not join the euro is to a large extent a matter of faith?
Yes, I think that is what you find. At the end of the day the costs and benefits of things like currency arrangements are material, but if you were to translate them into some calculus of equivalent effect on living standards, you would be hard put to make very large numbers. Politics inevitably tends to dominate in people's thinking. The debate we've had so far in this country has been quite unusual in stressing economics and it's because the political

debate is already cast in stone. Most people don't want greater integration into Europe in this country, politically, and therefore had the government said we think we should have the euro in order to politically integrate into Europe the British public would have said 'you must be joking'. We've got an economic debate and a future referendum on the economics, with the government not being upfront about the politics. They are giving themselves a chance to win on economics in order to obtain the political prize of joining in this uniting process in Europe in a fully committed way. Because they have got to have a referendum they are inevitably going to have politics in there, and public opinion quite clearly takes the view that politically they don't want to join. Economically they can't see much of a strong case. I would argue they are increasingly coming to the view that economically it's a negative. You will never convince the ones that are politically committed, just as you will never convince the ones that are politically committed against. If the Franco/German plans go ahead for a United States of Europe and the Convention goes through, there's likely to be a wider debate, beyond the euro, about the merits of European Union more generally. But that debate has not yet been engaged.

6. Euro-area enlargement and the accession economies

6.1 INTRODUCTION

In 2004 the 15-strong European Union (EU) admitted 10 new countries into membership: Cyprus and Malta, and from Central and Eastern Europe, the Czech Republic, Estonia, Hungary, Latvia, Lithuania, Poland, Slovakia and Slovenia. In 2007 Bulgaria and Romania also became EU members, forming an EU27. Presently, Croatia, the Former Yugoslav Republic of Macedonia, and Turkey are all candidate countries for EU membership (see Figure 6.1). The pool of potential euro-area members is clearly expanding. The purpose of the present chapter is to review the major issues underlying euro adoption for the EU accession economies.

As discussed in Chapter 5, of the original EU15, three countries have not as yet joined the euro area. Denmark and the UK have negotiated opt-outs which allow them to delay euro adoption until a time of their choosing. Sweden, on the other hand, has a *derogation* from its obligation to join the euro area which will be – in euro-speak – *abrogated* (that is, rescinded) as soon as it fulfils the Maastricht criteria. However, Swedish public opinion is presently set against the euro and accordingly, although the Swedish economy has achieved a high degree of sustainable convergence with the euro area, the Swedish government has so far chosen not to participate in the exchange rate mechanism (ERM II). In the present circumstances it seems unlikely that Sweden, Denmark or the UK will adopt the euro anytime soon.

This is decisively not the case for the accession economies, three of which – Slovenia, Cyprus and Malta – have already fulfilled the Maastricht criteria and adopted the euro. Like Sweden, *all* new EU members are obliged to actively pursue euro-area membership, and, indeed, all appear actually committed to doing so, albeit with varying degrees of progress.

Source: European Commission.

Figure 6.1   EU27 and candidate countries

Table 6.1 (column 1) summarizes the positions of each of the 12 accession economies with respect to the euro area. As noted, Slovenia, Cyprus and Malta are members. Lithuania made an application for membership alongside Slovenia but very narrowly failed to meet the reference rate for the Maastricht inflation criterion. We discuss this failed application in more detail below as it raises some interesting questions about the standards required of the accession countries in their attempts to join the euro area. In addition to Lithuania, three other economies – Estonia, Latvia and Slovakia – are participants in ERM II, making them prime candidates for early membership; recall that a two-year untroubled 'service' in ERM II is a Maastricht criterion. Estonia and Slovakia have published specific dates by which they hope to introduce the euro (2011 and 2009, respectively). Finally there are five economies – the Czech Republic, Bulgaria,

Table 6.1   *The accession countries and the euro area*

	Exchange rate regime	Monetary policy type	Target date for euro adoption	Maastricht criteria at issue[1]
Successfully joined euro area				
Slovenia	Floating euro	Set by ECB	Joined Jan 2007	–
Malta	Floating euro	Set by ECB	Joined Jan 2008	–
Cyprus	Floating euro	Set by ECB	Joined Jan 2008	–
Application failed				
Lithuania	Currency board with euro since 2002; and in ERM II since June 2004	Exchange rate targeting	None set since failure of application in May 2006	Met all criteria except inflation; narrowly missed target
Joined ERM II				
Estonia	Currency board since 1992. Joined ERM II in June 2004	Exchange rate targeting	As soon as possible; 2011 is realistic	Inflation
Latvia	Joined ERM II in May 2005; pegged to euro within +/− 1% fluctuation band	Exchange rate targeting	No specific date but 'it may happen in 2008'	Inflation
Slovakia	Joined ERM II in November 2005; +/− 15% fluctuation band; koruna revalued in 2007	Exchange rate targeting	1 Jan 2009	Inflation and deficit

Table 6.1   (continued)

	Exchange rate regime	Monetary policy type	Target date for euro adoption	Maastricht criteria at issue[1]
Outside ERM II				
Czech Republic	Floating	Inflation targeting; 3% +/− 1%; 2% from 2010 until euro entry	Preliminary date Jan 2010 withdrawn in 2006; no new date set	Deficit and ERM membership
Bulgaria	Currency board with euro	Exchange rate targeting	1 Jan 2010	n.a.
Hungary	Shadows ERM II but not a formal participant	Inflation targeting since 2001; 3% in medium term	None specified	All criteria
Poland	Floating	Inflation targeting: 2.5% +/−1%	None specified	Deficit and ERM membership
Romania	Floating	Inflation targeting +/− 1% around a disinflationary path	2014	n.a.

Note: [1] As recorded in ECB Convergence Reports, May and December 2006.

Hungary, Poland and Romania – that have yet to join ERM II, though two have established target dates for the adoption of the euro: Bulgaria in 2010 and Romania in 2014.

Table 6.1 also summarizes the preferred monetary policy regime of each of the accession countries. Recall that to meet the inflation criterion for euro-area membership, candidate economies have to reduce their inflation rates to not more than 1.5 per cent above the average of the best three inflation rates in the EU. The table shows that of the nine remaining candidate accession economies, five – Lithuania, Estonia, Latvia, Slovakia and Bulgaria – have elected to use exchange rate targeting as a mechanism for inflation control, while, in contrast, the other four – the Czech Republic, Hungary, Poland and Romania – follow a monetary regime of direct inflation targeting. Exchange rate targeting is in fact a *necessary* prelude to euro adoption because it also fulfils the ERM II membership criterion.[40] While this suggests that the ERM II members in Table 6.1 are in the ante chamber of the euro area and the inflation-targeting economies are more peripheral, in reality matters are a little more complicated. To understand why, we need to reflect a little more on the monetary policy regime choices that face the accession economies and the particular inflation context in which these choices are exercised.

6.2   ECONOMIC CATCH-UP, INFLATION AND THE ACCESSION ECONOMIES

It is widely acknowledged that in emerging from decades of central planning the accession countries of Central and Eastern Europe have some way to go before they achieve anything close to economic convergence with the EU15. Figure 6.2 shows GDP per capita for the EU15 and the CE10 between 1997 and 2008, with the EU27 set to 100.[41] It is evident that although income levels in the CE10 are still well below those prevailing in the EU as a whole and the EU15 in particular, the gap is not as wide as it was in the late 1990s. As the CE10 economies mature and become more deeply integrated with the rest of Europe it is expected that they will continue to converge with the original members of the EU. Figure 6.3 illustrates the higher growth rates achieved by the CE10 in comparison to the EU15 since 2000. However, this nascent convergence process is not costless in macroeconomic terms. An unfortunate consequence of such economic 'catch-up' is higher inflation which arises as a result of the so-called Balassa–Samuelson effect, after its discoverers, Bela Balassa and Paul Samuelson.

The Balassa–Samuelson effect results from rising productivity in the traded goods sector of a developing economy. It is this

[40] Note, however, that Bulgaria, even though it has a currency board with the euro, is not yet a formal participant in ERM II.
[41] The CE10 are the 10 Central and Eastern European economies that joined the EU in 2004 and 2007.

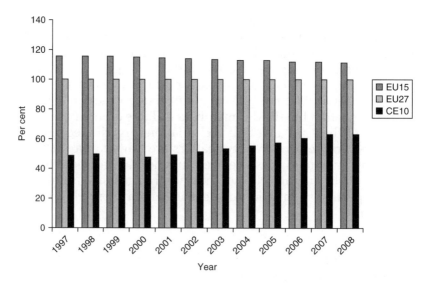

Note: * Purchasing Power Standards; 2007 and 2008 estimates.

Source: Eurostat.

Figure 6.2   GDP per capita in PPS* (EU15, CE10, EU27) (EU27=100)

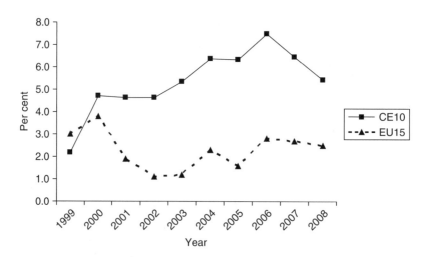

Note: * 2007 and 2008 estimates.

Source: Eurostat.

Figure 6.3   EU15 and CE10 real GDP growth rates, 1999–2008*

sector that is both exposed to competitive pressures from the economy's trading partners and most likely to benefit from inward investment, including the transfer of technology. The resultant higher productivity in the traded goods sector generates higher wages there. However, the difficulty arises when wages also increase in the economy's non-traded goods sector where there has been no commensurate increase in productivity – the outcome is that these 'unearned' wage increases force up the rate of price inflation in the non-traded goods sector and thus in the economy as a whole. Estimates of the Balassa–Samuelson effect suggest that the accession countries' inflation rates may be increased by between 1 and 3 per cent per year (see De Grauwe and Schnabl, 2005); and the problem is certainly acknowledged by the European Central Bank (ECB) in its series of convergence reports on the state of readiness of the accession countries for euro-area membership. For example, in pronouncing that Lithuania had failed to meet the reference rate of 2.6 per cent for inflation in its 2006 euro application (it could *not* have been closer: Lithuania's inflation rate was 2.7 per cent over the period in question), the ECB (2006a, p. 7) acknowledged that the Balassa–Samuelson effect would have a 'bearing on [Lithuanian] inflation for some years to come'.

Figure 6.4 compares the inflation performances of the EU15 and the CE10 between 1998 and 2006. It is evident from this figure that, following difficulties in the early stages of their transition from centrally planned to capitalist economies, the CE10 have largely managed to stabilize inflation at a little over 4 per cent. On the other hand, inflation for the EU15 is stable at around 2 per cent. The gap between the two rates may at least in part be accounted for by the Balassa–Samuelson effect which means that, at best, it will be difficult to close in the medium term. This in turn makes the inflation criterion potentially difficult to fulfil for the accession economies.[42]

One question that might reasonably be asked here is how did Slovenia, Cyprus and Malta manage to sidestep this problem and join the euro area so quickly after accession? Figure 6.5 shows that both before and after joining the EU in 2004, each of these countries was closer to the average EU per capita income level than the

---

[42] For a sceptical view of the relevance of the Balassa–Samuelson effect for the CE10, see Egert et al. (2003).

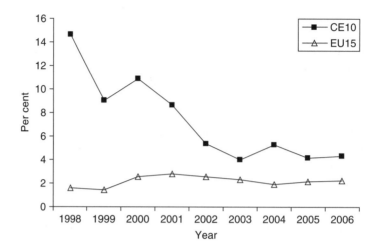

Source: Eurostat.

Figure 6.4   EU15 and CE10 price inflation, 1998–2006

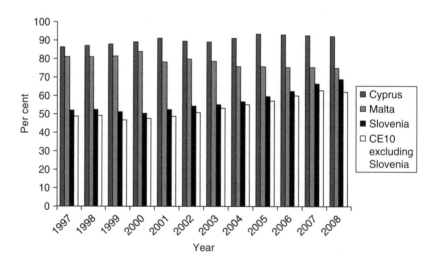

Note: * Purchasing Power Standards; 2007 and 2008 estimates.

Source: Eurostat.

Figure 6.5   GDP per capita in PPS* (Cyprus, Malta, Slovenia, CE10 excluding Slovenia) (EU27=100)

CE10 (excluding Slovenia), which meant that their room for economic catch-up was accordingly reduced, as were any attendant Balassa–Samuelson pressures. The ECB's May 2007 Convergence Report on the application of Cyprus and Malta to join the eurozone recorded that their inflation rates were 2.0 and 2.2 per cent, respectively, comfortably within the prevailing reference rate, then at 3 per cent.

It is the Balassa–Samuelson inflation context that makes the choice of monetary policy regime a delicate matter for the remaining members of the CE10 in their quest to join the euro area. Putting it simply, the accession economies (like all others) can elect to focus monetary policy – effectively the setting of interest rates – on *either* their exchange rate *or* their inflation rate; they cannot simultaneously target both of these variables. Thus, for example, the ECB's Convergence Report of December 2006 noted that while Latvia's exchange rate targeting strategy had maintained its currency, the lats, close to its ERM II central rate, the Latvian 12-month average inflation rate was 6.7 per cent – a long way above the then-prevailing Maastricht reference rate of 2.8 per cent. Had Latvia chosen to focus monetary policy on inflation control, it would almost inevitably have set interest rates incompatible with its preferred $+/-$ 1 per cent ERM II fluctuation band for the lats. In all likelihood the higher interest rates required to suppress inflation would have caused the lats to appreciate in value (Latvian long-term interest rates were well below the Maastricht reference rate at the time). To take a counter example, the same ECB report noted that Poland's inflation targeting strategy had produced an inflation rate of 1.2 per cent (which is in fact just below the Polish Central Bank's target range); however, its tight and credible monetary policy had also resulted in a relatively strong but volatile performance of the zloty against the euro, making early ERM II membership an unlikely prospect. Again, because monetary policy in Poland is focused on the inflation rate, it cannot simultaneously be used to positively condition the exchange rate.

Table 6.1 (column 2) shows that joining Latvia in exchange rate targeting are Lithuania, Estonia, Slovakia and Bulgaria. Of these countries, only Bulgaria is not yet also a participant in ERM II, although its currency board with the euro should make this step a formality. A currency board involves the complete underpinning of the monetary base of an economy with foreign currency and means that its central bank can never exhaust its foreign exchange reserves in the face of speculation against its chosen exchange rate; this makes a currency board a highly credible exchange rate regime. Note from Table 6.1 that Lithuania and Estonia have also tied their currencies to the euro using currency board arrangements, while Latvia has a tightly defined peg to the euro; only Slovakia targets the normal $+/-$ 15 per cent ERM II fluctuation band.

Exchange rate targeting potentially offers the accession economies two things. First, as noted, it enables them to meet the ERM II membership criterion. Second, in theory, it should also help them control inflation and therefore contribute towards the attainment of a second Maastricht criterion. This is because the adoption of a fixed exchange rate requires an economy to mirror the monetary policy of the country to whose currency it is tied. In the case of the CE10, the currency is the euro and the economy is the euro area. Thus the monetary policy practised by the ECB is the model for Lithuania, Estonia, Latvia, Slovakia and Bulgaria to follow. These countries cannot adopt policies divergent from the ECB's because these would tend to cause their currencies to drift away from the euro. In effect, then, they have imported the ECB's monetary policy and surrendered their monetary independence. This should be a desirable move because the ECB is a credible and independent institution running a sound low inflation monetary policy.

Yet what is collectively interesting about these exchange rate targeting economies is the Maastricht criterion they all appear to be struggling to attain – the final column of Table 6.1 shows that all are having difficulties with inflation control. It is not hard to understand why. Their monetary strategies are focused on the exchange rate and all, to a greater or lesser degree depending on their scope for economic catch-up, are experiencing Balassa–Samuelson symptoms, expressed here in relatively high inflation. Ordinarily, exchange rate targeting would be an effective means of inflation control, but the Balassa–Samuelson effect renders it insufficient. Were these economies to take the obvious step and tighten monetary policy they might well bring down inflation, but quite possibly at the expense of ERM II membership. In this context it would be almost churlish not to sympathize with Lithuania's failed euro application. Shaving just 0.1 per cent off inflation would have seen its candidacy fully Maastricht compatible. The difficulties inherent in balancing inflation fanned by the Balassa–Samuelson effect and ERM II membership have caused some commentators to suggest that the position of the accession countries in respect of euro-area admission is more demanding given the 'softer' admission questions asked of the original incumbents. The ECB's claim is that all EU members should receive *equal treatment* in their progress towards the euro area, but this ignores the changes in Europe's circumstances that the creation of the euro has itself brought about (Kenen and Meade, 2003). To give one example, the reference inflation rate that Lithuania missed by a whisker was, following the stipulations laid down in the Maastricht Treaty, constructed using the average rate of the three best-performing EU countries over the previous 12 months: these were Finland, Poland and Sweden. But at the time only Finland was actually a eurozone member. Thus a telling hurdle placed in front of a euro-area applicant was that it was insufficiently convergent with Poland and Sweden – two economies *outside* the euro area. When Finland was on course for euro adoption in the 1990s, it simply had to demonstrate convergence with those with whom it wished, economically speaking, to get into bed (as at that time did all other EU economies).[43] In this sense, the euro admission bar has arguably been raised for the accession economies.

Such action could be defensible in circumstances where new members posed a threat to the coherence or integrity of the euro area but this is unlikely in the case of the accession economies, given their small size. Figure 6.6 indicates that Lithuania would have contributed just 0.6 per cent to euro-area GDP had its 2006 application been successful. The euro area is clearly dominated in GDP terms by just five economies. The combined output of France, Germany, Italy, the Netherlands and Spain accounts for 82 per cent of the euro-area total.

Lithuania's application experience produced the following cryptic comment from the Chairman of the Bank of Lithuania: 'It would be useful to discuss the procedure for the calculation of the reference value in the future to avoid ambiguities and doubts'. This is not special pleading but a request that the Maastricht criteria, *post* the creation of the euro, be interpreted in a more sensible way.

One possibility, which reflects the fact that the euro area now actually exists, would be to use the ECB's own inflation target as the basis of the Maastricht reference rate for inflation. Recall that this requires that euro-area inflation should be below but close to

---

[43] As noted in Chapter 5, Denmark and the UK negotiated opt-outs from the obligation to join the euro area but Denmark was fully convergent and the UK absent only from ERM II at the time of the euro's launch.

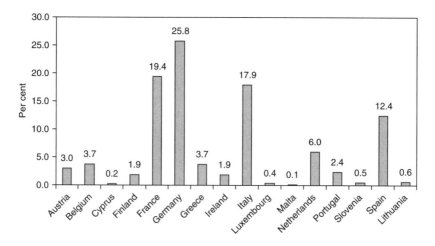

Source: International Monetary Fund.

Figure 6.6   *Euro-area GDP shares, 2006 (including Lithuania)*

2 per cent. If the reference rate was 1.5 per cent above this target, its maximum would be 3.4 per cent (1.9 + 1.5). This rate, or something close to it, would be one way to reconcile the need for the accession economies to demonstrate their sustainable convergence with the euro area (rather than the less relevant EU27) while allowing for the Balassa–Samuelson effect. Alternatively, a reference rate could be calculated on the inflation records of the three best-performing economies in the *euro area*, rather than in the EU as a whole. Neither of these approaches would offend the ECB's principle of equal treatment; they treat the EU15 before the creation of the euro and the CE10 after it in an *equivalent* manner (see Kenen and Meade, 2003). Figure 6.7 compares the actual inflation reference rate with those based on the ECB's target and on the three best-performing euro-area economies; note that had either of the last two been applied in 2006, Lithuania's application for euro-area membership would have been successful.

Should the interpretation of the reference rate for inflation not be amended, the immediate alternatives open to the CE10 are none too palatable. One suggestion is that exchange rate targeting economies might be forced to endure a 'transitional recession' to get their inflation rates sufficiently under control, but this has obvious and perhaps unacceptable costs in terms of lost output and higher unemployment (see Buiter and Grafe, 2002). Another

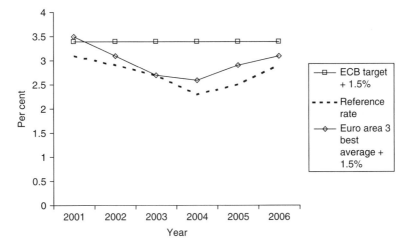

Source: Eurostat.

Figure 6.7 Inflation reference rates

convoluted and hardly logical option is that they temporarily forsake their carefully chosen and eminently sensible exchange rate targets in favour of a rapid dose of inflation targeting therapy before leaping back into ERM II and, hopefully, two years later, the eurozone. Whether such criterion juggling, or – to push the analogy – plate spinning, would be successful must be open to severe doubt. For economies with currency board arrangements that actually make them *de facto* members of the euro area, this kind of strategy would border on the bizarre.

Matters *may* be a little more clear-cut for the inflation-targeting group among the CE10. From Table 6.1 these are: the Czech Republic, Hungary, Poland and Romania. While their chosen monetary policy regime makes it probable that they will meet the Maastricht inflation criterion, the Balassa–Samuelson effect for these economies is likely to be expressed in appreciating and more variable exchange rates that may raise questions about their capacity to successfully participate in ERM II. Again, prior to the creation of the euro, this was not an issue. The euro area's originating economies were not subject to Balassa–Samuelson pressures and the peer group against which their sustainable exchange rate convergence was assessed was much more homogeneous. However, by using the full range of the normal +/− 15 per cent fluctuation band of ERM II, the inflation targeting countries among the CE10 may be in a position to meet the, for them, more demanding inflation criterion while simultaneously preserving ERM II membership (Buiter and Grafe, 2002).[44] But this is by no means certain. The exchange rates of the CE10, as economies in transition from central planning to capitalism, are both volatile and particularly liable to speculative assault (Wyplosz, 2003). Whether they can all survive a two-year passage through ERM II must, unfortunately, remain an open question.

Table 6.2 summarizes the most recent official positions, as estimated by the ECB, of the non-euro accession economies in respect of the inflation criterion, and confirms the inflation difficulties experienced by the ERM II exchange rate targeting economies. Inflation rates in Estonia, Latvia and Slovakia were considerably above the reference rate, while, as noted, Lithuania's inflation was narrowly above the reference rate prevailing at the time of its euro-area application. Of those economies outside ERM II, the Czech Republic and Poland met the inflation criterion, while Hungary did not.

If the inflation and exchange rate criteria are posing problems for many of the accession economies, what of the interest rate and debt-and-deficit criterion? Table 6.2 shows that the interest rate and debt criteria were met by all of the listed accession economies, with the exception of Hungary, which met neither. The deficit-to-GDP criterion was met only by Lithuania, Estonia and Latvia. All this suggests that the three Baltic countries are indeed primary candidates for euro-area membership in meeting all criteria except – for understandable reasons – inflation. Slovakia, too, though narrowly failing to match the 3 per cent of GDP deficit reference rate (and with a slight deficit problem), may yet have a realistic chance of meeting its stated 2009 euro-area target. Each of the three non-ERM II economies listed in Table 6.2 – the Czech Republic, Hungary and Poland – has breached the 3 per cent of GDP deficit threshold and been subject to the excess deficit procedure by the European Commission. For the moment then, the relatively poor condition of their public finances, coupled with ERM II membership issues and, in Hungary's case, a debt problem, makes the euro-area candidature of these countries a

---

[44] The same may be true for Slovakia, the only wide-band ERM II member. However, note from Table 6.2 that Slovakia, too, has struggled to bring inflation close to the reference rate.

Table 6.2   *The accession countries and the euro area: inflation, interest rate and debt and deficit criteria*[1]

	Inflation (reference rate 2.8%)	Interest rates (reference rate 6.2%)	Deficit (reference rate 3% of GDP)	Debt (reference value 60% of GDP)
Application failed				
Lithuania	2.7 (ref. rate 2.6 at May 2006 application)	3.7 (ref. rate 5.9 at May 2006 application)	0.5	18.7
Joined ERM II				
Estonia	4.3	n.a. but 'no indications of a negative assessment'	2.3	4.5
Latvia	6.7	3.9	*Surplus* of 0.1	12.1
Slovakia	4.3	4.3	3.1	34.5
Outside ERM II				
Czech Republic	2.2	3.8	3.6	30.4
Hungary	3.5	7.1	7.8	61.7
Poland	1.2	5.2	2.5[2]	42.4

Notes:

[1] Excludes Bulgaria and Romania, not members of the EU until 2007.

[2] Poland is in fact judged to be in an excess deficit situation under the Stability and Growth Pact. The inclusion of certain pension fund liabilities would add 1.9 per cent to this figure, giving an overall deficit of 4.4 per cent, i.e., above the 3 per cent reference rate.

Source: ECB Convergence Reports, May and December 2006.

rather distant prospect. Given their recent accession to the EU, the same conclusion probably applies to Bulgaria and Romania.

However, before we become too pessimistic here, it should be noted that weakness in public finance is not the exclusive preserve of the accession economies. Table 6.3 shows that Germany, Greece, Italy and Portugal have each struggled with the deficit criterion and moved into excess deficit positions. These countries have also breached the 60 per cent debt threshold – Greece and Italy spectacularly so. While the Maastricht criteria are now irrelevant as admission tickets for the euro-area incumbents, these indifferent performances do undermine any notion that the ambitions of the

Table 6.3   *Selected euro-area economies' deficit and debt positions,*
                 2005

	Deficit (reference rate 3% of GDP)	Debt (reference value 60% of GDP)	Excess deficit situation since abrogated?
Germany	−3.2	67.9	Yes in 2007
Greece	−3.7	109.5	Yes in 2007
Italy	−4.3	108.5	No
Portugal	−6.0	65.5	No

Source: European Commission.

accession economies for euro-area membership are unrealistic. Moreover, recall from Chapter 3 the observation that the Maastricht criteria were in some respects only loosely applied when the state of readiness of the founding members to actually launch the euro was judged. For example, only four of the original 11 euro-area members managed to meet the 60 per cent debt threshold (Baldwin et al., 2001). Once again, it appears that more is being asked of the accession economies in their obligation to join the euro area than was asked of the original members.

6.3   REAL CONVERGENCE AND THE ACCESSION ECONOMIES

We noted in Chapter 3 the discontinuity between the 'nominal' Maastricht criteria and the 'real' optimum currency area factors – such as trade integration and labour market flexibility – that would determine whether or not the euro would prove to be a long-term success. It is, then, perhaps reassuring to learn that the accession countries are clear about the need to address both the nominal entry conditions and the real criteria that will underpin their effective integration with the euro area. Thus, for example, the Czech government and Czech central bank have jointly acknowledged that the loss of an independent monetary policy will require the Czech economy to exhibit a high degree of flexibility if it is to cope with future economic shocks. With interest rates set by the ECB and fiscal freedoms limited by the Stability and Growth Pact, the burden of adjustment will fall on the Czech labour market in particular. However, the authorities

Table 6.4   Costs of euro adoption cited by selected Eastern accession economies

	Danger of asymmetric shocks in the face of lost monetary independence	Labour market rigidities
Czech Republic	✓	✓
Estonia	Discounted for this small open economy	And sufficient flexibility in the labour market
Hungary	✓	✓
Latvia	Largely discounted for this small open economy	And sufficient flexibility in the labour market
Lithuania	Discounted for this small open economy	And sufficient flexibility in the labour market
Poland	✓	✓
Slovakia	✓	✓

admit that the labour market is presently characterized by low-mobility, real-wage inflexibility and overall rigidity. Their conclusion is that 'the overall ability of the Czech labour market to absorb shocks thus remains limited and efforts must be made to enhance it' (Czech Government and Czech National Bank, 2007, p. 6). On the other hand, the same report notes that the high and increasing openness of the Czech economy and the significant trade relationships it has with the euro area potentially make euro adoption an immensely attractive step. Currently, the euro area and EU provide markets for, respectively, 60 and 85 per cent of total Czech exports. At the same time, 50 per cent of Czech imports come from the euro area and 70 per cent from the EU.

Table 6.4 summarizes the optimum currency area real convergence issues for several of the accession economies as they themselves perceive these issues. It is apparent that Hungary, Poland and Slovakia share the Czech Republic's concern over the readiness of their labour markets to rise to the challenge posed by the loss of an independent monetary policy. To exemplify, in the case of Poland the Polish central bank has commented: 'Wage rigidity indices for Poland are amongst the highest in the OECD [Organization for Economic Cooperation and Development] countries. It means that after joining the single currency area, Poland may, in this respect, face considerable consequences of giving up monetary policy autonomy' (National Bank of Poland, 2003, p. 26).

The Baltic countries, however, do not share such anxieties. The benefits of monetary independence are not significant for small open economies like theirs and, in any case, with either currency boards (Lithuania and Estonia), or a hard peg to the euro (Latvia), these economies have already opted to embrace the monetary policy of the euro area. In the words of the Estonian central bank: 'Accession to the euro area will not entail an economic policy adjustment. . . . We are already now very closely involved in the monetary policy of the euro area through the currency board arrangement and therefore giving up independent currency rate and interest rate policies does not pose an issue for us' (Bank of Estonia, 2007, p. 22). Moreover, the Baltic countries also appear to have reasonable confidence in the flexibility of their labour markets.

If the potential costs of euro-area membership are perceived unevenly across the accession economies, the potential benefits – which primarily hinge on the extent of intra-European trade – are unambiguously significant. Figure 6.8 shows the trade shares of the non-euro CE10 economies with the EU27. In all except two

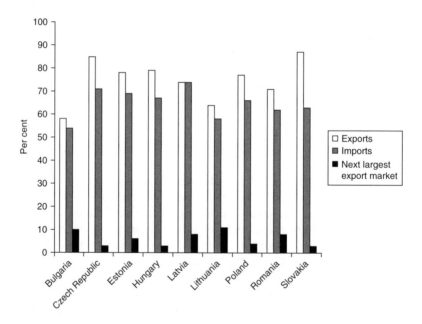

Source: World Trade Organization.

Figure 6.8   Accession economies' share of trade with EU27, 2005

instances, the EU27 provides a market for at least 70 per cent of the exports of these economies and for all the EU is over-whelmingly the major trading partner; the general case for membership of a growing euro area is very strong indeed. The next largest export market for each economy is shown for comparative purposes.

Table 6.5 complements this evidence in disentangling some of the particular advantages that the Eastern accession economies expect euro-area membership to bring. In all cases the major microeconomic boons of reduced exchange rate risk and price transparency are cited. In addition, only Latvia fails to explicitly reference the minor benefit associated with the elimination of transaction costs. The fourth column of Table 6.5 summarizes other membership advantages identified by the accession economies. Estonia, Latvia, Slovakia and Hungary each mention specific improvements in their growth performances; Lithuania and Latvia expect greater macroeconomic stability; while the Czech Republic, Bulgaria and Poland all anticipate lower interest rates.

6.4   CONCLUDING REMARKS

It seems clear that the accession economies wish to fulfil their obligation to join the euro area and would reap considerable benefits in so doing. Of the 12 new EU members, three have already successfully adopted the euro, while the Baltic countries and Slovakia have potentially placed themselves in an advanced position to do the same by joining ERM II. However, Lithuania has had a recent application for membership narrowly rejected and this failure – reflecting inflationary pressures at least in part associated with the Balassa–Samuelson effect – suggests that there may be serious structural obstacles to extending the euro area in Eastern Europe. A more sympathetic interpretation of the Maastricht criteria – such as that extended to the original euro countries – may improve matters. Of the five non-ERM accession economies, the Czech Republic, Hungary and Poland have as yet no target date set for euro adoption and each is presently short on at least two of the Maastricht criteria. Once these economies join ERM II, they too will come under Balassa–Samuelson pressures without the option to allow exchange rate appreciation to take the strain. The most recent newcomers to the EU, Bulgaria and

Table 6.5 *Benefits of the euro cited by the Eastern accession countries*

	Transaction cost elimination	Reduced exchange rate risk	Price transparency	Other cited advantages for each listed accession economy
Lithuania	✓	✓	✓	Small open economy highly integrated with EU – strong candidature for the euro area, fostering macro stability and real economic convergence
Estonia	✓	✓	✓	Protect against external risks as member of large currency union, e.g., danger of capital inflow reversals. Loss of monetary sovereignty explicitly cited as *not* an issue. IMF estimates that euro accession may increase Estonian GDP by 3–20% over 20 years
Latvia		✓	✓	6–19% increase in Latvian GDP over the long term
Slovakia	✓	✓	✓	A range of indirect benefits including: foreign trade growth; increased inflows of foreign direct investment; 7–20% increase in Slovakian GDP over 20 years
Czech Republic	✓	✓	✓	Lower interest rates; real convergence with EU average income levels
Bulgaria	✓	✓	✓	Lower interest rates
Hungary	✓	✓	✓	Increased financial and economic stability; additional growth of 0.6–0.9% annually
Poland	✓	✓	✓	Reduced macroeconomic risks, e.g., lower interest rates than with zloty as credibility is enhanced

Romania, have target dates of 2010 and 2014, respectively; given the need for two years' service in ERM II, the former is perhaps a little ambitious.

Given the Balassa–Samuelson issue there is a clear case for rethinking the Maastricht inflation criterion as it applies to the accession economies. Moreover, in a general climate of 'integration fatigue', of which the travails over the European constitution *manqué* is but the latest example, the European Council, Commission and Central Bank are perhaps unwise not to actively encourage wider and deeper integration among a new Eastern constituency that still has an appetite for the European project.

We conclude this chapter with an interview with Andrzej Wojtyna, a macro economist and central banker from Poland.

ANDRZEJ WOJTYNA

Andrzej Wojtyna is Professor of Economics and Head of the Macroeconomics Department at the Cracow University of Economics, Poland. Since 2004 he has been a member of the National Bank of Poland's Monetary Policy Council (MPC). He is best known for his work on the development of modern macroeconomics and macroeconomic policy analysis.

We interviewed Professor Wojtyna in his office at the Cracow University of Economics on 7 December 2007.

At the outset it is important for the reader to appreciate that the views expressed in this interview are your own and not the official views of the National Bank of Poland.
Sure.

Having noted this, can you give us a flavour of your experiences as a member of the Monetary Policy Council of the National Bank of Poland?
Well for a macro economist I think it's the ideal job as you're involved not just in policy analysis but also policy making. Policy making involves making decisions and the internal rules for our Monetary Policy Council do not allow abstentions from voting. This institutional rule is important because without it you could have two members of the MPC voting in favour of an interest rate rise, one against and seven members choosing to abstain. [*Laughter*] Our rules also ensure individual accountability as the voting record of MPC members is published after six weeks. This means that financial market analysts know who are the so-called doves and hawks. For me this ornithological approach to policy making is not the right one, but I accept that is how MPC members are classified. Another very exciting aspect of being a member of the MPC is the interaction we have with participants in financial markets. Initially this was very new to me. We frequently meet with people from different banks and foreign institutions. For example, we meet with people from the City of London, including customers of investment banks. Another interesting aspect of the job is that it involves speaking to the press about our decisions and about our views of the state of the economy.

What have been the main economic challenges for Poland during its transition from a centrally planned to a market economy?

With the benefit of hindsight I think that institutional change was the most difficult task because it involved a real systemic change. By that I mean not only moving from a planned to a market system but also moving from state to private ownership. This involved the dilemma of which institutions should be imported and which should be built from scratch, and the problem of making such institutions compatible. The slowing down of the privatization process opened another source of problem concerning the corporate governance of state-sector enterprises. This exposed difficult connections between the political sphere and the economy, where, for example, people are appointed from only one party to serve on managerial or supervisory boards of state-sector enterprises. In general, then, I would say that one of the main challenges has been the increasing role of political economy factors and the unclear links that arise between the state and the private sector. Another important challenge involved avoiding 'third way' proposals in our transition.

When do you expect the concept of transition to pass into history for Poland and other members of the CE10?
I think we should give up talking about transition. I accept that it is difficult to find a clear watershed for its passing but you can always choose an arbitrary one. For example, both the millennium and the EU accession in 2004 provided good opportunities to pronounce the death of transition. For me we should just acknowledge that we now experience problems similar to those experienced in Latin American countries or typical emerging-market economies

Although Poland is committed to join the euro, no target entry date has yet been set. Can you tell us a little about Poland's present euro-area ambitions?
I think that to some extent there has been a political correctness factor operating in Poland. In recent years our President and his twin brother the Prime Minister – who is now head of the opposition after the recent election – have been euro sceptics. Given this situation I suspect that some economists have been reluctant to express their support for joining the euro. Interestingly, there has been a decrease in popular support for the euro over the last year even though earlier it was growing. A number of factors could help explain why this has happened, including: the stance on the

euro taken by the President and his brother; fear of higher prices and a decrease in incomes if we join the euro; the fact that we have performed well outside the euro area – we now have a strong currency, low and manageable inflation, high, sustained and well-balanced growth; fear of loss of national identity etc. Perhaps not surprisingly the question of whether and when we should join the euro was not part of our recent election debate. It is as if there has been a silent agreement between the rival parties not to get involved in what is a technical issue. For this reason it is very difficult to be precise about when Poland will join the euro. Poland and Ukraine have won the organization of football's 2012 Euro Cup. One of the ideas circulating in the media immediately after was that Poland might enter the eurozone in the same year. However, some opposing arguments have been raised that to improve our infrastructure and build more football stadiums over the next four years or so will require increased expenditure which may be difficult to reconcile with the Maastricht deficit-to-GDP criterion. My overall impression is that in the public debate the short-run costs and political aspects have so far been overemphasized, whereas long-run benefits have been neglected. We need to restart the debate with a bigger role played by experts.

As a successful inflation-targeting economy, Poland has had to tolerate a relatively variable exchange rate performance against the euro. To what extent does this strategy make ERM II membership difficult to attain?
Right now I don't see volatility of our exchange rate as a big problem. Over the last 12 months or so our exchange rate has been fairly stable. Furthermore, the more recent appreciation of the zloty should help us fight inflation, though it may pose some problems for exporters. The danger is that we may enter ERM II following a currency appreciation much above its equilibrium level and we take the market rate as the rate for conversion. We would then have to wait until factor productivity growth, along with slower wage rate growth, restored competitiveness. This could be a long and painful process. For this reason, membership of the eurozone should not be thought of as some kind of automatic, miracle story for the Polish economy.

Although inflation has risen more recently, for many years Poland had one of the lowest inflation rates in the EU. How might one explain this given the likely presence of a Balassa–Samuelson effect in Poland?

Empirically I think there is growing consensus that the Balassa–Samuelson effect has been smaller during transition for all countries, including Poland, than expected, even though it will be much more important in ERM II and in EMU [economic and monetary union]. There are a number of global factors which could help explain why inflation has been lower than expected. Certainly the impact effect of higher energy prices on consumer prices has been much weaker than previous episodes of oil hikes might have suggested. Although these factors are complex and are difficult to disentangle, I think it is more important to find out what role global factors have played in keeping inflation low, rather than focus on the Balassa–Samuelson effect. In Poland, despite the demand for labour growing at a rate of more than 4 per cent month after month and there being a net migration of workers to other EU countries we have not experienced, until very recently, a rapid increase in wages. Of course the fairly restrictive monetary policy stance of the previous Monetary Policy Council, which to some extent we have continued, has contributed to our record of low inflation, but that is only part of the story. So the global factors have kept wages in check. Now our inflation has accelerated and again this is due to a global factor – a structural increase in demand for food.

Do you share the perception that the euro area is a harder club to join for the post-2004 EU economies than it was for the EU15?
I would say, yes and no. [*Laughter*] Yes in the sense that the Maastricht criteria were initially interpreted in a relatively relaxed way. For example, in the case of Italy and Belgium it was accepted that despite being double the 60 per cent limit their debt-to-GDP ratios were moving in the right direction. The problem comes when very strict interpretations of the criteria are applied resulting in a country being left outside the club. As an example of this I think that Lithuania has been treated in a harsh and rather unfair manner. The reason I would say no to your question is that we did a lot of the groundwork preparing for EU accession. This gave an impetus to the Polish economy. By now with more determination we could have been in ERM II. Even the fiscal adjustment necessary to get our budget deficit below 3 per cent wouldn't have been a big problem if our political parties had been in favour of joining the euro, as was the Slovak case. Despite quite strong political differences in Slovakia, when it comes to joining the euro they talk with one voice. So I don't think that the Maastricht criteria will present a big problem for Poland as long as we are determined to

join. You may not be aware of this but we already have a debt criterion written into our Constitution which provides fiscal discipline. Of course the Constitution could be changed by a democratic majority of three-fifths within parliament. If this were to happen then for young democracies like Poland the eurozone could provide an alternative anchor to ensure fiscal discipline.

Are the most serious obstacles to Poland's membership of the euro area to be found in optimum currency area theory rather than in the Maastricht criteria?

Actually I don't think that either are very serious obstacles. The Maastricht criteria are real obstacles in the sense that they are institutional devices which must be met. But if you look at the concept of obstacles in a broader sense then our time horizon lengthens. Obstacles may arise later on after we have joined the currency union. For that reason I'm more concerned with what may happen after we join the single currency. For example, following an asymmetric shock, the ECB's monetary policy stance could prove to be pro-cyclical for Poland. Another obstacle could arise if Poland enters with too strong a currency. As I mentioned earlier, this could involve a long period of painful adjustment during which time support for the euro could decline.

The EU is now Poland's main export market. How optimistic are you that this trade could be further enhanced by Poland joining the single currency?

I'm quite optimistic. In Poland we still have some considerable room for catching up in terms of the openness of our economy – measured in terms of imports and exports as a percentage of GDP – compared, for example, to Hungary and the Czech Republic. I believe in the argument that eliminating transaction costs and exchange rate risk and uncertainty enhances trade. This has been supported by empirical studies. In my opinion having a single currency will sharpen our competitive edge.

As the largest of the accession economies, do you think Poland has different macroeconomic policy priorities than, say, the much smaller and more open Baltic states?

I don't think so. In my opinion size by itself is not the main consideration. Of course if your institutions lag behind in terms of best practice then for a large country it's more difficult to coordinate inter-regionally and so on. What matters more from a macroeconomic standpoint is the choice of exchange rate regime. This has led to some of the problems the Baltic states have experienced in maintaining macroeconomic stability. Once your currency is linked with the euro you can get uncontrolled expansion if interest rates set by the ECB are too low. I think that Poland was both very wise and lucky to have had a genuine flexible exchange rate over the last 10 years. This has helped us a lot to avoid macroeconomic disequilibria. However, at the same time we have missed an opportunity to gather experience with currency market interventions which may be useful while in ERM II.

The main costs of joining a currency union concerns the problem, for participating countries, of dealing with shocks without the use of independent monetary policy. How important is this argument for Poland?
Clearly there have been different experiences in the eurozone. For example, I think that the Irish case shows that this process can be manageable so that you can grow much faster than, let's say, the core of the eurozone, but with slightly faster inflation. On the other hand, you have the case of a country like Portugal where there was a pre-entry investment boom followed by a post-entry investment bust. Irrespective of whether or not Poland joins the euro, to keep our economy on a stable and high growth path will require certain reforms and disciplines involving, for example, the labour market and deregulation.

Arguably, because of the euro, the countries in which the currency circulates have fewer concerns over the exchange rate as a generator of general and particular macroeconomic shocks. Given the Polish experience, what is your view of this attribute of EMU?
Our currency has been fairly stable. The real appreciation of the zloty in the last few years has, for example, been slower than in the case of the Czech, Slovak or Hungarian currencies. The appreciation of the zloty has been in line with positive changes in productivity and, in consequence, we have not experienced major disturbances in the current account of our balance of payments which is now close to a deficit of 4 per cent of GDP. Nobody would have expected this 10 years ago when in the mid-90s we had similar rates of growth – between 6 and 6½ per cent per annum – and our current account deficit was approaching 9 per cent.

*To what extent has the Polish labour market experienced difficulties fol-
lowing a net migration of workers to other EU member states?*

One of the problems in answering your question is that we don't
have detailed information on the characteristics of the migrants
by age, gender, skill, active v. non-active etc. Certainly the problems we've experienced in the Polish labour market have not
been uniformly distributed. For example, there are shortages for
certain specialist skilled workers required in producing medium-
tech consumer durables. In western parts of Poland close to the
German border, where this production is concentrated, there
have been skilled labour shortages. So far this has not been translated into strong inflationary wage pressure. One of the problems
we face is that domestically we have very low geographical
mobility of labour combined with high international mobility of
labour. This suggests that there might be a threshold for wages,
which we've not yet reached, before there is sufficient incentive
to trigger much higher domestic geographical mobility of labour.
In contrast, the opportunity to earn much higher wages in Britain
and Ireland, which is seemingly above this threshold, has triggered a high international mobility of labour.

*Despite recent improvements Poland still has one of the highest unem-
ployment rates in the EU. In your opinion what measures are needed to
remedy this situation?*

Well I don't think that there are any easy solutions. I believe there
are some myths that our labour market is very inflexible. These
include the type of traditional arguments often put forward in
Western Europe in the debate on unemployment, such as the role
of unemployment benefits. In Poland many of these types of
argument are simply not applicable. For example, only something like 10 per cent of the unemployed in Poland receive unemployment benefit. What we observe are marked geographical
disparities in unemployment. In the eastern part of Poland,
unemployment is twice the national average. In large cities and
in many parts of western Poland you often have labour shortages, especially of skilled workers. One of the main problems is
our low labour participation ratio, as is the case in Romania and
Bulgaria. In Poland's case this can in large part be explained by
past policy mistakes. After transition there was a push for people
to choose early retirement. Many people retired too early. This
has proved to be a disaster and has created a budget burden for
the younger generation. It's fine saying that what we need to

reduce unemployment is more active labour market policies. But in practice such policies are not always that easy to implement. For example, how do you convince people to participate in retraining? You need to have experienced civil servants to run those projects. Attempting to tackle the problem of unemployment in Poland is a very complicated issue.

One final question. When do you think Poland will join the euro and do you think it should?
I believe Poland should join the euro. As to when? The official position of the Monetary Policy Council is that, taking into account the costs and benefits, adoption of the euro in the near future would be favourable. The final decision, though, regarding the date belongs to the government.

7. Reflections on the future of the euro

7.1 INTRODUCTION

In this concluding chapter we review the performance of the euro area and consider the medium to long-term prospects of the new currency. The euro is close to its tenth birthday and to date its record is in many ways at least respectable. But what judgements will be passed in another 10 years, or on the fiftieth anniversary of the euro's launch? Of course, we can only be speculative in trying to answer such questions. However, we do have some theoretical terrain on which alternative futures for the euro and euro area might be mapped. In what follows we sketch out three possible scenarios using optimum currency area theory and some other theoretical and empirical considerations. Each scenario gives a *flavour* of what, in generalized circumstances, might happen to the euro. Our speculations are just that; they are not predictions of what will happen should certain events come to pass. However, before we discuss possible alternative futures for the euro, it will be helpful to review the broad parameters of the development of the euro area to date.

7.2 THE EURO IN ITS FIRST DECADE

7.2.1 The Euro's Launch and the Behaviour of the Euro Exchange Rate

As noted in Chapter 3, the Maastricht criteria that determined the eligibility of the original euro-area countries to adopt the new currency at its 1999 launch were, as Paul De Grauwe notes in our interview with him at the end of Chapter 2, 'leniently applied' because the political determination that the euro *would* happen was so strong. In fact, only Luxembourg and France managed to meet all the criteria, each of the other nine economies that were to form the euro area from the start fell short in at least one respect or more (see European Monetary Institute, 1998). Indeed, this occurred even after the application of what Feldstein (1997) has called 'gimmicks' to try to ensure that countries would be in the required shape for the decision period of 1997. For example, the French government's coffers were boosted by 0.5 per cent of GDP as a result of a partial privatization of France Télécom. The improved public finance position allowed France to record deficit-to-GDP and debt-to-GDP ratios of 3 and 58 per cent, respectively – just under the Maastricht 'wire'.

The political indulgence of creative accounting of this kind might not have inspired great confidence that the euro would enjoy an untroubled introduction to the world economy. Some American commentators in particular doubted that the currency would even appear. Robert Mundell, the original optimum currency area theorist whom many regard as the father of the euro, recalls a bet he made in 1992 with the renowned international macro economist, Rudiger Dornbusch, over whether or not plans for the single currency would indeed come to fruition. Dornbusch was sceptical but Mundell won the bottle of fine wine that was at stake (Vane and Mulhearn, 2006). Similarly, in 1996 Milton Friedman argued that, because European economies were unlikely to undermine the authority of their central banks, actually creating the euro 'was an impossible thing to do' (Snowdon and Vane, 1999, p. 140). Other commentators expressed the view that the introduction of the euro would create potentially deep conflicts within Europe over, for example, higher unemployment arising from optimum currency area failings. Economic conflict between Europe and the US was also possible in the event that the European Union (EU) responded to stagnation by trying to bolster its economy using protectionist trade policy (see Feldstein, 2000).

But in the end the euro's debut was relatively benign. Remember this was an entirely new supranational currency; there had been nothing else like it before, yet it emerged without any technical difficulties: the European Central Bank (ECB) described the process as a 'resounding success' (see Issing, 2000). There was, however, some concern over the initial weakness of the new currency as it fell sharply against the dollar, from $1.18 at its launch to a low of around $0.82 towards the end of 2000. The euro also fell against most other major currencies over this period. As Figure 7.1 shows, the euro did not climb consistently above the one-dollar mark again until the first half of 2003. This initial slide in the euro's value was a boon to the international

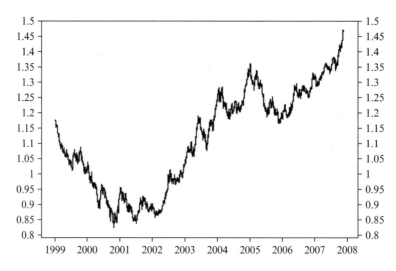

Source: European Central Bank.

Figure 7.1 Nominal exchange rate: US dollars per euro, 1999–2007

price competitiveness of euro-area firms, but it also posed a potential threat to the credibility of the new currency and was potentially a source of inflationary pressure (via higher import prices). It was evident at the time that the ECB harboured some concerns about the depreciation. In November 2000, it confirmed that it had intervened in the foreign exchange markets by buying euros to prop up the currency's value.[45] There were also attempts to discreetly 'talk up' the euro. In December 2000, as the euro touched a new low, Wim Duisenberg, the ECB president, gave a speech which included the following passage:

> I believe that the attractiveness of a currency depends crucially on the under-lying policies for economic growth in the country, or countries, concerned.
>   What I can say with confidence, is that the euro is playing and will con-tinue to play a role in offering new and good investment opportunities, including for investors based outside the euro area.

Duisenberg, like all central bankers, had to some extent to keep his remarks cryptic for fear the markets might react adversely to some perceived nuance in his words; however, his subtext seems reasonably clear – the euro-area economy is fundamentally

[45] ECB Press Release, 3 November 2000.

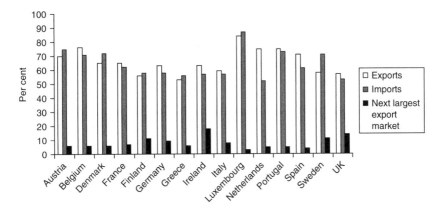

Source: World Trade Organization.

Figure 7.2 EU15 share of trade with EU25, 2005

sound and the medium-term health of its currency is therefore robust.

Figure 7.1 also shows that from its nadir in 2000 and 2001, the euro has since appreciated, with some interruptions, to a record high against the dollar of around $1.47 towards the end of 2007. While this might be better for the credibility of the currency – and the euro's recovery was welcomed by Duisenberg 'as a contributing force for keeping inflation under control'[46] – the downside is the potential damage a strong euro inflicts upon the external trade and growth performance of its member economies. Indeed, it seems clear that the ECB is now prepared to try to 'talk up' the dollar. Duisenberg's successor as ECB president, Jean-Claude Trichet, has recently endorsed the US authorities' claim that a 'strong' dollar is in the United States' interests.[47]

Cohen (2007) has suggested that the appreciation of the euro may cause particular difficulties for some smaller more open economies – such as Finland and Ireland – that trade more heavily outside the euro area. Figure 7.2 illustrates his point. While 63 per cent of Irish exports are to other EU economies, Ireland's next largest export market – the US – accounts for a further 18 per cent. Similarly, of Finland's exports, more than 55 per cent are intra-EU, but 11 per cent are sold in the Russian

46 ECB press conference, Frankfurt am Main, 9 January 2003.
47 ECB press conference, Frankfurt am Main, 8 November 2007.

Federation. Intra-euro-area currency stabilty may have its price for these countries in trading difficulties with other important markets if the euro is more unstable against the dollar and the rouble than were the punt and the markka (the Irish and Finnish former currencies). Interestingly, from Figure 7.2, this argument also appears to apply to the UK and Sweden, both of whom trade heavily with the US (respectively, 14 and 11 per cent of their exports are sold there). In our interview with him about the wisdom of UK euro-area membership, this was a telling point against the euro for Patrick Minford.

However, taking the period since 1999 as a whole, it is probably reasonable to conclude that the fluctuations in the euro's value are not a matter of *primary* concern and, indeed, may not even be considered novel in the sense that the German mark previously moved against the dollar by at least as much (Verdun, 2007). This is apparently the ECB's position given that it has no declared exchange rate policy. As discussed in Chapter 4, the Maastricht Treaty determined that the ECB's primary objective would be to maintain price stability in the euro area. The ECB subsequently decided that this objective should be interpreted as an inflation rate less than, but close to, 2 per cent over the medium term. As interest rate setting by the ECB is focused on inflation it cannot simultaneously address the euro's exchange rate, though clearly monetary policy in the euro area will have an affect on the euro's external value. Reflecting on his practical experience as a member of the Bank of England's Monetary Policy Committee, Willem Buiter (see interview at the end of Chapter 5) makes an important and revealing point in this regard. The context is the Bank's hope and expectation in the late 1990s that the British pound would depreciate from its then overvalued level to alleviate pressure on UK manufactured exports. But, frustratingly, the pound stayed strong. Buiter's conclusion: 'The exchange rate was not an instrument, the exchange rate just happened to us'. The ECB evidently has some grounds for feeling the same way.

7.2.2 Inflation in the Euro Area

Given the ECB's conception as an institution for the delivery of price stability, it is important that we consider the euro area's inflation experience to date. Figure 7.3 shows the record to be satisfactory in the sense that euro-area inflation has been low and relatively stable. However, it is also clear from the figure (on which,

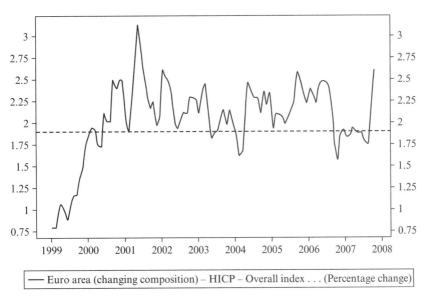

Source: European Central Bank.

Figure 7.3   Inflation in the euro area, 1999–2007

for illustration, we have imposed an 'implicit' inflation target ceiling of 1.9 per cent) that the ECB's stated objective that inflation should be below but close to 2 per cent has not been achieved with any great regularity. The obvious issue here is whether or not this is a problem. It is clear from the history of ECB monthly monetary policy pronouncements that there has been a consistent expectation that the objective *would* be met. For example, in 2001 and 2002 the ECB supposed that the inflation rate would soon fall below 2 per cent and remain there. However, by 2003 and through to 2004 it was apparent that the attainment of the target had been delayed by *inter alia* adverse food- and oil-price developments, though the expectation was that 'HICP [Harmonized Index of Consumer Prices] inflation would fall below 2% in the course of 2005 if no further adverse shocks occurred'.[48] More recently, similar problems have led the ECB to conclude that 'we expect the HICP inflation rate to remain significantly above 2% for the coming months before moderating again in the course of 2008'.[49] Not surprisingly, in the light of the inflation target's elusiveness

[48] ECB Press Conference, Frankfurt am Main, 2 December 2004.
[49] ECB Press Conference, Frankfurt am Main, 8 November 2007.

the ECB president has been questioned about its realism. His standard response has mirrored the most recent pronouncement, which runs as follows: '[the target is] Certainly not unrealistic. It is our definition of price stability. We are credible in the delivery of price stability in the medium run and we have a transitory [inflation] phenomenon. Full stop'.[50]

One difficulty here, as we briefly noted in Chapter 4, section 4.1.3, is that unlike, for example, Sweden and the UK, the euro area has adopted an asymmetric inflation target: inflation needs to be *below* 2 per cent. The Swedish Riksbank and the Bank of England both have symmetrical 2 per cent targets. For them, an inflation performance like the euro area's would appear much more acceptable as inflation rates *above* 2 per cent are not intrinsically problematic. However, we also noted in Chapter 4 that in some views, the ECB appears to operate in practical terms as if 2 per cent were indeed the midpoint of a symmetrical inflation range. If this is the case, the authorities may be reluctant to admit as much for fear that the credibility of monetary policy may be undermined. Certainly, what is not in doubt is that the ECB's intention that monetary policy should firmly anchor medium- and long-term expectations of inflation on price stability has been realized (European Central Bank, 2006b). Firms and workers in the euro area are attuned to low and stable inflation and build the assumption that this will continue into their price-setting and wage-bargaining behaviour; accordingly – conditioned by an appropriate monetary policy – inflation remains low.

7.2.3   Unemployment and Output in the Euro Area

Figure 7.4 compares unemployment in the euro area, the three largest euro-area economies (France, Germany and Italy), and the US and UK. Since 1999 it is clear that average euro area unemployment has generally been around 3 percentage points higher than the two non-euro-area economies at any given time. However, on current projections, the gap may narrow to about 2 per cent in 2007. This in part reflects the broad upward trend in euro-area economic growth since the middle of 2003 (see Figure 4.1). Unemployment in Germany and Italy is expected to be below the euro-area average in 2008, but unemployment in France appears set to remain stubbornly high.

---

[50] Jean-Claude Trichet, ECB Press Conference, Frankfurt am Main, 8 November 2007.

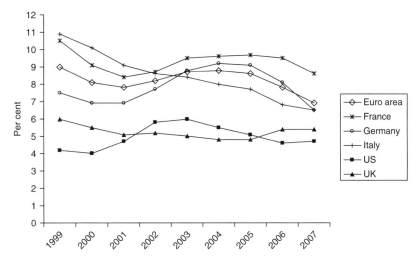

Note: * 2007 estimate.

Source: International Monetary Fund.

Figure 7.4 Unemployment in the euro area, US and UK, 1999–2007*

A legitimate question here concerns the possible role of euro-area institutions and policies in unemployment underperformance. One pejorative view is that the euro is indeed culpable: because of its optimum currency area failings, some economies have simply been saddled with depressive monetary policies unsuited to their particular circumstances. Figures 7.5 and 7.6 show the respective paths of euro-area interest rates and French real economic growth since 1999. Were France not in the euro area would it have chosen to make the eight successive interest rate increases implemented by the ECB since December 2003, given its underwhelming growth record and seemingly intractable unemployment? As inflationary pressures in France had been weak and the French inflation rate below 2 per cent, the answer is almost certainly no: the French economy required lower not higher interest rates. Should this state of affairs persist or even worsen into the long term, it is possible to envisage a case for France to *leave* the euro area: effectively, the cost–benefit membership decision would be reversed as the slow growth and high unemployment costs of an unsuitable monetary policy outweigh the euro area's market-enhancing benefits. De Grauwe (2006)

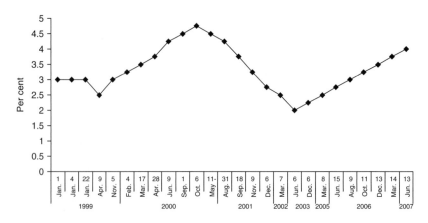

Source: European Central Bank.

Figure 7.5   ECB main interest rate, 1999–2007

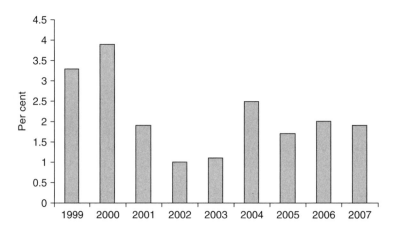

Note: * 2007 estimate.

Source: International Monetary Fund.

Figure 7.6   Real GDP growth in France, 1999–2007*

argues that this kind of problem highlights a basic design fault in
the euro's architecture. This is the absence of a sufficient degree
of political integration that would facilitate the creation of a
European-level authority – a government really – that could use
fiscal policy (taxing and spending) to improve conditions in
asymmetrically depressed euro-area economies. De Grauwe

points out that such an agency would also be in a position to react to shocks to the euro area as a whole, offering the possibility of stabilization policies for output and employment that the ECB, given its price-stability mandate and lack of fiscal powers, cannot countenance. Both these forms of fiscal discretion are possible – and happen – in, for example, the United States where they raise the overall cohesion and stability of the American economy; however, given the near collapse of the momentum for further integration in Europe they are unlikely to be on the EU agenda even in the medium term.

It is important not to be too Cassandra-like here. Although the euro area has performed relatively poorly in growth and unemployment terms since its creation and its members' experiences have been uneven, there has not been any *telling* shock or problem of asymmetry that has in any way threatened the project as a whole. Countries still want to join rather than leave. Moreover, adjustments to the ECB's monetary strategy and the Stability and Growth Pact have been implemented in the light of some combination of experience and expediency; and on balance these changes have been broadly welcomed. It is true that some large non-euro-area economies – such as the US and the UK – have perfomed better since 1999 (see Table 7.1) but, as Nickell (2006) suggests, this may reflect positive real shocks arising from the application of information and communications technology in the US, and improved labour market flexibility in the UK, rather than any pronounced shortcomings in the euro area itself.

It should also be acknowledged that, counter to some expectations, the ECB has, within its purely monetary competencies, reacted as promptly and appropriately as any other central bank to such shocks as have occurred in the world economy in the last decade. Cohen (2007, p. 8) argues that the euro area appears 'remarkably unprepared to cope with any wider instability that might erupt in international finance'. His point is that the division of responsibility between the ECB and individual member states in the event of a crisis is unclear. Yet, in August 2007, when a wave of illiquidity in the euro money market (crudely, commercial banks were short of cash: tensions in the US 'sub prime' mortgage market impeded the usual lending that continually takes place between financial institutions) threatened to turn into a full-blown commercial banking crisis, the ECB injected a sum of €95 billion in overnight loans to the European banking sector, followed by further sizeable injections over the next few days,

Table 7.1   *Macroeconomic performances, 1999–2008 (per cent,*
            annual averages)*

	Inflation	Unemployment	Real GDP growth
Euro area	2.05	8.07	2.13
United States	2.66	5.03	2.64
UK	1.61	5.26	2.74

Note: * 2007 and 2008 estimates.

Source: International Monetary Fund.

and again in September and October (see González-Páramo, 2007). This action preserved the orderly operation of the euro money market and was praised, not least in the UK where politicians were quick to castigate the Bank of England for failing to take equally decisive action.[51]

All this suggests that, while the euro area and its institutions have not produced dazzlingly optimum performances, nor have there been any incontrovertible disasters. Given the halting progress of Europe towards monetary union – starting meaningfully with the Barre Memorandum as long ago as 1969 – and the hugely ambitious nature of the project, a measured conclusion might be: so far so good. One could add the rider, 'with room for improvement', but this, surely, would apply to all economies.

7.3   POSSIBLE SCENARIOS FOR THE EURO AREA

7.3.1   An Optimum Currency Area Context

We turn now to informed speculations about the future of the euro and euro-area economies. A crucial issue here is the extent to which the euro area approximates, or by virtue of its creation and development comes to approximate, an optimum currency area (OCA). In Chapter 3, section 3.4, we noted that Robert Mundell's pioneering work identified three main criteria that could be used to assess whether or not countries may collectively form an OCA. The first of these was the extent of trade integration between

---

[51] See evidence given by senior Bank of England staff to the House of Commons Treasury Committee, 20 September 2007.

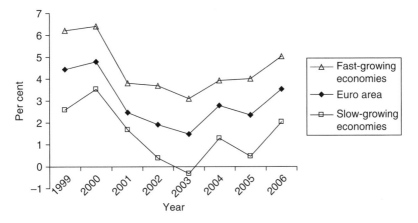

Note: Fast-growing economies: Greece; Spain; Ireland; Luxembourg; Finland. Slow-growing economies: Germany; Italy; Portugal.

Source: International Monetary Fund.

Figure 7.7   Real GDP growth in the euro area, 1999–2006

prospective members. The key benefits of price transparency and reduced exchange rate risk arising from the adoption of a single currency can only be fully realized by countries that trade heavily with one another. The UK and Paraguay, for example, are not good potential single currency partners because their mutual trade is negligible. On the other hand, the deep and extensive trading relations between the countries of Europe – as shown in Table 3.1 – makes this region a good OCA candidate: *existing* economic relations between European economies may be greatly enhanced by a single currency. The same reasoning may eventually underpin aspirations for currency sharing by other groups of economies that trade heavily with one another. East Asia is one regularly touted candidate for such a move.

The remaining two OCA criteria identified in Chapter 3 were the degree of symmetry evident in economic shocks and business cycles between countries, and the flexibility – that is, the efficiency – of members' labour markets. On the basis of the development of the euro area to date, it seems clear that there have been notable differences in macroeconomic achievement between member countries, not least in terms of economic growth. Figure 7.7 depicts annual real GDP growth for separate groups of fast- and slow-growing euro-area economies, as well as growth in the euro area as a whole. The figure makes clear that average growth rates in Germany, Italy and Portugal have been substantially and consistently below rates achieved in Greece, Spain, Ireland, Luxembourg and Finland. It is also evident that business cycles in the euro area are fairly closely aligned: the slowdown between 2000 and 2003 was experienced right across the euro area, as was the halting recovery thereafter.

This makes it possible to interpret the last two OCA criteria a little differently. Given that there *is* unevenness in economic performance between euro-area economies and the fact that, although their business cycles appear symmetrical, they may well be subject to discriminatory country-specific shocks in an unknowable future, to what extent can the euro area rely on labour market flexibility as a mechanism for the restoration and maintenance of a satisfactory macroeconomic performance for its members, both individually and collectively? If there is sufficient responsiveness in euro-area labour markets, then the euro area may indeed claim the status of an OCA with an assured future; if not, its integrity could be under threat in the medium to long term.[52]

Interestingly, our interviewees take a range of positions on this crucial question. Charles Wyplosz memorably calls the euro area's failure to attend to the structural impediments of its labour markets 'the original sin of the monetary union'. In his view the euro area is *not* an OCA and this is certainly at least a potential problem. Both Nick Crafts and Niels Thygesen agree, with the latter arguing that: 'the flexibility of the labour market is, in the long term, a very important criterion for the success of EMU'. However, in his view this 'is not something that immediately threatens monetary union. It would take a long time for these tensions to build up to such an unacceptable level that they would blow up the whole system'. Paul De Grauwe is less sanguine. He points out that because member economies retain sovereignty in a range of areas – in fiscal policy, and in wage and social policies – there is *bound* to be divergence. This is where his noted proposal for a government at the European level comes in. The fiscal

---

[52] It is also important that the markets for goods and services behave in a competitive manner. The Single European Act (1986) was intended to ensure that they did, but the European Commission (2007) has recently acknowledged that there are still price rigidities in services in particular. In our interview with him, Niels Thygesen made the telling remark that monetary integration in Europe has overtaken market integration: 'We have now got one money, but do we have one market?'.

strategy of such an agency would be a much more reliable means of underpinning euro-area cohesion than would the vagaries of euro-area labour markets, the efficiency of which is at least open to question. Finally, Willem Buiter takes a refreshingly different approach to the whole OCA question. He argues that labour market flexibility and the exchange rate flexibility that is lost in monetary union are hardly good substitutes for each other. An ideally managed exchange rate permits an economy to quickly achieve relative cost or price changes *vis-à-vis* its competitors. Buiter suggests that to achieve the same thing through labour mobility, the process would need to be reversible through the economic cycle: an economy would lose labour during the economic downswing, and gain it during an upswing. His point is that '[v]ery few countries have significant labour mobility at cyclical frequencies', and certainly not the US which is indisputably a coherent monetary union. The implication is that either the US is not an optimum currency area, or an optimum currency area is possible without this kind of labour mobility. Buiter holds to the latter position. Of course, he does not deny that improved labour market flexibility is desirable, but its absence in a particular form does not undermine the credentials of the euro area as an OCA.

7.3.2   Is There Sufficient Labour Market Flexibility in the Euro Area?

We saw in Chapter 3, section 3.3, how labour market flexibility is supposed to operate in the euro area. In sluggishly growing member economies, as output slackens and unemployment increases, wages will begin to fall. Lower wages mean that firms' wage costs are reduced, allowing them to raise output and cut prices. This stimulates demand both internally and, importantly, from consumers in other parts of the euro area as the economy in question gains competitiveness relative to other member economies. The crucial point here is that it is wage flexibility that is at the heart of a spontaneous recovery process. If wages are less flexible then this so-called 'competitiveness channel' takes much longer to work; in this case there may be significant losses in output and persistently high unemployment. Finally, where wage flexibility is complemented by labour migration, any initial reduction in unemployment may be tempered somewhat as unemployed workers move and take jobs in other euro-area economies.

For faster-growing economies the process is reversed. A boom entails a loss of national competitiveness as wages and prices rise. Demand will then fall and the level of economic activity should slacken back towards the euro-area average. Again, labour migration may temper the amplitude of any boom as unemployed workers from other parts of the euro area move to fast-growing economies seeking better employment opportunities.

To what extent have these processes been evident in the early history of the euro area? Work by the European Commission suggests that in certain cases the competitiveness channel may be working quite well. For example, in the Netherlands an above-average growth performance around the time of the euro's birth pushed up both wages and inflation. The associated loss of competitiveness and fall in corporate investment caused demand to slacken and created a climate in which wage restraint was possible. After two years of subdued economic activity in 2002 and 2003, the Dutch economy recovered so that by 2006 growth was exactly at the euro-area average.

Unfortunately, as Figure 7.8 suggests, this experience has not been a general one. The figure depicts real effective exchange rates for selected euro-area economies. These are measures of economies' competitiveness based on unit labour costs. Higher labour costs per unit of output indicate a fall in competitiveness for an economy relative to its main trading partners, while lower labour costs per unit of output indicate improvements in competitiveness. We know from Figure 7.7 that Germany, Italy and Portugal have consistently been the three slowest-growing euro-area economies since the advent of monetary union. Figure 7.8 implies that their responses to this situation have not always been appropriate. On the one hand, significant wage moderation in Germany led to a steady improvement in competitiveness and a recovery in growth in 2006 close to the euro-area average (see Figure 7.9). However, in Italy and Portugal competitiveness continued to deteriorate despite a sluggish growth performance; consequently, as Figure 7.9 also shows, recovery was much less pronounced. The European Commission suggests that part of the problem lies in the mosaic of wage sensitivities that covers the euro area. In Germany, for example, wages appear to be reasonably well attuned to the German economic cycle; but in Italy and Portugal, among others, there is downward wage rigidity during periods of slow growth. The Commission concludes that in these and similar economies, unemployment may have to increase

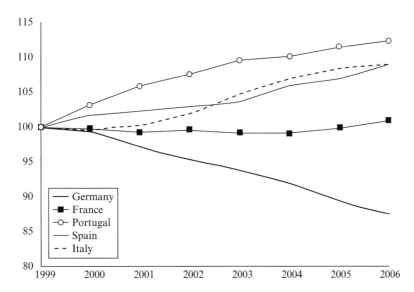

Note: The real effective exchange rate is based on unit labour costs. An increase is equivalent to a deterioration in cost competitiveness.

Source: European Commission (2007).

Figure 7.8 Real effective exchange rates (index 1999 = 100)

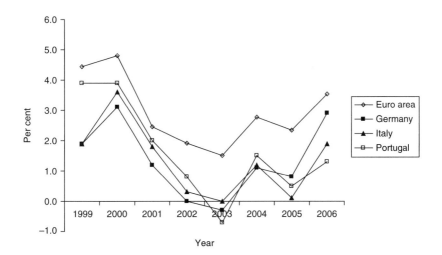

Source: International Monetary Fund.

Figure 7.9 Real GDP growth, selected economies, 1999–2006

more emphatically to produce improvements in competitiveness (European Commission, 2006). Taking all the countries represented in Figure 7.8, the broad conclusion would seem to be that although the competitiveness channel appears to be functioning in Germany and Spain – the latter requiring a moderation in competitiveness to take the edge off a lengthy period of higher-than-average growth – in Italy and Portugal it is not. The position of France is to some extent indeterminate: it has lost ground on Germany but its steady real effective exchange rate has allowed it to gain against Italy, Portugal and Spain.

If there are unresolved issues about wage flexibility in the euro area, what of the possibilities of adjustment afforded by labour migration? Here again the evidence is mixed. As noted in Chapter 3, section 3.1.1, the Single European Act (1986) provided for the free movement of labour in the EU. This created the opportunity for increased migration in Europe, as for EU citizens the right to work was extended from their own country to the

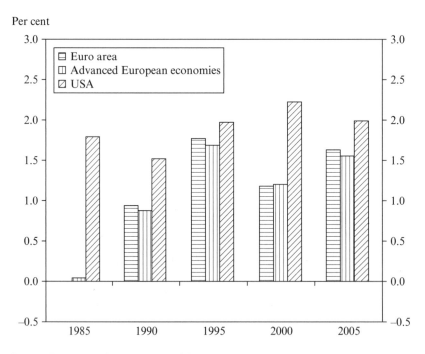

Source: International Monetary Fund (2007).

Figure 7.10   Net migration/population, 1985–2005

entire Union. Figure 7.10 indicates that the opening up of labour markets in this way enabled migration in Europe to increase from very humble beginnings in the 1980s to close to the levels of migration to (not within) the US by 2005. However, it is generally recognized that intra-euro-area migration continues to lag a long way behind inter-state migration in the US (International Monetary Fund, 2007).

Our question at the beginning of this section asked if there was sufficient labour market flexibility in the euro area. On the basis of the evidence presented here and elsewhere we can say that, for *some* economies, the answer is a qualified yes: the competitiveness channel does appear to be working. However, because of downward wage ridigities, a number of other euro-area economies face the prospect of prolonged periods of slow growth and high unemployment before competitiveness *may* be restored (so far this has not happened for Italy and Portugal). Nor is there, at present, much solace to be found in the possible contribution that labour migration might make to easing this burden. Overall, then, it seems reasonable to conclude that the OCA credentials of the euro area have yet to be fully established in the sense that some economies may find the disadvantages of membership particularly pronounced. This, of course, is not the same as saying that members may leave: as Niels Thygesen argues, such an issue is for the very long term.

Moreover, the euro area is a dynamic and developing collective. The obvious rejoinder to a counsel of OCA despair is for member states to continue to engage in reforms that will improve the functioning of their labour markets. This has been done with some success by several EU and euro-area economies. In a review of the experiences of Denmark, Ireland, the Netherlands and the UK, Annett (2007) found that, while the particulars of labour market reform differed between countries, the outcome achieved in all cases was wage moderation: precisely the competitiveness channel that the euro area needs to open up. To give one example, in the Netherlands, agreements between the authorities and trade unions were reached that produced tax cuts for labour in exchange for lower wage claims. This approach was complemented by modifications to the unemployment benefits system designed to improve the incentive to work. Unfortunately, for the moment, the European Commission's view is that labour market reforms – often politically controversial and bitterly contested – are not high on the policy agendas of other euro-area member states: in fact: 'they are doing little in the way of reforms that could raise the euro-area's adjustment capacity and that are therefore important for the smooth functioning of EMU [economic and monetary union]' (European Commission, 2007, p. 36). The euro area as an OCA still seems some way off.

We now turn to possible scenarios for the future of the euro area.

7.3.3   The Euro Area as an Optimum Currency Area

Let us begin with the most benign prognosis: that euro-area members embrace the reform challenges that presently beset their labour markets and, in time, come to meet the optimum currency criteria we discussed earlier. This means that the decision to surrender monetary sovereignty will not prove to be too costly because the market efficiency of member states will underpin their future performance, irrespective of the kinds of shock to which Europe is exposed. To revisit a familiar phrase: one size should fit all. In such circumstances, the doubts about monetary union will melt away as members reap the real benefits of improved material prosperity.

A growing and prosperous euro area would be an attractive community to join. Already, three of the 12 post-2004 accession economies have entered the euro area and one – Lithuania – has had an application narrowly refused. We could expect many more of the accession economies to firm up their membership plans, as, presumably, would the EU candidate countries once EU membership had been secured. It is possible, then, to begin to speculate about something approaching a 24-member euro area. However, note from Figure 7.11 that the GDP contribution that the accession economies may make to the euro area is relatively modest. All nine that are presently outside the euro area account for about 11 per cent of the EU27's GDP, whereas the UK alone accounts for about 15 per cent. Were the UK to take up membership – and since 1997 it has been committed to joining a *successful* monetary union – the euro area would just surpass the US as the world's largest economy. Adding Denmark and Sweden would produce a euro area of 27 countries.

Yet there are obvious obstacles to such enlargement, several of which we have already discussed: for example, the particular difficulties faced by the CE10 in seeking to adopt the euro (see Chapter 6, sections 6.2 and 6.3); and the strains on policy making

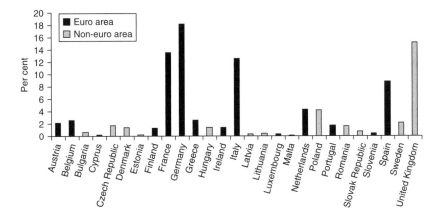

Source: International Monetary Fund.

Figure 7.11   EU27 GDP shares, 2006

that come when there are many contributors to the process rather than a few (see Chapter 4, section 4.1.3). One related issue we have not yet touched on is the possible politicization of euro-area policy making. This may not be on any current agenda but it is possible in the future that an enlarged and successful euro area may be receptive to suggestions that it could do more than simply deliver low and stable inflation. There is evidence of similar hubris in earlier stages of European monetary history – recall, from Chapter 2, section 2.5, the unforeseen and unfortunate consequences of the exchange rate market-defying Basle–Nyborg agreement for the exchange rate mechanism (ERM I). Should future policy makers in the euro area threaten to compromise inflation control in the pursuit of other objectives, one outcome could be murmurs from Germany and perhaps the Netherlands about their stake in monetary union, which is decisively founded on the principle of low and stable prices. Most reflections on possible defections from the euro area focus on the hypothesis that stagnant economies wishing to free monetary and fiscal policy from, respectively, ECB control and European Commission sanction, will be the most likely to consider leaving. This may be true but other kinds of discontent are still possible.

Finally, we should be clear what a well-functioning euro area offers. It is not a system for promoting convergence and equality between economies; rather, monetary union provides a stable and open macroeconomic framework within which the economic potentialities of member states can be most productively developed. This is clearly of benefit to the established industrial economies, but perhaps it is even more attractive to the economies of Eastern Europe that were denied such opportunities for several decades after 1945.

7.3.4   The Euro Area with Limited OCA Credentials

A second general scenario for the euro area might involve continued development in something like its present form, with structural problems – particularly but not exclusively in labour markets – raising some questions over its OCA status and long-term integrity. However, in the short to medium term we could still expect to see several of the accession countries adopting the euro. These would be most likely to come from the group of ERM II members, together with Bulgaria, which has a currency board with the euro, and Hungary, which shadows ERM II (see Table 6.1). In the absence of any marked improvement in the euro area's collective performance, Denmark, Sweden and the UK are likely to continue to retain their own national currencies. Overall, then, we may expect the euro area to add perhaps four or five new members over the next 10 or so years, though given their small size they will not add significantly to its total GDP.

If labour market flexibility cannot be relied upon to protect the integrity of the euro-area, arguments for further political integration of the kind advanced by Paul De Grauwe may gain ground. A euro-area institution with powers to tax and spend could provide fiscal transfers to support and reform less-competitive European regions. But, again, how realistic is such an ambitious strategy? There are few signs that the popular jaundice with the integration project will ease anytime soon. This makes it not impossible that, in the long term, some member states may consider leaving the euro area: the prime candidates would be economies that *consistently* failed to realize the adjustment opportunities presented by the competitiveness channel discussed earlier.

But leaving the euro area is likely to be messy: certainly far more difficult than joining in the first place. A leaver, abandoning its chosen macroeconomic and – to some extent – microeconomic strategies, would be admitting economic and political failure, and the process would inevitably be highly destabilizing.

The motive for reassertion of national monetary policy would be to loosen it – interest rates and the exchange rate would both fall. However, the difficulty here is that the policy change would presumably arrive at the end of long and open national and euro-area discussions; it would, in other words, be fully anticipated. As Milton Friedman pointed out more than 50 years ago, currency devaluations engineered by governments in response to economic difficulties are inevitably crisis-ridden because they present a secure profit opportunity for speculators (see Friedman, 1953). If Italy, say, were to contemplate seceding from the euro area, Italian residents and firms would have a huge incentive to shift what money they could into non-Italian banks prior to its conversion into lira and inevitable fall in value, switching back into lira – and profiting in the process – after the devaluation. In the worst case this could engender an economy-wide bank run of catastrophic proportions (Eichengreen, 2007). It may also be doubtful that a leaving country would actually resolve its central difficulties by reasserting monetary independence. A lower interest rate and cheap currency are probably not the answer if an economy's real problem is a deep-seated lack of competitiveness.

On the other hand, the secession of a chronically poor performing member might not be a wholly bad thing for the rest of the euro area. Remember that an OCA comprises a group of economies that can benefit from a shared currency. The loss of a member with severe structural problems in its labour markets may leave the euro area looking and behaving more like an OCA than before; jettisoning weak economies potentially strengthens the collective integrity of those that are left.

7.3.5   The Euro Area with Severe OCA Weaknesses

Were the euro area to be buffeted by a series of asymmetric shocks in combination with undiminished structural weaknesses in its labour and other markets, the medium to long-term result could well be pressures leading to the fragmentation of the monetary union. Effectively, member economies, despite their extensive trading relations, would be economically just too unalike to share a common monetary policy, a commonly regulated fiscal framework and, possibly, a currency riding consistently high against, for most, their second most important trading partner: the US (recall Figure 7.1). In this scenario, secessions by poorly performing economies might be at least contemplated sooner rather than later.[53] While the euro area could still add one or two more members in the short term, the broad implication is that, overall, the union would not grow as some established participants made their uneasy preparations to leave.

The crucial issue would then become the reaction of the euro-area institutions and member states to this threat to the integrity of monetary union. If this was to reaffirm the independence of the ECB and endorse its declared strategies, the likelihood is that the euro area will continue to lose members until it assumes the proportions of a (much-reduced) OCA, possibly centred on Germany, the Netherlands and some other contiguous states that are comfortable with, or at least prepared to tolerate, monetary rectitude. On the other hand, if the response was to try to placate discontented members by loosening monetary policy and introducing a political dimension to the ECB framework, the result might be disquiet and threats to leave on the part of Germany, the Netherlands and others. Either way, the euro area would have a greatly diminished and chaotic future, and this is before the political ramifications of either shake-out are considered: a doomsday scenario indeed.

7.4   CONCLUDING REMARKS

At present it is fair to say that, of our three possible futures for the euro area, the second looks the most probable. This means that, in the medium to long term at least, European monetary union is secure and the euro is likely to grow, modestly, in geographical coverage and international stature. Given the immense ambition, and sheer scale of the whole project, this is no small achievement and almost certainly something with which the architects of the euro would have been content. Note, too, that these architects have a long lineage, stretching back to Churchill, Monnet and

---

[53] Though falling far short of calls for France's withdrawal from the euro area, the 2007 campaign for the French presidency produced interesting agreement between opposing candidates that the French economic agenda has not been best served by the policies of the ECB. Thus, Nicolas Sarkozy argued that, 'We have built the world's second currency and we are the only region in the world that obstinately refuses to make the currency serve growth and employment. It cannot go on'. Segolene Royale was equally critical of the extent of the influence of euro-area institutions on the French economy: 'It is not up to [ECB president] Trichet to decide the future of our economy, but to democratically elected French leaders'.

Schuman, whose contributions we reviewed in Chapter 1. The concern of these visionary leaders was to reshape the history of a war-torn continent. In a world where internecine conflicts continue to rage, it is to their and others' eternal credit that Europe is today a place of peace and prosperity.

Bibliography

Adams, W.J. (1989), *Restructuring the French Economy*, Washington, DC: Brookings Institution.

Alesina, A. and L.H. Summers (1993), 'Central Bank Independence and Macroeconomic Performance: Some Comparative Evidence', *Journal of Money, Credit and Banking*, **25** (2), May, 151–62.

Annett, A. (2006), 'Enforcement and the Stability and Growth Pact: How Fiscal Policy Did and Did Not Change Under Europe's Fiscal Framework', IMF Working Paper No. WP/06/116.

Annett, A. (2007), 'Lessons from Successful Labour Market Reformers in Europe', IMF Policy Discussion Paper No. 07/1.

Annett, A., J. Decressin and M. Deppler (2005), 'Reforming the Stability and Growth Pact', IMF Policy Discussion Paper No. PDP/05/2.

Bacchetta, P. and E. van Wincoop (2000), 'Does Exchange-rate Stability Increase Trade and Welfare?', *American Economic Review*, **90** (5), December, 1093–1109.

Badinger, H. (2005), 'Growth Effects of Economic Integration: Evidence from the EU Member States', *Review of World Economics*, **141** (1), April, 50–78.

Badinger, H. and F. Breuss (2004), 'What Has Determined the Rapid Postwar Growth of Intra-EU Trade?', *Review of World Economics*, **140** (1), 31–51.

Baldwin, R. (2006), 'The Euro's Trade Effects', ECB Working Paper No. 594.

Baldwin, R., E. Berglof, F. Giavazzi and M. Widgren (2001), 'Nice Try: Should the Treaty of Nice be Ratified?', *Monitoring European Integration*, 11, Centre for Economic Policy Research, London.

Bank of Estonia (2007), *Report on the Adoption of the Euro*, May.

Barro, R.J. and D.B. Gordon (1983), 'Rules, Discretion and Reputation in a Model of Monetary Policy', *Journal of Monetary Economics*, **12** (2), September, 101–21.

Boughton, J.M. (2001), *Silent Revolution: The International Monetary Fund 1979–1989*, Washington, DC: IMF.

Broadberry, S.N. and N.F.R. Crafts (1996), 'British Economic Policy and Industrial Performance in the Early Post-war Period', *Business History*, **38** (4), October, 65–91.

Buiter, W.H. and C. Grafe (2002), 'Anchor, Float or Abandon Ship: Exchange Rate Regimes for the Accession Countries', *Banca Nazionale del Lavoro Quarterly Review*, **221**, June, 1–32.

Cecchini Report (1988), *The European Challenge 1992: The Benefits of a Single Market*, Aldershot: Gower Press.

Cohen, B.J. (2007), 'The Euro in a Global Context: Challenges and Capacities', forthcoming in K. Dyson, *The Euro at Ten*, Oxford: Oxford University Press.

Cottarelli, C. and J. Escolano (2004), 'Assessing the Assessment: A Critical Look at the June 2003 Assessment of the United Kingdom's Five Tests for Euro Entry', IMF Working Paper, WP/04/116.

Crafts, N.F.R. (1995), 'The Golden Age of Economic Growth in Western Europe, 1950–1973', *Economic History Review*, **48** (3), August, 429–47.

Crafts, N.F.R. (1996), 'Deindustrialisation and Economic Growth', *Economic Journal*, **106** (434), January, 172–83.

Crafts, N.F.R. (1998), *The Conservative Governments' Economic Record: An End of Term Report*, London: Institute of Economic Affairs.

Czech Government and Czech National Bank (2007), *The Czech Republic's Updated Euro Area Accession Strategy*, 29 August.

De Grauwe, P. (2006), 'What Have We Learnt about Monetary Integration since the Maastricht Treaty?', *Journal of Common Market Studies*, **44** (4), November, 711–30.

De Grauwe, P. and G. Schnabl (2005), 'Nominal Versus Real Convergence – EMU Entry Scenarios for the New Member States', *Kyklos*, **58** (4), 537–55.

Delors Report (1989), *Report on Economic and Monetary Union in the European Community*, Luxembourg: Office for Official Publications of the European Communities.

Dominguez, K.M.E. (2006), 'The European Central Bank, the Euro, and Global Financial Markets', *Journal of Economic Perspectives*, **20** (4), Fall, 67–88.

EC Commission (1977), *Report of the Study Group on the Role of Public Finance in European Integration (MacDougall Report)*, Brussels: EC Commission.

Egert, B., I. Drine, K. Lommatzsch and C. Rault (2003), 'The Balassa–Samuelson Effect in Central and Eastern Europe: Myth or Reality?', *Journal of Comparative Economics*, **31** (3), 552–72.

Eichengreen, B.J. (2007), 'The Breakup of the Euro Area', NBER Working Paper No. 13393, National Bureau of Economic Research, Cambridge, MA.

European Central Bank (2004), *The Monetary Policy of the ECB*, Frankfurt am Main, Germany: European Central Bank.

European Central Bank (2006a), *Convergence Report*, May, Frankfurt am Main, Germany: European Central Bank.

European Central Bank (2006b), 'Measures of Inflation Expectations in the Euro Area', *Monthly Bulletin*, July, 59–68.

European Commission (1990), 'One Market One Money: An Evaluation of the Potential Benefits and Costs of Forming an Economic and Monetary Union', *European Economy*, **44**, October.

European Commission (2006), *Adjustments in the Euro Area*, Brussels: European Commission.

European Commission (2007), *Annual Report of the Euro Area – 2007*, SEC (2207) 550, Brussels: European Commission.

European Monetary Institute (1998), *Convergence Report*, March, Frankfurt am Main, Germany: European Monetary Institute.

Feldstein, M. (1997), 'The Political Economy of the European Economic and Monetary Union: Political Sources of an Economic Liability', *Journal of Economic Perspectives*, **11** (4), Fall, 23–42.

Feldstein, M. (2000), 'The European Central Bank and the Euro: The First Year', *Journal of Policy Modelling*, **22** (3), May, 345–54.

Frankel, J.A. and A.K. Rose (1998), 'The Endogeneity of the Optimum Currency Area Criteria', *Economic Journal*, **108** (449), July, 1009–25.

Frankel, J.A. and A.K. Rose (2002), 'An Estimate of the Effect of Common Currencies on Trade and Income', *Quarterly Journal of Economics*, **117** (2), May, 437–66.

Friedman, M. (1953), 'The Case for Flexible Exchange Rates', in M. Friedman (ed.), *Essays in Positive Economics*, Chicago: University of Chicago Press, 157–203.

Gillingham, J.R. (2006), 'The German Problem and European Integration', in D. Dinan (ed.), *Origins and Evolution of the European Union*, Oxford: Oxford University Press, 55–81.

González-Páramo, J.M. (2007), 'The Euro Area Economy and the Financial Markets', Speech given at the University of Coruna, 11 October.

Gray, W.G. (2006), '"Number One in Europe": The Startling Emergence of the Deutsche Mark, 1968–1969', *Central European History*, **39** (1), March, 56–78.

Gros, D. and N. Thygesen (1998), *European Monetary Integration: From the European Monetary System Towards Monetary Union*, 2nd edn, London: Longman.

HM Treasury (2003), *UK Membership of the Single Currency: An Assessment of the Five Economic Tests*, Cm 5776, London: HMSO.

HM Treasury (2004), *The Stability and Growth Pact: A Discussion Paper*, London: HMSO.

HM Treasury (2006), *Convergence Programme for the United Kingdom: Submitted in Line with the Stability and Growth Pact*, London: HMSO.

House of Commons (2000), 'What Would the Euro Cost British Business?', *Trade and Industry Committee Report*, Cmnd. HC755.

International Monetary Fund (2007), *Regional Economic Outlook: Europe*, Washington, DC: IMF.

Issing, O. (2000), 'Europe's Challenges after the Establishment of Monetary Union: A Central Banker's View', Speech given at the CSO-IFO Conference on Issues of Monetary Integration in Europe, Munich, 1 December.

Kenen, P.B. and E.E. Meade (2003), 'EU Accession and the Euro: Close Together or Far Apart?', Policy Brief, Washington, DC: Institute for International Economics.

Kydland, F.E. and E.C. Prescott (1977), 'Rules Rather than Discretion: The Inconsistency of Optimal Plans', *Journal of Political Economy*, **85** (3), 473–91.

Lane, P.R. (2006), 'The Real Effects of European Monetary Union', *Journal of Economic Perspectives*, **20** (4), Fall, 47–66.

McCallum, J. (1995), 'National Borders Matter: Canada–US Regional Trade Patterns', *American Economic Review*, **85** (3), June, 615–23.

Miller, V. (2000), 'The Danish Referendum on Economic and Monetary Union', Research Paper 00/78, London: House of Commons Library; available on www.parliament.uk.

Miller, V., C. Taylor and E. Potton (2003), 'The Swedish Referendum on the Euro', Research Paper 03/68, London: House of Commons Library; available on www.parliament.uk.

Minford, P. (2002), *Should Britain Join the Euro? The Chancellor's Five Tests Explained*, IEA Occasional Paper 126, London: Institute of Economic Affairs.

Minford, P., D. Meenagh and B. Webb (2004), 'Britain and EMU: Assessing the Costs in Macroeconomic Variability', *World Economy*, **27** (3), March, 301–58.

Mundell, R.A. (1961), 'A Theory of Optimum Currency Areas', *American Economic Review*, **51** (4), September, 657–65.

Mundell, R.A. (1973), 'A Plan for a European Currency', in H.G. Johnson and A.K. Swoboda (eds), *The Economics of Common Currencies*, London: George Allen & Unwin, 143–73.

National Bank of Poland (2003), *A Report on the Costs and Benefits of Poland's Adoption of the Euro*, Warsaw: National Bank of Poland.

Nickell, S. (2006), 'Discussion of Charles Wyplosz's paper on European Monetary Union: The Dark Sides of a Major Success', *Economic Policy*, **21** (46), April, 247–53.

Rose, A.K. (2000), 'One Money, One Market: The Effect of Common Currencies on Trade', *Economic Policy*, **15** (30), April, 9–45.

Rose, A.K. and E. van Wincoop (2001), 'National Money as a Barrier to International Trade: The Real Case for Currency Union', *American Economic Review*, **91** (2), May, 386–90.

Roseveare, D., W. Leibfritz, D. Fore and E. Wurzel (1996), *Ageing Populations, Pension Systems and Government Budgets: Simulations for 20 OECD Countries*, OECD Economics Department Working Paper No. 168, Paris: OECD.

Scammell, W.M. (1987), *The Stability of the International Monetary System*, Basingstoke: Macmillan.

Scheller, H.K. (2006), *The European Central Bank: History, Role and Functions*, Frankfurt am Main, Germany: European Central Bank.

Snowdon, B. and H.R. Vane (1999), *Conversations with Leading Economists*, Cheltenham, UK and Northampton, MA, USA: Edward Elgar.

Thom, R. and B. Walsh (2002), 'The Effect of a Currency Union on Trade: Lessons from the Irish Experience', *European Economic Review*, **46** (6), June, 1111–23.

Thygesen, N. (2004), 'Perspectives on Europe's Monetary Unification', Farewell Lecture, University of Copenhagen, 10 December, EPRU-Analysis No. 23, Copenhagen: Economic Policy Research Unit.

Vane, H.R. and C. Mulhearn (2006), 'Interview with Robert A. Mundell', *Journal of Economic Perspectives*, **20** (4), Fall, 89–110.

Verdun, A. (2007), 'Economic Developments in the Euro Area', *Journal of Common Market Studies*, **45** (s1), September, 213–30.

Wyplosz, C. (2003), 'Accession Countries and ERM II', Briefing Notes to the Committee for Economic and Monetary Affairs of the European Parliament, Geneva: Graduate Institute of International Studies.

Wyplosz, C. (2005), 'Fiscal Policy: Institutions Versus Rules', *National Institute Economic Review*, **191**, January, 64–78.
Wyplosz, C. (2006), 'European Monetary Union: The Dark Sides of a Major Success', *Economic Policy*, **21** (46), April, 207–61.

Time line of key events in the history of European economic, monetary and political integration

1946

Winston Churchill's 'United States of Europe' **speech** delivered at the University of Zurich.

1950

May   **Schuman Declaration** presenting Jean Monnet's plan for the unification of key sectors of the French and German economies, and inviting the participation of other European nations.

July   **European Payments Union** created to enable balance-of-payments adjustment, facilitate currency convertibility, and promote trade in Europe.

1952

July   **European Coal and Steel Community (ECSC)** is established. Founded by the Treaty of Paris (1951), the ECSC developed a common market in the production, and trade, of coal and steel between its six member countries (Belgium, France, Germany, Italy, Luxembourg, and the Netherlands – known collectively as the Six).

1955

Messina Conference of the Six agrees to develop common institutions and gradually merge their economies.

1957

March   **Treaty of Rome** is signed. The Treaty, which
                        came into force on 1 January 1958, provided for
                        the gradual development of a customs union
                        between the six founding members of the ECSC
                        involving a commitment to free trade between
                        the countries concerned, together with common
                        external tariff arrangements with the rest of
                        the world. The Treaty established the **European
                        Economic Community (EEC)** – a customs union,
                        which became popularly known as the Common
                        Market – and the **European Atomic Energy
                        Community (Euratom)**.

1964

May   **Committee of Central Bank Governors** of the
                        member states of the EEC is formed.

1969

October   **Barre Memorandum** explores the possibilities of
                        intensifying monetary cooperation in Europe.

December   **Community Heads of State and Government
                        summit in The Hague** agrees that a plan for eco-
                        nomic and monetary union for the Six should be
                        drawn up.

1970

                        Werner Report expressed an intention to achieve
                        monetary integration in Europe through a single
                        currency, or irrevocably fixed exchange rates, by
                        1980.

1971

                        Collapse of the **Bretton Woods System** of fixed
                        exchange rates.

1972

April   **'Snake' Fixed Exchange Rate System** is intro-
                        duced. The system entailed a set of bilateral

bands limiting fluctuations between the currencies of the member states of the EEC.

1973

January — **Membership of the three European Communities is enlarged from 6 to 9 countries** with the inclusion of Denmark, Ireland and the UK.

April — **European Monetary Co-operation Fund** established.

1979

March — **European Monetary System (EMS)** is instituted. The EMS sought to create a 'zone of monetary stability' in Europe via EEC members maintaining low and stable inflation rates and stable exchange rates against one another. The key feature of the EMS entailed the **exchange rate mechanism (ERM)**: a fixed, but adjustable, exchange rate initiative among participating member countries. Member countries maintained exchange rate fluctuations within a band 2.25 per cent above, and 2.25 per cent below, the official parities. Up to 1990, Italy used a wider band of fluctuation ($+/-$ 6 per cent) – this wider band was also adopted by Spain (1989), the UK (1990) and Portugal (1992) when they joined the system.

1981

January — **Membership of the three European Communities is enlarged from 9 to 10 countries** with the inclusion of Greece.

1986

January — **Membership of the three European Communities is enlarged from 10 to 12 countries** with the inclusion of Spain and Portugal.

February — The **Single European Act (SEA)** is signed. The SEA, which came into force on 1 July 1987, sought to develop the EEC from a customs union into a 'single' common market by providing for the free internal movement of capital, labour, goods and services by the end of 1992. The SEA also expressed an ambition for the revival of plans for a European single currency.

1987

September   **Basle–Nyborg Agreement** is signed. The agreement greatly strengthened the resources that participating members of the ERM could deploy in defence of agreed exchange rate parities.

1989

Delors Report is published. The Delors Committee was set up by the European Council in 1988 to study and propose concrete stages leading towards economic and monetary union (EMU).

June   **European Council** agrees on the realization of EMU in three stages.

1990

July   **Stage one of EMU** begins.

December   **Intergovernmental Conference** is launched to prepare for stages two and three of EMU.

1992

February   **Treaty on European Union (TEU)**, also known as the **Maastricht Treaty**, is signed. The Treaty, which came into force on 1 November 1993, created the European Union (EU) consisting of three pillars: the European Communities (ECSC, EEC and the Euratom – the EEC was renamed the European Community); a common foreign and security policy (CFSP); and police and judicial cooperation in the fields of justice and home affairs (JHA).
                The Treaty established that the second stage of

EMU would begin on 1 January 1994 with the establishment of the European Monetary Institute (EMI). It also confirmed that the final stage of EMU would begin *no later than* 1 January 1999 with the launch of a single currency and the establishment of a central European bank, and identified the 'convergence criteria' to be satisfied before the then-15 individual member states of the EU would become eligible to join the then un-named single currency.

September   First wave of **ERM crises**. Prompted by the inflationary implications of German reunification in 1990, the 1992 crisis witnessed the suspension of sterling's and the lira's membership of the ERM.

1993

August   The **ERM** is 'effectively' **abandoned**. Following the decision of the European Union Council of Economics and Finance Ministers (ECOFIN) to widen the band of exchange rate fluctuation from $+/-$ 2.25 per cent to $+/-$ 15 per cent, the ERM was transformed from a fixed, but adjustable, exchange rate regime (with a maximum range of exchange rate fluctuation of 4.5 per cent for the majority of participating countries), to a quasi-flexible exchange rate regime (with a maximum range of exchange rate fluctuation of 30 per cent).

1994

January   **Stage two of EMU** begins and the **European Monetary Institute** (the forerunner of the European Central Bank) is established.

1995

January   **Membership of the EU is enlarged from 12 to 15 countries** with the inclusion of Austria, Finland and Sweden.

December   **Madrid European Council** meeting. The meeting agreed further details for the third and final stage of EMU, which would begin on 1 January 1999. Decision made to call the new single currency the euro.

1997

June/July   **Stability and Growth Pact (SGP)** agreed by the European Council. The SGP effectively rolled forward previously agreed (at Maastricht) limits on the deficits and debts of participating countries in order to ensure continuing fiscal prudence after the introduction of the euro.

October   **Treaty of Amsterdam** is signed. The Treaty, which came into force on 1 May 1999, amended both the Treaty establishing the European Community and the TEU.

1998

June   **European Central Bank (ECB)** and the **European System of Central Banks (ESCB)** are established. Membership of the ESCB consisted of the national central banks (NCBs) of the then-15 EU member states.

1999

1 January   **Stage three of EMU** begins. The euro becomes the single currency of the euro area; 11 EU member states (Austria, Belgium, Finland, France, Germany, Ireland, Italy, Luxembourg, the Netherlands, Portugal and Spain) who satisfied the Maastricht criteria and who wished to participate in full European monetary union commenced the irrevocable fixing of their exchange rates to the euro; the ERM ceased to exist and **ERM II established**; the ECB assumes responsibility for a single monetary policy in the euro area.

2001

1 January **Euro area enlarged from 11 to 12 countries** when Greece enters the third and final stage of EMU and becomes the 12th EU member state to adopt the euro.

February **Treaty of Nice** is signed. The Treaty, which came into force on 1 February 2003, amended both the Treaty establishing the European Community and the TEU and paved the way for EU enlargement.

2002

1 January **Euro coins** and **banknotes** are introduced in 12 EU member states.

End February The **euro** becomes the **sole legal tender** in the euro area.

2003

November The **SGP** falls into **disarray**.

2004

May **Membership of the EU is enlarged from 15 to 25 countries** with the inclusion of Cyprus, the Czech Republic, Estonia, Hungary, Latvia, Lithuania, Malta, Poland, Slovakia and Slovenia; **membership of the ESCB is enlarged from 15 to 25 NCBs**: inclusion of the NCBs of 10 new EU member states.

October Treaty establishing a **Constitution for Europe** is signed and came into force on 1 November 2006.

2005

July **Revised SGP** comes into force.

2006

Lithuania's application for euro-area membership narrowly rejected on the inflation criterion.

2007

1 January   **Euro area enlarged from 12 to 13 countries** when Slovenia adopts the euro.

January   **Membership of the EU is enlarged from 25 to 27 countries** with the inclusion of Bulgaria and Romania; **membership of the ESCB is enlarged from 25 to 27 NCBs**: inclusion of the NCBs of two new member states.

2008

1 January   **Euro area enlarged from 13 to 15 countries** when Malta and Cyprus adopt the euro.

Name index

Subject index